MOTOROLA *XOOM*™ FOR DUMMIES®

by Andy Rathbone

WILEY

Wiley Publishing, Inc.

MOTOROLA XOOM™ For Dummies®

Published by
Wiley Publishing, Inc.
111 River Street
Hoboken, NJ 07030-5774

www.wiley.com

Copyright © 2011 by Wiley Publishing, Inc., Indianapolis, Indiana

Published by Wiley Publishing, Inc., Indianapolis, Indiana

Published simultaneously in Canada

For general information on our other products and services, please contact our Customer Care Department within the U.S. at 877-762-2974, outside the U.S. at 317-572-3993, or fax 317-572-4002.

For technical support, please visit www.wiley.com/techsupport.

Wiley also publishes its books in a variety of electronic formats and by print-on-demand. Not all content that is available in standard print versions of this book may appear or be packaged in all book formats. If you have purchased a version of this book that did not include media that is referenced by or accompanies a standard print version, you may request this media by visiting http://booksupport.wiley.com. For more information about Wiley products, visit us www.wiley.com.

Library of Congress Control Number: 2011930298

ISBN 978-1-118-08835-7 (cloth); ISBN 978-1-118-12162-7 (ebk); ISBN 978-1-118-12163-4 (ebk); ISBN 978-1-118-12164-1 (ebk)

Manufactured in the United States of America

10 9 8 7 6 5 4 3 2 1

WILEY

About the Author

Andy Rathbone started geeking around with computers in 1985 when he bought a 26-pound portable CP/M Kaypro 2X. Like other nerds of the day, he soon began playing with null-modem adapters, dialing computer bulletin boards, and working at Radio Shack.

He wrote for various techie publications before moving to computer books in 1992. He's written the *Windows For Dummies* series, *Upgrading and Fixing PCs For Dummies, TiVo For Dummies, PCs: The Missing Manual,* and many other computer books.

Today, he has more than 15 million copies of his books in print, and they've been translated into more than 30 languages. You can reach Andy at his website, www.andyrathbone.com, where he answers a reader's question online each week.

When not geeking around with consumer electronics, Andy plays ukulele and tries to remember the songs he learned last week.

Author's Acknowledgments

Special thanks to Dan Gookin, Matt Wagner, Tina Rathbone, Katie Mohr, Rebecca Senninger, Bethany Hiitola, and Kathy Simpson.

Thanks also to all the folks I never meet in editorial, sales, marketing, layout, graphics, and manufacturing who work hard to bring you this book.

Publisher's Acknowledgments

We're proud of this book; please send us your comments at http://dummies.custhelp.com. For other comments, please contact our Customer Care Department within the U.S. at 877-762-2974, outside the U.S. at 317-572-3993, or fax 317-572-4002.

Some of the people who helped bring this book to market include the following:

Acquisitions and Editorial

Project Editor: Rebecca Senninger

Acquisitions Editor: Katie Mohr

Copy Editor: Kathy Simpson

Technical Editor: Bethany Hiitola

Editorial Manager: Leah Cameron

Editorial Assistant: Amanda Foxworth

Sr. Editorial Assistant: Cherie Case

Cartoons: Rich Tennant
(www.the5thwave.com)

Composition Services

Project Coordinator: Patrick Redmond

Layout and Graphics: Samantha K. Cherolis

Proofreader: Toni Settle

Indexer: Sherry Massey

Publishing and Editorial for Technology Dummies

    Richard Swadley, Vice President and Executive Group Publisher

    Andy Cummings, Vice President and Publisher

    Mary Bednarek, Executive Acquisitions Director

    Mary C. Corder, Editorial Director

Publishing for Consumer Dummies

    Kathleen Nebenhaus, Vice President and Executive Publisher

Composition Services

    Debbie Stailey, Director of Composition Services

Contents at a Glance

Table of Contents

Introduction

*W*elcome to *MOTOROLA XOOM For Dummies,* your look-it-up-and-find-it guide to the Motorola Xoom tablet.

Your Motorola Xoom crosses the boundary between smartphone and netbook, giving you a large but lightweight screen on which to display all your books, magazines, newspapers, movies, and digital photos.

When you're not buried in your media, your Motorola Xoom also lets you keep tabs on your friends through video chats, e-mail, Twitter streams, and Facebook updates.

This book helps you do all that and more with either a Wi-Fi Xoom or a Xoom with a data plan.

The official name of the tablet in your hands is the MOTOROLA XOOM. I occasionally refer to it that way, but mostly, I call it the Xoom.

About This Book

Like all *For Dummies* books, this book is a reference. Don't bother trying to read it from cover to cover. Instead, flip to the chapter or section that contains the information you need at the time, follow the steps to accomplish your task, and then put the book aside and get back to work. These tasks, for example, are explained clearly, each in its own section:

- Turning your Motorola Xoom on and off
- Setting up your Internet connection
- Typing without a keyboard
- Sending and receiving e-mail
- Browsing the web
- Downloading and running apps
- Taking and sharing photos and videos
- Backing up and password-protecting your Motorola Xoom

Don't bother memorizing anything. Just flip to the page you need, read the explanation or follow the steps, and get on with your life. Unlike user manuals, this book lets you skip the dry, boring stuff and simply get things done.

When the book tells you to do something specific, you see numbered steps. A specific step may look like this:

2. Touch the Microphone icon.

This step tells you to touch the little picture of the microphone on the screen.

Finally, you find a full table of contents in the front of the book for general reference and an index in the back for more detailed searches.

And You, Dear Reader . . .

Chances are good that you already own a Motorola Xoom or are thinking about buying one. You probably know what you want to do with a tablet computer. Unfortunately, the Xoom doesn't always do what you want it to do, and that's why you've picked up this book.

Although I assume that you want to know about the Xoom, I don't assume that you have a data plan — a monthly fee paid to a cellular carrier for Internet access. The Xoom comes in a Wi-Fi—only flavor, meaning that it can slurp up the Internet through the wireless networks available in many homes, offices, coffee shops, and airports but can't access the Internet from cellphone towers.

If one of the features in this book requires a data plan, I say so — and also tell you how to get around the need for a data plan.

I also assume that you have — or plan to get — a Google account. Your Google account's username/password combination unlocks many features, including its apps for e-mail, calendar, contacts, and backup.

How This Book Is Organized

This book is broken into five main parts, each of which explains how to perform specific tasks on the Motorola Xoom.

Part 1: Introducing the Motorola Xoom

This part of the book introduces the Xoom and its parts. It walks you through removing the Xoom from the box, removing the packaging, and charging the Xoom for the first time. It describes how to add more storage space by inserting a new memory card.

Part I also explains how to turn the Xoom on and off, and control it by touching or typing on its screen. Finally, it explains all your Xoom's lights, buttons, and ports, and translates the messages displayed on different portions of the screen.

Part II: Staying Connected

Like a car without a freeway, the Xoom doesn't really shine until it's connected to something — another computer, the Internet, another gadget, or your friends. In this part of the book, you discover how to connect your Xoom with the Internet, your computer, and a data service (if you've paid your cellular provider for its data plan).

Part II explains how to stay connected with your friends on your Xoom, through e-mail, contact lists, Google Calendar, and your social networks. It also describes how to connect the Xoom with keyboards and headphones, should you feel the urge to do so, as well as how to connect it to your high-definition television set, home stereo, and digital camera.

Chapter 9 explains how to use *apps:* small programs that came with your Xoom or that you can download online.

Part III: Digesting Media

Unlike PCs and laptops, tablets work best by letting you consume information created by other people. This part of the book explains all you need to know about listening to music, watching movies and photos, reading books, and navigating with maps.

Part IV: Tweaks

Eventually, some part of the Xoom will need a tweak, either to make it run faster or mesh with your needs more tightly. In this part, you find out how to change your Xoom's settings, as well as customize its appearance and behavior. You see how to keep your Xoom running smoothly and how to fix it when the going gets rough.

Finally, if something truly awful happens, this part explains how to perform a factory reset, which lets you start from scratch.

Part V: The Part of Tens

These easily digestible nuggets of information work well in a list format: Ten Essential Free Apps, Ten Essential Tricks 'n' Tips, and Ten Handy Accessories. (Check out the Bluetooth keyboard that lets your Xoom move one step closer to a laptop.)

Icons Used in This Book

Like all *For Dummies* books, this one contains four standard icons.

The Tip icon calls out special time savers or easier ways to do things.

Do these important things, and your life will be easier.

Don't do these things, or both you and your Xoom will regret it.

Don't bother reading these sections unless you're looking to boost your nerd cred.

Other icons in this book's margins represent the different icons that appear on your Xoom's screen. When one of the steps tells you to touch a certain icon, you see that icon both next to the step in the book and on your Xoom's screen.

Where to Go from Here

If you can keep your hands off your shiny new Motorola Xoom for a while, start flipping through the pages. The index pinpoints pages with specific information; the table of contents guides you toward more general coverage.

Or simply start browsing in the first chapter, flipping pages until you've fully charged your newly purchased Motorola Xoom. Enjoy!

Part I
Introducing the Motorola Xoom

The 5th Wave   By Rich Tennant

©RICHTENNANT

"Of course your Xoom lets you watch videos, listen to music, and surf the web. But does it shoot silly string?"

In this part . . .

Welcome to the world of the Motorola Xoom. (It's pronounced *zoom* because *exhume* lacks sparkle.)

Consider this part of the book to be your care-and-feeding guide, designed to help you through the first few days after you bring home your new Xoom. It explains how to charge it for the first time, how to handle its first waking words, and how to carry on a conversation through its touchscreen.

Finally, after you've met your Xoom's first needs, find out in this part how to make the thing start meeting your own.

v minutes.

Start Here

In This Chapter

▶ Removing the Xoom from its box

▶ Giving the battery a charge

▶ Identifying the Xoom's pieces

▶ Getting the computer drivers and software you need

▶ Checking your Xoom for missing features

▶ Inserting memory and SIM cards

*T*he Motorola Xoom is a tablet computer — a new breed of computer that resembles a laptop with a lopped-off keyboard, which you control by poking the screen with your fingers. Your Xoom tablet is many things rolled into one: a music player, movie viewer, e-book reader, web browser, and e-mail system.

It's quite intelligent, actually. It listens to your commands and dutifully trots off to do your bidding — be that bidding fetching the latest news or grabbing your e-mail. What it won't do, unfortunately, is extricate itself from its box, set itself up, and tell you whether anything's missing.

That's where this chapter comes in. It explains how to remove your shiny new tablet and accessories from the box, charge its battery, and peel away the plastic packaging film. If you bought a memory card to add more storage space, this chapter also explains how to maneuver that tiny card into the even tinier spot in your Xoom.

While you wait for your Xoom's battery to charge, read how to prepare your desktop computer to recognize your Xoom, making the first Xoom–computer hookup much less awkward.

Finally, this chapter explains why certain things may be mysteriously missing from your Xoom and (if Motorola's promises come true) when those items will magically appear.

The Grand Unboxing

The Xoom's gray cardboard box opens much like a box of candy. Pull off the top, and the Motorola Xoom sits inside, neatly wrapped in plastic and sitting on top of a pile of goodies.

Here are the sweet things hiding inside the box:

Your Motorola Xoom: Your Xoom tablet can be either of two models. One type can access both Wi-Fi and cellphone towers for "always on" Internet. The other model connects to the Internet only through Wi-Fi networks.

And which version sits in your hands? You can tell by looking at the white bar-code-ridden sticker on your Xoom's cardboard box, shown in Figure 1-1, as well as the sticker on the back of the Xoom's plastic wrap.

Look for the letters *MZ* followed by three numbers to see the model number, which determines how the device can connect with the Internet. Here's the rundown:

Model Number	Capabilities
MZ600	United States: Verizon Wireless data service and Wi-Fi
MZ601/MZ603	Asia/Europe: AT&T and Sprint data service and Wi-Fi
MZ604	All regions: Wi-Fi only; no cell data service

If you're in the United States, for example, a model MZ600 Xoom can connect to both Wi-Fi *and* the cellphone network (if you pony up the money to your cellular carrier for a data plan, that is). The MZ604, by contrast, costs less because it's limited to Wi-Fi Internet access.

Manuals: You'll probably find the following manuals and papers inside the box:

- *Master Your Device:* This 20-page manual explains the basics of your Xoom. It's too skimpy to be of much use.

- *Future Ready:* This pamphlet, if included, explains that your Xoom can be upgraded to 4G (a topic that I cover in this chapter's "Checking Your

Xoom for What's Missing" section). You can also find instructions online at `www.verizonwireless.com/xoom4glteupgrade`.

✔ *Important Consumer information:* Here's some oh-so-boring information about Federal Communications Commission rules and regulations.

✔ *Consumer Information about Radio Frequency Emissions and Responsible Driving:* This booklet contains even *more* boring information about radio-frequency emissions, as well as common-sense warnings about playing with your Xoom while driving.

✔ *Product Safety and Warranty Information:* This item explains that the glass will break when the Xoom is dropped, among other things, and that you shouldn't try to dry a wet Xoom in a microwave oven. Your eyes may light up when you read about the warranty, though: It's for one year, detailed in five pages of fine print.

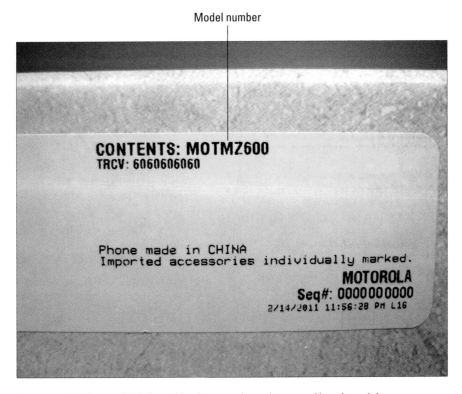

Model number

CONTENTS: MOTMZ600
TRCV: 6060606060

Phone made in CHINA
Imported accessories individually marked.

MOTOROLA
Seq#: 0000000000
2/14/2011 11:56:28 PM L16

Figure 1-1: The letters *MZ* followed by three numbers show your Xoom's model.

Micro USB cable: The bundled USB cable has a normal USB port on one end and a tiny micro USB port on the other end. (Don't confuse *micro* with *mini* when you're shopping for a replacement or second cable.) To transfer files between the Xoom and your PC, plug the tiny end into the bottom of your Xoom and the large end into your PC. (I cover file transfers in Chapter 5.)

Unlike most gadgetry, the Xoom can't charge its battery through its USB cable. The USB cable *only* lets you transfer files and other information. To charge your Xoom, you must use either the bundled AC adapter or the car charger that's sold separately.

Charger (AC adapter): Like most chargers, the Xoom's charger is a black boxy thing known as a "wall wart" with a long black cable. The black boxy end plugs in to the wall; the cable's tiny pinlike plug fits into the tiniest hole in the bottom of your Xoom. Examine that tiny pinlike plug closely. If you buy an auto charger, you'll need one with that same-size plug.

To keep the charger as small as possible, the outlet's prongs fold inward when not in use. You can flip them in and out fairly easily with your fingers.

Charging the Battery

Your Xoom's battery may be partially charged on arrival. To eliminate potential problems, though, you should fully charge the battery before turning on your Xoom.

Should I keep my Xoom plugged in?

Extending your Xoom's battery life will quickly become a priority. Should the battery die while you're on the road, your tablet would turn into an expensive Etch A Sketch, so it's tempting to leave it plugged in all the time while you're at home.

Resist that temptation, though. Your Xoom's batteries are designed to be charged to the brim and then fully run down. If you leave the Xoom plugged in, the batteries can become lazy and stop holding their full charge as long as they should.

So charge your Xoom, use up the batteries, and then leave the tablet plugged in overnight to recharge fully. Don't leave it plugged in constantly when you're using it at home.

To charge the battery, follow these steps:

1. **Fold out the charger's prongs so that they extend from the charger's base.**

   The charger is cleverly designed to slip easily into suitcases; its prongs fold into a notch on the charger itself. Pull the prongs outward, and they snap into place.

2. **Push the charger's prongs into the wall outlet.**

   Any wall outlet will do; you don't need a three-prong outlet.

   If the charger covers both outlets, turn the charger around so that it's facing away from the other outlet. That leaves you room to plug in a second gadget.

3. **Plug the charge cable's tiny prong into the tiny charger port on the Xoom's bottom side, as shown in Figure 1-2.**

   On the bottom of your Xoom, you'll spot a tiny hole that matches the pinlike plug on the end of your charger's cable. Push the plug into the hole until it snaps into place.

Figure 1-2: Push the tiny prong on the end of the charger cable into the tiny hole on the bottom end of your Xoom.

When it's plugged in, the Xoom shows its first signs of life: A little light near the charger's plug begins glowing. This light glows a frightening red when the battery's power drops below 15 percent, turns white when battery power ranges from 15 percent to 95 percent, and shines bright green when the battery charge is 95 percent or greater.

If your battery ever drops below a 4-percent charge level, your Xoom turns off automatically. If you want to keep working, you must plug your Xoom into a charger.

4. **Keep charging until the little light turns green, which can take one to three hours.**

5. **Unplug your Xoom and start playing with it as I describe in the next chapter.**

 ✓ The charger light comes on only if your Xoom is *turned off* while charging.

 ✓ Unlike most portable gadgets, your Xoom hides its battery deep within its innards, where you can't remove or replace it even if you want to. You need to take your Xoom to an authorized Motorola service center to have the battery replaced.

 ✓ Motorola warrants that your battery will hold at least 50 percent of its charge within your first year of purchase.

Should your battery go bad or not hold a 50-percent charge within a year, contact Motorola to have it replaced. You can visit the Support area on Motorola's Xoom web page (www.motorola.com/xoom) or call Motorola directly at (800) 734-5870.

Peeling Off the Plastic

While you're waiting for your Xoom to charge, peel off the protective screen covering on its front and back. Grab the plastic by one corner and give it a slow pull, as shown in Figure 1-3. The front covering comes off fairly easily and in one piece.

The plastic surrounding the back and sides probably breaks into pieces, making your job a little tougher.

 ✓ You can leave the front cover on, if you want, for use as a screen protector. The cover isn't designed for that purpose, though, so it not only obscures the screen, but also makes your front-facing camera shots a little blurry.

TIP

✔ Little labels on the plastic covering the front screen point out the positions of your Xoom's volume switch, webcam, webcam light, notification light, and charging light. (I point out all those things and more in Chapter 3.)

✔ The plastic surrounding the back and sides probably breaks into pieces when you remove it, making your job a little tougher.

Figure 1-3: Grab hold of the plastic by the corner and carefully peel it off your screen.

Downloading USB Drivers and Software for Your Desktop Computer

Your Xoom works as a self-contained unit; you never need to connect it with your desktop computer or laptop. But if you want to transfer large files between your Xoom and your desktop computer, you want to connect the two devices. (I explain how to connect your Xoom with a computer to transfer files in Chapter 5.)

You'll run into problems if you simply plug your Xoom into your computer or laptop, however. Computers won't always recognize a Xoom when it's plugged in.

So while you're waiting for the battery to charge, download and install this software on your desktop computer.

Windows XP, Windows Vista, or Windows 7 USB drivers: Windows PCs usually recognize USB gadgets as soon as they're plugged in to a USB port. The Xoom's an exception; it requires special USB drivers. The easiest way to install those USB drivers is to download and run MotoHelper software from this page on Motorola's website:

```
www.motorola.com/Support/US-EN/Support-Homepage/Software_and_
                Drivers/USB-and-PC-Charging-Drivers
```

Mac OS X computers: Download Android File Transfer from the Android website:

```
www.android.com/filetransfer
```

Download and install the right software for your type of computer — MotoHelper for Windows PCs or Android File Transfer for Mac OS X computers. Then, when you connect your computer and your Xoom in Chapter 5, they'll embrace like old friends.

Checking Your Xoom for What's Missing

Although you paid full price, you may not have received everything as advertised. The Xoom was missing a few things when it first shipped.

If your Xoom didn't come with the following items, you have one of those first Xooms. You can get most of these things fixed for free by Motorola, though. Here's the scoop:

Memory-card support: Your Xoom comes with a slot along its top side where you can slip in a memory card. Adding a 32GB memory card, for example, would double your Xoom's storage space to 64GB. Unfortunately, your Xoom can't recognize any SD cards. Google promises to issue a free update to let the Xoom notice and begin using those cards. (I describe how to insert memory cards later in this chapter.)

To see whether your Xoom has received the update for memory card support, touch Apps⇨Settings⇨Storage. If your SD Card update has arrived, that screen will list an entry for External Storage.

Adobe Flash support: Although Motorola made Flash a major selling point, the Xoom doesn't support Flash out of the box. Without Flash, you won't be able to view some websites and web videos. (Fortunately, the lack of Flash support also means that you can't see annoying ads on many websites.)

To download your Xoom's Adobe Flash update, visit the Android Market, covered in Chapter 9, and download Flash Player by Adobe Systems.

4G support: Many cellular carriers are rapidly updating their cellphone networks to something called 4G, which is faster than the current 3G speed. Your Xoom doesn't support 4G, but Motorola promises to upgrade your Xoom to 4G for free. The catch? You must mail your Xoom to Motorola inside a prepaid box and wait about six business days for its return. For more details, visit Verizon's "getting ready" page here:

```
http://support.vzw.com/information/xoom_grg.html
```

Music store: Google mentioned that it would provide a Xoom music store where you could buy music online and send it straight to your tablet. The music store wasn't finished before the Xoom hit the shelves, but Google will most likely send it in a free update. When it does, you'll find it in the Android Market, described in Chapter 9.

HDMI cable: A little jack on the bottom of your Xoom lets you plug in an HDMI cable and connect your Xoom to a high-definition television (HDTV) set. Motorola didn't toss a cable into the box, though, nor did they promise one. But if you want to view your Xoom on an HDTV set, you must buy your own HDMI cable. It's a special cable with a micro HDMI plug on one end and a normal HDMI plug on the other. (I explain how to connect your Xoom to a HDTV in Chapter 5.)

Accepting updates

When Motorola, Google, or one of their partners finishes an update for your Xoom, they send the notice to your Xoom. The update notice subsequently appears on your screen the next time your Xoom connects with the Internet, either through Wi-Fi or your cellular provider's data plan.

When you spot an Android Update notice, touch the button labeled Install or Restart & Install to begin installing the update.

By accepting the updates, you keep your Xoom up-to-date with today's ever-changing technology for as long as possible.

Upgrading Storage with a Memory Card

Your Xoom comes with 32GB of storage. That's enough for about 20,000 e-books, 2,500 songs, or a half-dozen high-definition movies. Songs, books, and movies come in different sizes, of course, so your own mileage may vary.

Need more storage space? You can add it by buying a memory card and sliding it into the card slot on your Xoom. The Xoom requires either a *microSD* (Micro Secure Digital) or *microSDHC* (Micro Secure Digital High Capacity) memory card, like the one shown in Figure 1-4. Commonly used in cellphones and some small digital cameras, these fingernail-size pieces of plastic come in sizes of 2GB, 4GB, 8GB, 16GB, and 32GB.

What's the difference among Wi-Fi, 3G, and 4G?

Wi-Fi, 3G, and 4G all refer to different ways to access the Internet. The biggest difference? The speed at which information can flow into your Xoom.

Speed isn't a big deal when you're merely browsing websites, but you need speed for downloading large files or watching Internet video. Without fast speeds, your YouTube video will keep stopping and starting, waiting for more data to arrive.

Here's the rundown:

✔ **Wi-Fi:** The fastest speed, Wi-Fi lets gadgets talk through the same wireless networks computers have been using for years. If you've set up a wireless network in your home, your Xoom can use that network. Alternatively, you can drop by a coffee shop that offers Wi-Fi and access the Internet that way. Wi-Fi is almost always faster than 3G, and it's not subject to any data-plan limits imposed by your cellphone provider.

✔ **3G:** Most *smartphones* — phones that let you chat with your friends *and* access the Internet — send and receive information at 3G (third-generation) speeds. Although it's not as fast as wireless, 3G was once considered to be the fastest you could expect from a cellphone's data connection.

✔ **4G:** As technology races ever forward, the new 4G (fourth-generation) networks scoot Internet information to phones and tablets up to ten-times more quickly than 3G networks. 4G networks work in only a few dozen major cities right now, but 4G is the future. Verizon, for example, promises to switch all its towers to 4G by the end of 2013.

Straight out of the box, Motorola's Xoom works at either Wi-Fi or 3G speed, switching to whatever's faster at the time. Motorola says it will update your Xoom to 4G capability for free if you mail your Xoom to Motorola for an update. (I explain more about 4G upgrades in "Checking Your Xoom for What's Missing" earlier in this chapter.)

Figure 1-4: You can add memory with a microSD or microSDHC memory card up to 32GB.

The Motorola Xoom won't recognize memory cards until Google releases an update, which should arrive in your Xoom automatically. I describe how to check for updates in Chapter 16.

To insert a memory card into your Xoom, follow these steps:

1. **Turn off your Xoom.**

   Hold in the power button until the Xoom asks, "Would you like to shut down?" Touch OK to shut down, and wait until the screen goes blank.

2. **Slide the slot cover out from the top of the Xoom, and set it aside.**

   Place a fingernail in the little notch, and pull the little black plastic tray straight out. The tray will hold either a SIM card or a little clear plastic SIM-card placeholder. Set the tray aside, being careful not to let the SIM card or placeholder fall out. (If it falls out, align the card's notch with the notch in the tray; that lines everything up so that the card fits correctly.)

   Now that you've removed the tray with the SIM card, you need to remove the little plastic placeholder for the memory card, which hides inside an even *smaller* slot.

3. **Turn your Xoom with the glass face down; then pull out the clear plastic memory-card placeholder, as shown in Figure 1-5.**

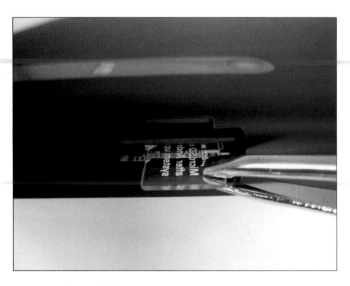

Figure 1-5: Place the Xoom glass side down on a towel, and pull out the clear placeholder card with tweezers.

You'll probably need tweezers for this delicate operation, as you're working in *very* cramped quarters.

As you remove the plastic placeholder, note the position of the plastic card's notches; the notches on your memory card must face in the same direction for the card to fit.

4. Slide the new card into the now-vacant slot.

The card fits in only one way, so if it's not sliding in smoothly, flip it over and try again. Again, tweezers may help you position it just right, as shown in Figure 1-6.

5. Slide the tray back into the slot.

Make sure that the tray contains either the plastic SIM placeholder or, if you've upgraded your Xoom to 4G speed, the actual SIM card.

 ✔ The memory card fits in only one way: the right way. If it's not fitting in smoothly, make sure that you're sliding it into the right slot.

 ✔ The notches of the card must line up with the notches inside the slot. You may need to turn the card upside down for it to fit.

What's new in Android 3.0?

Your Xoom runs Google's Android 3.0 operating system. Like Windows on a PC, Android controls your Xoom, runs programs, juggles memory and storage space, and keeps things running smoothly.

Android 3.0 introduces some improvements over earlier Android versions, which lived primarily on cellphones. If you've already used Android on a cellphone, here are the improvements you'll notice in Android 3.0:

- Support for larger screens
- New music player and music store
- New video player, video recording software, and video editor

- Three-dimensional desktop for easier navigation
- Web browser with tabbed pages, automatic form fill, bookmark syncing with Google Chrome, and private browsing
- Video chat support through Google Talk and similar chat programs
- Support for a larger keyboard and faster, more powerful hardware

Google will undoubtedly keep tweaking Android 3.0, so don't be surprised when an update arrives to give your Xoom more features or fixes existing problems.

Figure 1-6: Slide the memory card into the tiny slot until it stops.

What's New in Android 3.1?

Shortly after your Xoom connects with the Internet through either Wi-Fi or your cellular data plan, you'll see updates waiting to be downloaded. Always download the updates, as they add new features to your Xoom and fix old problems.

The biggest update, Android 3.1, arrived in May, 2011. Once downloaded and installed, Android 3.1 adds these enhancements to your Xoom:

Support for USB accessories: Your Xoom's USB port now lets you plug in keyboards, mice, joysticks, and digital cameras for viewing or transferring photos.

Scrollable recent apps display: Pushing the Recent Apps button, covered in Chapter 3, fetches thumbnail photos of your five last-used apps. The list now scrolls, letting you see more apps.

Resizable widgets: Information-filled windows called *widgets*, which I cover in Chapter 9, constantly update their information. The update lets you adjust a widget's size, letting you decide how much information it should display.

Mouse support: Plugging in a mouse places a mouse cursor on the screen, letting you point at, tap, select, drag, and scroll through items onscreen.

Enhanced browser: Faster than before, the browser now lets you save pages for offline viewing, handy when traveling through areas with no Internet coverage.

Fully searchable contacts: You can now search any text on a contact's page, not just his or her name.

To see the version of Android running on your Xoom, touch Apps➪Settings➪About Tablet. The version number appears in the Android Version area, shown in Figure 1-7.

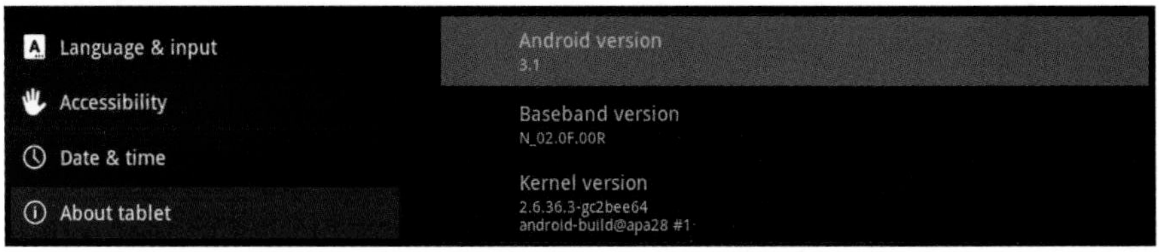

A Language & input	Android version 3.1
✋ Accessibility	
🕐 Date & time	Baseband version N_02.0F.00R
ⓘ About tablet	Kernel version 2.6.36.3-gc2bee64 android-build@apa28 #1

Figure 1-7: The Android Version area displays your current version of Android.

2

Setting Up Your Motorola Xoom

*W*hen most people learn to drive, they practice by driving in a parking lot, usually with an anxious parent clutching the passenger seat.

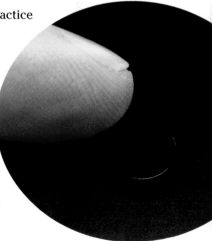

Driving certainly isn't the only activity that requires practice and training. The salespeople at your local electronics store, for example, began training to use the Motorola Xoom three days before the little gizmos went on sale at their stores.

Their training probably involved how to shuttle you to the cash register fastest. This chapter offers far more practical training.

Now that you've charged your Motorola Xoom, as described in Chapter 1, you're ready to take it for its first test drive — figuring out the ignition lock, making sure the papers are in order, and turning it off again so you can catch your breath.

Setting Up a Google Account

Before you even turn on your Xoom, you should create a Google account, and here's why: Google created the operating system that runs the Motorola Xoom, and your entire Xoom experience centers on your Google account.

A Google account gives you e-mail (called Gmail) and a place to store your contacts and appointments. When that information's in your Google account, it automatically appears on your Xoom; you needn't reenter it.

It's much easier to create a Google account on a desktop PC, but if you want to give it a try on your Xoom, head to `http://mail.google.com/mail/signup`.

To create a Google account on your desktop computer, head to `www.google.com`; click the words *Sign In* in the top-right corner of the page; and then follow the instructions to create a username and password. Now you'll have that precious Google account to enter when you set up your Xoom as I show you later in this chapter.

You also get these benefits with a Google account:

- **Back up your info:** Your Google account lets you back up your Xoom to Google's servers. If you lose or damage your Xoom, your information will reappear on your new device as soon as you enter your Google username and password.

- **Sync with other Android devices:** If you own an Android phone, your Google contact and calendar information automatically appear on your phone as well.

- **Sync with everything:** If you ever update your information on any device, that information automatically updates itself on *all* your Google devices: your PC, Xoom, and Android phone.

Turning on Your Motorola Xoom

Unlike most gadgets, the power button isn't in an easily accessible location. That button's on the back, about an inch from the top-right corner and almost directly behind the Motorola logo on the front of the device.

To turn on your Xoom, press and hold the power button on the back of your tablet, as shown in Figure 2-1. (Look for a little padlock on the button.)

Figure 2-1: To turn on your Xoom, press and hold the power button on the back.

After a second or two, the round red Motorola/Batman logo appears, along with the words *DualCore technology.* A few seconds later, a glowing, purple honeycomb appears. Before any bees emerge, the honeycomb melts away, and about 30 seconds later, your Xoom's alive and waiting for your first touch.

✔ Be sure to charge the device with its bundled adapter, as described in Chapter 1, before starting to play with it. The Xoom doesn't always come out of the box fully charged.

✔ You need to hold down the power button for only a few seconds when you start the Xoom. Most of the time, your Xoom will simply be *sleeping,* not turned off. When it's sleeping, a quick push of the power button wakes it back up.

✔ Your Xoom goes to sleep quite frequently. You'll find yourself pushing that button again and again, wondering why it's not located on the easier-to-reach *front* of the Xoom. (I explain how to change your Xoom's napping behavior in Chapter 15.)

Completing Initial Setup

After you've charged your Xoom (see Chapter 1) and turned it on (see the preceding section), the screen asks you to follow a series of steps. These steps introduce you to your Xoom and give it permission to know certain things about you and about its location.

There's nothing really creepy in this arrangement. After all, a friend who knows nothing about you won't be as helpful as one who knows some basic information, and your Xoom's certainly trying to help you navigate life.

If the screen goes blank while you're following these steps, don't worry; your dutiful Xoom has just fallen asleep to extend its battery life. Nudge it awake by pressing and releasing the power button on the back.

1. **Change the language, if necessary.**

   In the United States, the Xoom comes set up for English menus. To change the language, touch the word *English* and then touch the name of your own language in the drop-down menu.

2. **Touch the word Start and wait patiently for a cellular connection. If you're not paying a cellular provider for a data plan, touch Skip. Touch Next when activation is complete.**

   If you touch Start, your tablet immediately tries to activate your data-plan service with your cellular provider. If your Xoom lacks a data plan, touch Skip to bypass activation.

   When you see the words *Activation Complete,* your Xoom has connected successfully with your cellphone provider (see Figure 2-2).

   If activation fails, touch Back to try again. (You may need to be closer to a cellphone tower.) If activation *still* fails, move on to the next step to try to make a Wi-Fi connection.

   Even if your Xoom activates through a cellular provider, you will still want to set up a Wi-Fi connection in the next step. (You *need* a working Internet connection to set up your Xoom.)

3. **Set up a Wi-Fi network and then touch Next.**

   If it *still* fails, click Next to try to connect to a Wi-Fi connection. The Wi-Fi setup screen appears, listing all the Wi-Fi networks within range. Touch an existing network (and type a password, if requested) to connect to the Wi-Fi network.

   Is no Wi-Fi network available? Touch Skip for now, and set up your Wi-Fi connection later (see Chapter 5).

Figure 2-2: Touch Next when activation is complete.

4. **Approve or disapprove of Google's location service; then touch Next.**

   Before your Xoom can help you with basic searches, it needs to know your location. After all, you don't care about ATMs that *aren't* nearby.

   Google offers two location-based options:

   - *Allow Google's Location Service to Collect Anonymous Location Data. Collection Will Occur Even When No Applications Are Running:* Approving this lets Google update its cellular and Wi-Fi location maps as you travel, speeding up your location-based searches.

   - *Allow Google to Use Location for Improved Search Results and Other Services:* If you plan to travel, choose this option as well. When Google knows your location, it can provide quick searches for "Closest gas station" or "Closest restaurant with extra-crispy fries".

   If you think that Google's a stalker by wanting to know your location, deselect either option, or both options, by touching the checked boxes. When you search later, you can manually choose to give Google access to your location.

5. **Touch Next to sign in with your Google account information or create a new account. Or click Skip to create an account later.**

Google created your Xoom's software, so it's no surprise to find that your Xoom relies heavily on Google's services. A Google account gives you e-mail; automatic backups of your Xoom's bookmarks, apps, and settings; and access to many other features — if you don't clear the approval check box.

Whether you enter your Google account information now or choose Skip, you end up at the Xoom's home screen (see Figure 2-3). If you want to jump right into exploring the home screen, turn to Chapter 3.

If you enter your Google account, Google silently begins stocking your Xoom with your contacts, calendars, and e-mails.

Figure 2-3: When you finish making choices, you land at Xoom's home screen.

✔ It's much, much easier to set up a new Google account on a desktop computer. That keyboard's much faster, and setting up an account can require lots of typing before you find a username that's not already taken.

✔ Chances are, your Xoom will download a few updates when you complete the setup process. Be sure to approve each update, as each update adds important features to your Xoom.

✔ If you have a Wi-Fi network in your home or office, be sure to set up your Wi-Fi connection, covered in Chapter 5. Wi-Fi works faster than a cellular connection, and it's free.

✔ To enter a Google account in your Xoom later, visit Chapter 6, where you enter your Google account information to create an e-mail account.

✔ Were you unable to find an Internet connection? Your Xoom will repeat some of these steps the next time you turn it on or wake it up. Your Xoom *needs* the Internet to download software updates, bug fixes, and other information.

✔ After you complete these steps (and find an Internet connection), you needn't be bothered with them again. You can still change your Xoom's language (which I cover in Chapter 15) and Wi-Fi choices (which I cover in Chapter 5) in the Xoom's settings area.

Locking, Unlocking, and Password-Protecting Your Xoom

When it's ignored for a few minutes, your Xoom acts like a cat: It goes to sleep. To rouse it from its slumber, press the power button on the back-right corner of the Xoom's case (refer to Figure 2-1 earlier in this chapter).

The Xoom wakes instantly, showing its ever-so-easy-to-break lock screen: a padlock icon enclosed in a tiny circle (see Figure 2-4). Touch the lock icon and drag it in any direction; then let go. You're inside your Xoom.

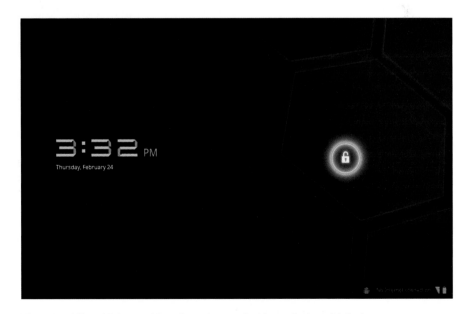

Figure 2-4: When it's ignored for a few minutes, the Xoom displays this lock screen.

Encrypting your Xoom

Adding password protection protects your Xoom from most office pranksters and casual handlers. To secure your information to the fullest extent, however, encrypt it. *Encryption* is a process that turns all your data into gibberish; you have to enter a secret code to see the real data. This process may be overkill for most people, but if your Xoom carries information more important than vacation photos and casual correspondence, encryption protects it from all but the most dedicated prying eyes.

Encryption takes an hour or more and requires your Xoom to have a fully charged battery *and* to be plugged in to its charger. Keep your Xoom plugged in until the screen says that the encryption process is complete. If your Xoom loses power during this process, you'll lose some or all of your data.

To encrypt your Xoom's data, follow these steps:

1. **Touch the Apps button in the home screen's top-right corner.**

2. **Touch Settings; then touch Location & Security.**

3. **Touch Encrypt Tablet; then touch the Encrypt Tablet button.**

4. **Follow the onscreen instructions, including creating a password to access your information.**

5. **Write down that password, and keep it in a very, very safe place.**

   If you lose that password, you've also lost all the information in your Xoom. The only way out is a factory reset, which I cover in Chapter 16.

   The Xoom wakes up, asking for your preferred language, as in "Completing Initial Setup" at the beginning of this chapter.

Think about it, though. That simple lock won't stop your co-workers from getting inside your Xoom, either. Even worse, it won't stop somebody who's stolen your Xoom.

If you leave your Xoom without password protection, anybody can log on to your Xoom, read your e-mail, buy things from your accounts, and access your password-protected websites. To protect yourself from possible fraud, identity theft, and similar problems, set up a password immediately.

To protect itself from both office pranksters and ne'er-do-wells, you can enable different degrees of password protection that satisfy nearly anybody's convenience-to-security ratio.

To find a password level that meets your needs, follow these steps:

1. **Touch the Apps button in the top-right corner of the home screen (refer to Figure 2-3 earlier in this chapter).**

   The Xoom lists your currently installed apps. (I cover *apps* — small programs — in Chapter 9.)

2. **Touch the Settings icon; then touch Location & Security.**

   I cover the Settings area in Chapter 15.

3. **In the Lock Screen category, choose Configure Lock Screen.**

   The Xoom presents five levels of security, ranging from Off (which never locks the screen at all) to Password (which requires you to type a password for entrance).

   For a good compromise between security and convenience, choose Pattern. That setting requires you to slide your finger around a grid of dots in a certain direction to gain entrance. It's quick to use, easy to remember, and difficult for others to guess. In fact, if intruders can't guess it within five attempts, they must wait 30 seconds before trying again, slowing them down significantly.

4. **Choose your level of security, and touch Next.**

5. **Reenter your new password so that the Xoom knows you remember it.**

6. **Touch Confirm to finish.**

   Your new security level appears the next time your Xoom wakes up from sleep or shutoff.

Entering Your Owner Information

Now that your Xoom is running, password-protected, and ready for action, complete one last step: Enter your owner information. The computer equivalent of a "If found, please return to" tag, this information appears on the lock screen whenever your Xoom's turned on.

To enter owner information in your Xoom, follow these steps:

1. **Touch the Apps button in the top-right corner of the home screen.**

2. **Touch the Settings icon; then touch Location & Security.**

3. **In the Lock Screen category, choose Owner Info.**

4. **Tap the words *Enter text to display on the lockscreen.***

   The Xoom's onscreen keyboard appears, as shown in Figure 2-5.

5. **Touch the keys to type the message you want strangers to see on your lost Xoom at the laundromat.**

   You can hunt-and-peck the keys or touch-type, pressing each letter.

6. **Touch any of the other settings in the left column to save your work and move on.**

I give full instructions for using the Xoom's onscreen keyboard in Chapter 4. (If you don't care for typing on glass, I also explain how to simply dictate to the Xoom so that it types for you.)

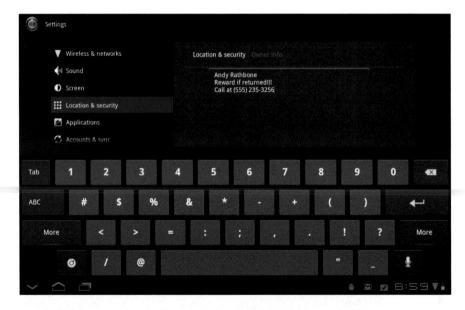

Figure 2-5: Type your name and contact information so that kind strangers can return your lost Xoom.

Turning Off Your Xoom

There's rarely a need to turn off your Xoom completely. The device watches its battery life more than you do. When it senses that you're doing something else, your Xoom simply goes to sleep. When you tap its power button, it wakes up instantly.

But if you *do* want to turn off your Xoom — perhaps because you're not going to use it for a while, or a flight attendant demands it — just hold in the power button on the back. The Xoom will ask, "Would you like to shut down?" (see Figure 2-6).

Touch OK to tell your Xoom to power down completely rather than just sleep.

✔ Your Xoom takes several minutes to power up again after being turned off. You don't want to turn it off and on again during the day; instead, let the Xoom simply go to sleep when it wants to.

✔ Powering off your Xoom also clears its memory of recently used programs. When you touch the Recently Used Programs button, nothing will appear.

Figure 2-6: To turn off the Xoom, hold down its power button and then touch OK.

How's a Xoom different from an Android smartphone?

The Motorola Xoom runs Android, which once was limited to cellphones, yet your Xoom can run apps written for Android smartphones. In fact, the Xoom resembles a huge cellphone. So exactly how *does* a Xoom differ from a cellphone?

There are four distinguishing factors:

✔ **The Xoom is bigger than a phone.** Unlike a cellphone, the Xoom doesn't limit your screen real estate. That makes the Xoom better for browsing websites and composing lengthy e-mails. Add a Bluetooth keyboard, and your Xoom's almost a full-fledged computer.

✔ **The Xoom can't make or receive phone calls.** When you sign up for a data plan, your Xoom receives a phone number, but it's just for billing purposes. If anybody tries to call your Xoom or send it a text message, you'll never know.

✔ **The Xoom can't vibrate.** You can set most cellphones to vibrate, letting you know silently that somebody's called or that a new message has arrived. Your Xoom doesn't have a built-in vibration feature, however. Apparently, the designers didn't think that you'd stuff it in a coat pocket and take it to the opera.

✔ **The Xoom runs Android 3.0.** The vast majority of smartphones still run Android version 2.0, 2.2, or 2.3, which are designed for smaller screens. Your Xoom runs the new Android 3.0, built specifically for tablets and their larger screens.

Otherwise, your Xoom is almost identical to an Android smartphone.

3

A Casual Walkthrough

In This Chapter

▶ Getting a grip on your Xoom

▶ Finding your Xoom's main parts

▶ Checking out the home screens

▶ Getting in touch with the navigation buttons

▶ Seeing notifications

Computers excel in certain niches. One computer can whip the experts on "Jeopardy!", for example, but it takes a completely different computer to win at chess and yet another to control the traffic lights at the intersection down the street.

Computers are so absorbed in their own unique problem-solving tasks that they pretty much ignore you. They never answer when you ask, "What does *this* button do?"

Because the Motorola Xoom's niche doesn't include self-awareness, this part of the chapter helps *you* figure out your Xoom's many parts: buttons, bars, lights, sensors, cameras, and icons. It describes how to hold the darn thing, gaze at the important areas of the screen, push the right plugs into the right holes, and decipher what those blinking lights are trying to tell you.

Holding Your Xoom

TV sets, radios, computers, and phones don't need "This Side Up" stickers, as it's obvious where to put them and how to hold them. The Motorola Xoom, by contrast, doesn't seem to care.

Sure, the screen points toward you, but otherwise, there's no recognizable feature that says, "Hold here." So how *do* you hold it?

Well, just pick it up and see which way feels right to you. No matter how you hold a Xoom, the screen orients itself to be right side up.

Try turning the Xoom around in your hands, first long side up and then wide side up. No matter which way you turn your Xoom, its screen always turns right side up, because the built-in compass always knows which way is up. (Also, when you're driving, the compass constantly updates a map to show the direction in which you're heading — a delight that I describe in Chapter 14.)

Depending on their current needs, people hold their Xooms in either of two ways:

- **Landscape mode:** Holding the Xoom with its Motorola/Verizon logos at the top gives you a wide viewing angle that's great for movies. It also lets you reach the power button easily, as your left index finger rests next to it.

  A few programs and features (such as the camera) run only in landscape mode, forcing you to hold your Xoom that way.

- **Portrait mode:** When the Xoom is held in portrait mode, its screen becomes taller and narrower. Portrait mode lets you see more of a web page, although the words and pictures shrink a bit. You can also see more words on an e-book's page, which minimizes page turning.

  Most apps available for the Xoom were originally written for cellphones, which is why some apps insist that you hold the Xoom in portrait mode. As tablets grow in popularity, more apps will support both landscape and portrait modes.

Simply put, there's no right or wrong way to hold a Xoom. Experiment by tilting from landscape to portrait mode, watching the changes, and choosing the mode that works best for what you're doing.

Don't want the screen to keep squirming in different directions? Lock it in place by touching Apps in the top-right corner, touching Settings, and touching Screen. Finally, touch the box next to Auto-Rotate Screen to remove the check. (Repeat these steps to toggle autorotation back on.)

Your Xoom's Parts: Buttons, Lights, Cameras, and Ports

Although your Xoom can speak — a helpful feature when it's guiding you through treacherous intersections in unfamiliar neighborhoods — it's mostly silent. That's a good thing, actually. Robots aren't very good at small talk.

Instead, your Xoom communicates mostly through a series of short beeps and blinking lights.

Unlike the lights you see flashing in science-fiction movies, the lights are quite understated. Nothing warns of pending explosions. Most of the communication comes from the main screen itself.

If you examine your Xoom closely, you'll spot not only lights, but also hidden cameras, a mysterious pair of unlabeled buttons, two speakers, and several unlabeled ports for plugging in cables. They're all identified and described in the next three sections.

Buttons, lights, and sensors

In a refreshing change of pace for gadgetry etiquette, there are only three hardware buttons. All the other buttons live on the screen itself, meaning that they disappear when the screen turns off.

Whether the screen's turned on or off, you'll usually see these few lights and buttons, as shown in Figure 3-1 and Figure 3-2.

- **Power button:** Covered in Chapter 1, this round button on the back (shown in Figure 3-2) turns on your Xoom or wakes it from sleep. You'll spend a lot of time pressing this button, as your lazy Xoom sleeps at any hint of neglect (to save battery life). A quick press of the power button wakes it back up; a long press turns it on or off.

- **Up/down volume buttons:** These buttons, located on the side near the Motorola logo, control the volume. Hold down or press the top button to increase the volume; press or hold down the bottom button to turn the volume down.

Down volume button
Up volume button
Memory card slot
Front-facing camera
Ambient light sensor
Headphone jack
Recording light
Notification light

Charging port
Micro USB port (black)
Charging light
Micro HDMI port (white)

Figure 3-1: Your Xoom's front.

✔ **Charging light:** This tiny light near the bottom edge (see Figure 3-2) glows only when the Xoom is turned off *and* being charged. It's red when the battery charge drops to its last 5 percent; white when the battery's powered between 5 percent and 95 percent; and a refreshing green when it's completely charged. I explain how to charge your Xoom in Chapter 1.

✔ **Notification light:** This light blinks slowly when something needs your attention — perhaps a newly arrived e-mail, an instant message, or a scheduled calendar event. It blinks only when your Xoom's sleeping, however, which lets your Xoom grab your attention without turning on the battery-hogging screen.

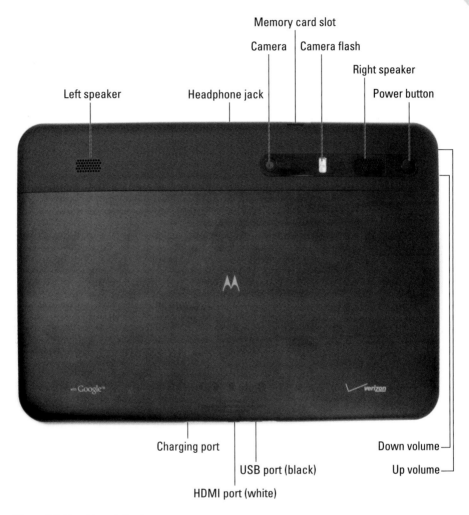

Figure 3-2: Your Xoom's back.

✔ **Live video/camera light:** This light glows red like a newsroom camera when you turn on your front-facing camera. (That way, you know when to smile.) The light doesn't glow at all when you switch to the back-facing camera. (I explain how to shoot photos and movies in Chapter 11.)

✔ **Ambient-light sensor:** This nearly invisible sensor along the top front edge constantly measures the surrounding light and automatically brightens or darkens the screen for best visibility.

Cameras and speakers

Your Xoom packs not one but *two* cameras and a set of stereo speakers to match. Both cameras can shoot photos and video, but they're meant for use in different situations.

Here's a quick rundown:

- **Front camera:** The 2-megapixel camera living on the top-front edge won't win any awards. It's more a vanity cam, designed for snapping quick Facebook profile photos and holding slightly blurred video chats with friends. (I describe video chats in Chapter 11.)

- **Back camera:** This higher-quality, 5-megapixel camera shoots both photos and high-definition video. Although awkward to hold, your Xoom's large screen helps you frame your photos more easily than the tiny screens on most digital cameras do. When a UFO finally lands across the street, you'll have high-definition footage to sell to CNN.

- **Stereo speakers:** Two speakers are mounted on back for stereo sound. Unfortunately, it doesn't record videos in stereo, but you'll hear stereo sound from any Hollywood-style blockbusters that you play back on your Xoom.

The rear-mounted speakers blast the sound *away* from you. For much better sound, plug your Xoom into a pair of desktop computer speakers or even a home stereo system.

I describe how to shoot still photos and video in Chapter 11.

Ports and their matching cables

The Xoom definitely took a tip from the cellphone playbook, because the connectors are about the size of a grain of rice. On the positive side, if you've bought a micro HDMI cable for a Droid X smartphone, that cable also works with the Xoom.

The bottom edge of your Xoom comes with the most connectors (see Figure 3-3), and the top edge offers two:

- **Micro USB port:** This tiny black port on the Xoom's bottom edge lets you transfer files between your Xoom and your Windows PC or Mac. The port is black so that you can distinguish it from the similarly shaped white micro HDMI port a quarter-inch away.

Unlike most USB gadgetry, the Xoom won't accept a charge from the USB port.

Your Xoom came bundled with one USB cable. If you buy a spare, be sure to buy a *micro* USB cable, not the more common *mini* USB cable.

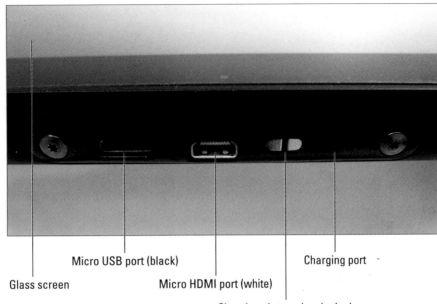

Micro USB port (black) Charging port

Glass screen Micro HDMI port (white)

Charging plates when in dock

Figure 3-3: You plug cables into these ports along your Xoom's bottom edge.

✔ **Micro HDMI port:** Also on the Xoom's bottom edge, this little white port lets you connect your Xoom to a high-definition TV set for showing off videos and photos, described in Chapter 5.

Your Xoom didn't come with a micro HDMI cable, though, so you'll need to buy one. Be sure to buy a *micro* HDMI cable rather than the more popular *mini* HDMI variety.

✔ **Microphone:** The Xoom has a tiny built-in microphone on its bottom edge. It's a little pin-prick of a hole living an inch to the right of the power jack.

✔ **Power jack:** On the Xoom's bottom edge, this small hole accepts the AC adapter's equally small plug to charge your Xoom as you slumber. (I describe how to charge your Xoom in Chapter 1.)

✔ **Memory-card slot:** This pull-out slot on the *top* of your Xoom contains clear plastic placeholders. Remove those plastic placeholders, and you can add two things: an extra memory card for extra storage and a SIM card if you upgrade to a cellular provider's faster 4G network. (I describe upgrading your Xoom with memory cards in Chapter 1.)

✔ **Headset jack:** The only connector on the Xoom's *top* edge, this little hole accepts standard mini headphones, the type bundled with MP3 players worldwide. For better sound quality, plug in desktop computer speakers. (You can also plug an iPod microphone in here for better recording quality.)

Welcome Home!: Touring the Home Screen

Your Xoom has lots of little lights, but you'll spend most of your time gazing at just one: Your Xoom's beautiful screen. The biggest light by far, the screen drains about 80 percent of your battery's power. That's why you have to forgive your Xoom for darkening the screen and sleeping so often.

Meeting the main home screen

When you first turn on and unlock your Xoom, you see the home screen, shown in Figure 3-4. The home screen works much like a traditional desktop; it's a workspace, free of coffee stains, that provides a home for your most important work tools. If you squint, it even looks a little like the Microsoft Windows desktop.

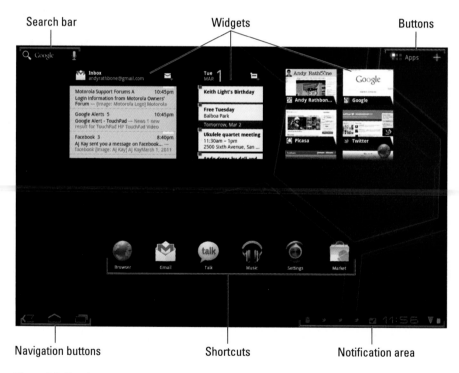

Figure 3-4: Your home screen appears whenever you turn on and unlock your Xoom.

Like any other desktop, it's completely customizable. You can make your home screen display your calendar, a list of your favorite programs (called *apps*) or perhaps views of your most-visited websites.

Whenever you turn on your Xoom, the home screen shows the following things:

- ✓ **Search bar:** Google's Search app lives in the top-left corner. It searches not only the Internet, but also everything stored on your tablet. To find something, tap the word *Google.* A keyboard appears, allowing you to type your search criteria. You can also touch the keyboard's microphone and tell the Xoom the term you want to find. (I cover the keyboard and microphone in Chapter 4.)

- ✓ **Shortcuts:** You create these push-button icons to launch different things: your favorite apps and websites, music playlists for road trips, or anything else you want to access quickly. Your Xoom comes preloaded with shortcuts to a web browser, Gmail, Google's Talk messaging program, a music player, e-book reader, and a shortcut to Google Market, for buying apps, books, and music.

- ✓ **Widgets:** These windows constantly update themselves with new information. A music widget, for example, displays information about the song you're currently playing, and a weather widget shows the current temperature. Some widgets are "stacked." YouTube's stacked widget, for example, lets you flip through your subscribed videos, much like flipping through cards in a Rolodex.

- ✓ **Navigation buttons:** These three ever-present buttons, which I discuss later in this section, help you navigate. From left to right, they're the Back, Home, and Recent Apps button, much like the ones found on earlier Android phones.

To return to the home screen, press the Home button, shown in the margin. The Back button returns you to your last-visited page, and the Recent Apps button fetches push-button thumbnails of your most recently used apps.

If your screen isn't bright enough, which frequently happens outdoors, crank up the brightness a notch. To do that, touch the Apps button, touch Settings, touch Screen, and touch Brightness. Clear the Automatic Brightness check box by touching it. Then slide the Brightness bar toward the right to make the screen brighter.

Getting to know the four other home screens

The desktop has plenty of room for storing various shortcuts, buttons, and widgets. But if you're feeling crowded, look to your four *other* home screens.

To see them, place your finger on the screen and drag to the left or right. As you drag, other screens come into view (see Figure 3-5) — two on the left side of the main home page and two on the right side of that page. To return to home central, press the Home button in the bottom-left corner.

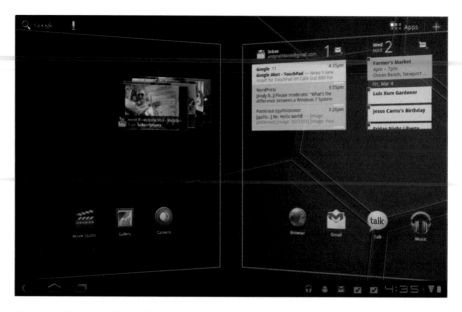

Figure 3-5: Drag your finger left or right to cycle among your home screens.

 Why does anybody need five screens? Your main home screen — the one you see when you press the Home button — should show your most important information, such as your e-mail inbox, upcoming appointments, and shortcuts to favorite programs.

You can make the home screens match your life rather than simply look pretty while sitting in Motorola's display kiosks. One of the four extra home screens can be dedicated to travel, for example, with shortcuts to maps, navigation aids, and hotel directories. Set aside another for work, with shortcuts to office programs, and yet another to videos and music. Keeping your home screens dedicated to different themes helps you stay organized.

✐ Dragging your finger on the screen, a task I cover in Chapter 4, is an integral way to move between items on your Xoom, be it flipping pages of a book, skipping through music during a song, moving down a long web page, or playing a game.

✐ I explain how to customize your home screens in Chapter 17.

Navigating with buttons

Most of your Xoom's buttons don't have physical counterparts. They live only when the screen's turned on. You use them by touching their little pictures, leaving an onscreen smudge mark with every tap.

Bottom-left corner

You'll become well acquainted with the bottom-left corner of the screen, which contains the buttons you'll touch most often. Here they are, from left to right:

✔ **Back/Close:** Depending on what you've just done, a press of the Back button returns to your last-visited website, closes a just-opened app, or moves back through a string of menus. When the Back button turns into the Close button — a downward-pointing triangle — you can press it to close the onscreen keyboard or remove a menu that's blocking the screen.

✔ **Home:** Touch this button to return to your main home screen, which is the desktop where you do most of your work.

✔ **Recent Apps:** This button displays thumbnail screen shots of the five apps you used most recently, as they appeared when you last used them. (You can still see that restaurant's phone number without having to reload the browser, for example.) To return to an app, just touch its thumbnail.

✔ **Menu:** This button appears only when you're running an app designed for an Android *mobile phone*. Those phones all came with four buttons, so the Xoom slips in this menu button to stay compatible. Pressing it brings up the menus for that older app.

Earlier versions of Android ran on tiny phones with tiny screens and limited room for buttons. To wring out the most functionality possible, the designers had some buttons perform different actions depending on whether they were pressed once, pressed twice, or held down for a second or two. The Xoom drops that behavior; it recognizes only a single press.

Top-right corner

The screen wears plenty of buttons down below but only two in the top-right corner, plus one that hides till you need it:

✔ **Apps:** *Apps* are mini programs that let you customize the Xoom to do your bidding. To see the preinstalled apps, tap the Apps button in the top-right corner of the screen. The Xoom immediately shows all your apps (see Figure 3-6).

To find and purchase more apps in the Android Market, tap the Market app's icon (refer to Figure 3-6). You can also send apps to your Xoom directly from your desktop computer's web browser by visiting the Android Market at `https://market.android.com`. (I describe apps — and show you how to download, launch, delete, and update them — in Chapter 8.)

✔ **Add:** This plus-sign button, shown in the margin, lets you customize your home screens by adding your favorite apps and shortcuts. (I discuss customizing in Chapter 17.)

✔ **Menu:** Hidden until it's needed, the Menu button fetches a menu for the currently running task, be it an app, widget, or web browser. This button is the *tablet* replacement for the Menu button on Android cellphones that lived in the bottom, left corner.

Figure 3-6: Touch the Apps button in the screen's top-right corner to see your apps.

Checking out the secret notifications panel

Located in the bottom-right corner of every screen, the notifications panel (refer to Figure 3-4, earlier in this chapter) is the Xoom's equivalent of a tap on the shoulder. Your dutiful Xoom always wants you to know the time, for example, so it places the clock in that corner.

When the Xoom notices other things, however, such as a newly received e-mail or a newly encountered Wi-Fi connection, the notifications panel displays a little icon to let you know. Touch that icon, and a pop-up window appears, showing more information about the notification (see Figure 3-7).

Figure 3-7: Touch an icon in the notifications panel for more information; click the X to close it.

If you've seen enough information, touch the pop-up window's little X to close the window and remove the icon. If you want to see more, as in the case of an e-mail message, just touch the pop-up window itself to see the message; then you can act on the e-mail or dismiss it as spam. (I cover e-mail in Chapter 6.)

When a cluster of notification icons appears, see all those icons quickly by touching the clock. You see not only the time, but also detailed information about every nagging icon, as shown in Figure 3-8. (Touch the Xs next to the notifications to close them one by one.)

Figure 3-8: Touch the clock, and the notifications panel lists all your notifications.

The notifications panel has one more trick up its sleeve. Touch the clock to bring up the panel shown in Figure 3-8; then touch the clock again. Wham! A list of handy settings appears (see Figure 3-9).

Here, you can switch quickly to airplane mode during flights, toggle your Wi-Fi connection or screen autorotate feature, change the screen's brightness, or turn off those annoying notification icons. You can also touch the Settings icon to access all your settings. (I cover the Settings area in Chapter 15.)

- The more you use your Xoom, the more you'll find yourself poking the notifications panel.

- When you watch a full-screen movie, the Xoom's bottom bar — including the buttons and the notifications panel — dims automatically so as not to interrupt your viewing pleasure. The buttons turn into tiny dots. Even if you can't see those dim dots, just poke in their general direction; the buttons reappear, letting you poke the right one.

Figure 3-9: Touch your notification panel's clock for access to frequently used settings.

Touching, Typing, and Talking to Your Xoom

In This Chapter

▶ Getting touchy with the screen

▶ Typing on the onscreen keyboard

▶ Checking your spelling as you type

▶ Cutting and pasting words

▶ Talking to your tablet

▶ Giving the Xoom voice commands

*L*ike most computers, the Motorola Xoom comes with a keyboard. Unlike most computers, the keyboard is made of glass, living directly on the screen. It pops up when needed and dutifully slinks away when you're through.

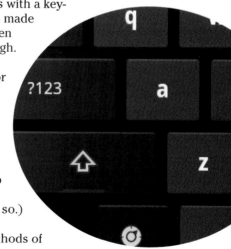

To type, you poke the glass keys with your fingers or thumbs. You can even touch-type, if you have small fingers.

If the onscreen keyboard is a little too clumsy, switch to Plan B: Touch the keyboard's little microphone icon and speak your commands. The Xoom carries them out. (Your commands will have to stop quite short of world domination, but the Xoom can dig up the closest coffee shop when you tell it to do so.)

This chapter covers both the typing and talking methods of making the Motorola Xoom do your bidding.

Touching the Screen

Most of your interaction takes place in the form of quick pokes on its Gorilla Glass screen. A soft touch with the end of a finger can accomplish an awful lot.

The Xoom recognizes much more than just finger jabs, though. Here's a breakdown of all the different finger movements your Xoom recognizes and when you should use them:

- ✔ **Tap:** The obvious choice, this gentle press-and-release movement lets you choose a specific item: an icon, a button, or a menu option. Most people tap with their index finger, but any digit does the trick.

  You needn't press hard. In fact, just holding your finger a fraction of an inch above the desired option will select it. Magic!

- ✔ **Double-tap:** Two taps in quick succession either zoom in or zoom out of an object. Double-tap an interesting area of a photograph or website to see a full-size view. Double-tap again to zoom back out, resizing the image to fit your screen.

- ✔ **Touch and hold:** Touching something and holding your finger pressed against the glass often brings up a menu. Touch and hold a word to select it for later copying and pasting, or touch and hold an unwanted photo, and then choose Delete from the pop-up menu. The touch-and-hold trick doesn't work on everything, but it's usually worth a try.

- ✔ **Drag:** Touch something and then drag your finger up, down, or sideways across the glass. Dragging your finger down a list or web page, for example, scrolls more portions of it into view. Dragging your home screen to the left or right reveals your other home screens, as described in Chapter 3. Also, touch the screen while a movie is playing, and a bar appears; drag the button on that bar to skip forward or backward through the movie.

- ✔ **Drag, hold, and drop:** This technique works much like dragging and dropping with a mouse, except that you use your finger. To move an icon on your home screen, for example, touch it, wait until it twitches, and then slide it with your finger to a new spot on the screen. When you lift your finger, the icon stays in its new resting place.

- ✔ **Flick:** Much like flicking a piece of dirt off the screen, flicking lets you scroll through a long list speedily. A quick flick keeps the list scrolling even after your finger leaves the glass. When your desired item scrolls into view, touch the screen again to stop the movement.

After you flick a list, a little bar appears along the list's edge, as shown in Figure 4-1. Drag that little bar up or down to move through the list quickly. As you drag the bar through an alphabetized list, a letter shows your location. When you spot the desired letter, remove your finger from the bar to stop scrolling at that spot.

✔ **Pinch:** Pinching works just like it sounds. When you pinch something on the screen, you zoom out. If you see only a person's large nose in a photo, for example, pinch the nose to shrink the photo and bring the rest of the face into view.

✔ **Spread:** The opposite of pinching, spreading involves placing two fingers together on the screen and then pulling them apart. When you're looking at a group photo, for example, spread your fingers over the person you want to see. As you spread your fingers, you zoom in to that portion of the image.

Pinching and spreading are easiest when you use an index finger and thumb.

Sliding bar

Current letter

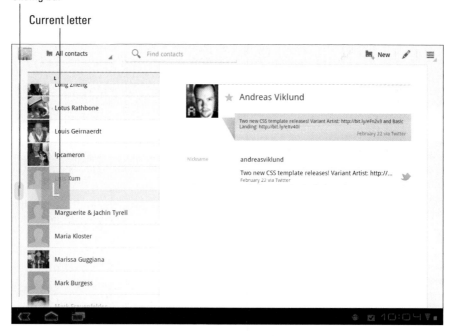

Figure 4-1: Flick the list and then slide the bar up or down to scroll by letter.

✔ **Rotate:** This technique lets you rotate Google's maps to a different view-ing position. Place two spread fingers on the screen and then rotate your hand, as though you're rotating a piece of paper on a table. The map moves along with your fingers. Remove your fingers to leave the screen in its new position. (I cover Google's maps in Chapter 14.)

Your Xoom won't recognize a plastic stylus, like the one you use to sign your name in the grocery-store checkout line, but it does recognize a stylus designed specifically for capacitive touchscreens. (Before pur-chasing a stylus, check its fine print to make sure it works on capacitive touchscreens.) A stylus lets you wear your gloves on cold days.

Working with the Glass Keyboard

Whenever you're expected to type something, you'll spot a familiar text box. But where's the keyboard? Touch inside the text box, and the onscreen key-board rears up, as shown in Figure 4-2. (To stow the keyboard away when you're through, press the Back/Return button, shown in the margin.)

Figure 4-2: Touch where you want to type, and the keyboard appears.

Just like a traditional keyboard, the keyboard lets you type letters, numbers, punctuation symbols, and even foreign characters.

- ✔ The keyboard is fairly intelligent and forgiving. Its built-in spell checker can be almost clairvoyant, as described in the next section.

- ✔ To end a sentence quickly, press the spacebar twice. That action adds a period and a space, and holds down the Shift key to capitalize the first word of your next sentence.

- ✔ As you type, your Xoom automatically capitalizes the first letter of your next sentence or paragraph, ensuring proper typography and nixing most Shift-key fumbles.

Fine-tuning the spell checker

Typing on a Xoom eventually confirms that a glass keyboard won't beat the real thing. Your Xoom knows this, so it watches your fingers and corrects your most obvious errors.

If you type *waterr* instead of *water,* for example, your Xoom notices your misspelling and, ever helpful, corrects the word automatically. It neither tells you nor asks permission; it just slips in the correct word.

This behavior however leads to a dilemma: What if you're describing an abstract art project called Waterr that you don't want autocorrected? Or what if your Xoom keeps changing your Ukrainian friend's last name?

You can always touch the Backspace key and change the autocorrection, but doing that becomes tiresome after a while. After all, aren't computers supposed to speed things up?

When you find yourself continually backspacing to correct the same overzealous correction, stop your Xoom's help by adding that troublesome word to its dictionary.

Follow these steps to stock your Xoom with words that it should leave uncorrected:

1. **Open the Settings area.**

   Touch the Apps button in the screen's top-right corner; then touch the Settings icon. (Consider putting a convenient shortcut to the Settings icon on your home screen, as I discuss in Chapter 17.)

2. **Touch Language & Input in the Settings area; then touch User Dictionary in the right panel.**

   The user dictionary appears, as shown in Figure 4-3. It's a sea of blank space until you begin adding words.

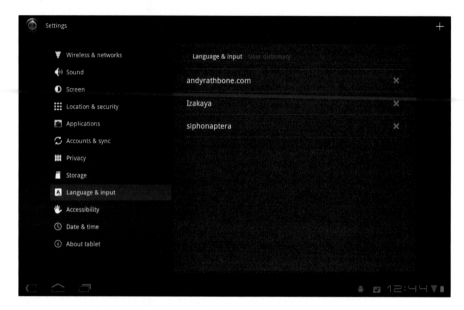

Figure 4-3: Add words to the user dictionary, and the Xoom stops trying to correct them automatically.

3. **Click the Add icon (shown in the margin) in the screen's top-right corner.**

   A screen appears to let you begin adding your own exceptions to your Xoom's dictionary.

4. **Type a word and touch OK to add it to the dictionary.**

   Your Xoom adds the word and retreats to Step 3. This time, however, the user dictionary lists the word you just added.

5. **Repeat Steps 3 and 4 until you've added all your words for this session. Then press the Home button, if desired, to return to your home screen.**

After you've added words to your dictionary, your Xoom no longer autocorrects them to something else. In fact, when you start to type some recognizable letters of your added word, Xoom jumps in, automatically finishing the word for you.

✐ Start stocking your user dictionary with your own last name, as well as your favorite abbreviations. Xoom owners in the workplace should also add the names of their company and products. Sprinkle in the names of your favorite ethnic restaurants, and you're off to a good start.

✐ Want to remove an unwanted word from the dictionary? In Step 2, touch the X next to the word (refer to Figure 4-3). The word drops from the list.

✐ You can add words to the user dictionary on the fly if you turn on the suggested-words list, which I cover in the next section.

Speeding up your typing

If your mind moves faster than your fingers can glide along the Xoom's keyboard, let your Xoom help you out. As you type, the Xoom can place a list of suggested words above the keyboard. With each letter you type, your Xoom lists words matching those letters (see Figure 4-4).

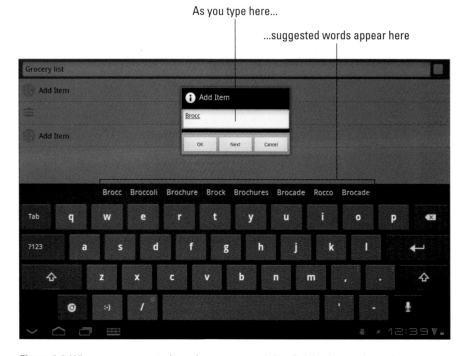

Figure 4-4: When your suggested word appears, touch it to finish what you're typing.

When you spot the word you're trying to type — *broccoli,* for example — touch it. Your Xoom instantly swaps that word for your first few pecks on the keyboard. Android phones have always had this suggested-words feature, but the Xoom comes with it turned off.

To turn on the suggested-words list, follow these steps:

1. **Open the Settings area.**

   Touch the Apps button in the screen's top-right corner; then touch the Settings icon.

2. **Touch Language & Input in the Settings area; then touch Configure Input Methods in the right panel.**

   The Android Keyboard Settings area appears.

3. **Touch Settings; then touch Show Correction Suggestions.**

   A pop-up menu appears.

4. **Choose Always Show.**

   Now, as you type, a list of suggested words appears above the keyboard, zeroing in on the word you're trying to type.

   ✔ To remove the suggested-words strip, follow these steps, but in Step 4, choose Always Hide.

   ✔ To show the suggested words only when you're holding the Xoom sideways (in portrait mode), choose Show on Portrait Mode in Step 4.

   ✔ Miss your keyboard's sound when you type a letter? While you're on the keyboard's Settings page, touch the box next to Sound on Keypress. That makes your Xoom click each time you touch a key.

   ✔ The suggested-words list has an added benefit: When you finish typing a word that wasn't suggested, touch and hold that word in the suggested words list until you see the word *Saved.* Your Xoom adds the word to your user dictionary (refer to "Fine-tuning the spell checker," earlier in this chapter) and includes it in the suggestions thereafter.

Typing special characters

Because the keyboard exists as lights on a pane of glass, the keys can change according to what you're trying to type. When you're typing a web address in your browser, for example, a key to the left of the spacebar types *.com* when you press it (see Figure 4-5). If you're typing an e-mail address, banned e-mail address characters like the exclamation point (!) disappear from the keyboard, thereby reducing misspellings.

TECHNICAL STUFF

Taming autocorrect's aggression level

Fulfilling the dream of students worldwide, your Xoom lets you choose how strictly it grades your spelling. To change the tightness of your Xoom's hair bun, touch Settings⇨ Language & input⇨Configure Input Methods⇨ Settings⇨Auto Correction. Then you can choose among three levels of spelling correction:

✔ **Off:** This setting disables autocorrection, leaving you on your own.

✔ **Modest:** This setting (the default) lets your Xoom autocorrect mostly short or commonly misspelled words. If you misspell a long,

uncommon word, the Xoom figures that you know what you're doing and leaves the word alone.

✔ **Aggressive:** This setting autocorrects both longer words and uncommon ones.

No matter what you choose, you can always backspace and overrule a correction.

Your best bet? Leave the autocorrect level set to Modest until you've stocked your user dictionary with most of your oddball words. Then switch to Aggressive to see whether you prefer it.

Figure 4-5: When you tap your browser's address bar, the lowercase keyboard sprouts a .com key to the left of the spacebar. Use it to enter website names quickly.

What if you want to enter characters that you *don't* spot on the keyboard? The Xoom handles that several ways. To access some common characters, press the ?123 key (shown at the far-left end of the keyboard in Figure 4-5). That key fetches the usual gang of numbers, as well as common punctuation symbols (see Figure 4-6).

Still not enough? Touch the More key (refer to Figure 4-6) to bring up more-esoteric symbols used for foreign currencies, mathematical equations, and other oddities (see Figure 4-7).

Figure 4-6: Touch the ?123 key to see this keyboard layout, featuring numbers and common punctuation symbols.

Figure 4-7: Touching the More key lets you type more esoteric symbols.

If that's *still* not enough, look closely at the keyboard back in Figure 4-5. See the little gray question-mark symbol in the top-right corner of the period key? That means tapping and holding the period key briefly creates a question mark rather than a period.

:-)

Similarly, the .com key and the smiley-face key (shown in the margin) have little gray ellipses on them. Tap and hold one of those two keys briefly to see the options shown in Figure 4-8. When the options appear, touch the character you want to insert.

- Some keys aren't marked with little gray options, but they reveal foreign-language equivalents. Tap and hold the n key, for example, to add the proper embellishment to *mañana*. You'll also find foreign variations by holding down any of the vowels, as well as by holding down the c key.

- When you're typing inside a website or within an e-mail, the .com key turns into a smiley-face key.

Figure 4-8: Touch and briefly hold the .com key or the smiley-face key to reveal a palette of options; touch the option you want to enter.

✔ A tap of the key shown in the margin brings up the keyboard's settings page.

✔ Touch the microphone key to dictate what you want to type, a technique described later in this chapter.

✔ To type fractions, tap and hold any of the number keys. Holding down the 1 key, for example, lets you type ¼, ½, and other common fractions. Other held-down number keys offer similar fractions, as well as exponents like 4^2.

Editing text

Your Xoom is meant more for reading than writing. Nonetheless, its Swiss-army-knife personality lets you select, cut, copy, and paste words. Editing is a little tedious, but if you simply must correct that e-mail before it goes out, you can use your Xoom's small set of editing tools.

The first step in editing text is selecting the portion that needs attention. To select text, follow these steps:

1. **Touch and hold the first word you want to select.**

   Your Xoom automatically grabs the word, isolating it between little movable bars.

   You can select only *text* — not images. To grab an image, hold your finger on it and then choose Copy from the pop-up menu.

2. **With your finger, drag the two bars inward or outward until they surround the text that you want to capture (see Figure 4-9).**

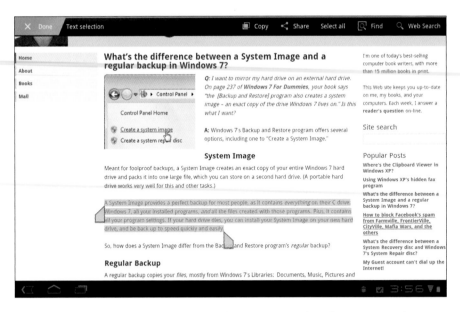

Figure 4-9: Touch a word, and when the selection bars appear, drag them to surround your desired words or letters.

Now that you've selected your text, you're ready to start fiddling. You can simply press the Backspace key to delete a misspelling that you've selected in an e-mail, for example. But if you're hankering for something a little fancier, look at the menu bar across the top of the screen. The menu bar's options vary slightly, depending on what you're editing, but you'll always see some of the following:

- **Copy:** Copy the information to the clipboard, where you can paste it elsewhere — even into a different application.

- **Cut:** Remove the selected information, placing it on the clipboard for pasting someplace else.

- **Share:** Fetch a menu that shows all the places you can send the information, usually through apps you've installed. You can post the selected information on Facebook, send it through Gmail, or tweet it on Twitter, for example.

- **Select All:** Disregard your neatly selected words and select all the text on the page.

- **Find:** Want to find another instance of your selected text on that page? Choose Find to search for a match.

✔ **Web Search:** This option tosses your selected text to Google, asking it to find matches on the web.

✔ **Done:** Choose this option when you're through with your operation and ready to move on.

Even if you don't see a menu across the top, these basic editing steps work in most parts of the screen:

✔ Want to paste something you've copied? Tap the screen where you'd like to paste it, either within the same program or in a different one. A little bar appears, with the word *Paste* hovering above it. Touch the word *Paste* (shown in the margin) to paste your clipboard's contents at the bar's location.

✔ You can drag and drop selected text to a different place onscreen. Touch and hold the selected text. When the highlighting disappears, a ghostly copy of the text appears. Drag that copy to its new location and then lift your finger to leave the text in the new location.

Replacing Typing with Talking

Every once in a while, you'll become a little frustrated with the slippery keyboard. Instead of cursing at it, try talking to it.

Your Xoom will listen to your voice, understand your words, and spell them out onscreen. It's pretty darn good at this. I sang to my Xoom once, and it picked up the lyrics.

Whenever you touch the microphone icon (shown in the margin), your Xoom is ready to listen. You'll spot this icon on just about every variety of keyboard.

To tell your Xoom what to enter as text, follow these steps:

1. **Touch any place on the screen that's expecting text.**

   You can be composing an e-mail, filling out a form, or working in any other place that expects incoming words. When you touch the text box, the familiar keyboard appears, ready for you to tap away.

2. **Touch the microphone icon.**

   This icon, usually located on the keyboard, launches the voice-input program (see Figure 4-10).

3. **Speak clearly and emotionlessly, like . . . well, like a robot.**

   If your Xoom catches your drift, it quickly spells out your speech as text.

   If it doesn't translate your speech into text, move to Step 4.

Figure 4-10: Speak slowly and clearly, and your Xoom will spell out your spoken words.

4. **Choose the right translation, if necessary.**

   Sometimes, your Xoom can't quite figure out what you're saying. When that happens, it lists what it *thinks* you said, as shown in Figure 4-11.

   Touch the right translation, and you're on your way. If your Xoom didn't understand, touch Cancel, and try again.

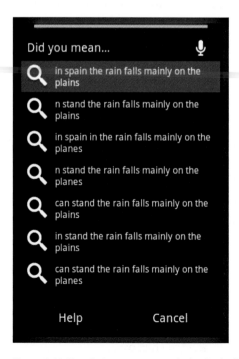

Figure 4-11: Touch the correct translation in the list.

Practice is the key to success here. Try talking to your Xoom in different ways. Try talking in smaller, partial sentences, waiting for the Xoom to transcribe your first few words before adding more. Eventually, you'll discover phrasing that lets the Xoom understand you most easily.

- ✒ When you use the microphone to fill out a form, your words appear in the form as text. Touch the keyboard's Enter key to send the information on its merry way.

- ✒ Train your Xoom to recognize your voice. Head to Setting⇨Language & Input⇨Voice Recognizer Settings. Then touch Personalized Recognition, and approve its use. Thereafter, Google compares your speech with the words you've verified, honing its recognition of your voice and storing those recognition patterns with your Google account.

- ✒ To add punctuation, speak the type of punctuation you want: comma, for example, period, or exclamation point.

- ✒ Your Xoom listens for only a few seconds before it translates what it's heard. You can't leave your Xoom in a front-row seat in a classroom, return in an hour, and expect to find a transcribed lecture. (Actually, you probably won't even find your Xoom, but that's another story.)

Commanding Thy Tablet to Do Thy Bidding

The microphone icon also lives next to Google's search box, located in the top-left corner of your home screen. That handy microphone handles two tasks: It lets you search the Internet by voice, and it lets you boss your Xoom around with a few key commands.

To search the Internet or make your Xoom follow a verbal command, follow these steps:

1. **Touch the microphone icon, and wait for the Speak Now box to appear.**

   The Speak Now box appears (refer to Figure 4-10, earlier in this chapter).

2. **Say your command, followed by your preference.**

   Just say a few words, and your Xoom loads your browser with relevant pages.

   Or, boss your Xoom around by saying any of the commands listed in Table 4-1.

Your Xoom carries out your command immediately, provided that it understands your request. You may need to choose the right translation, as shown in Figure 4-11, earlier in this chapter. If the Xoom doesn't come up with the right translation, touch Cancel to start over.

Table 4-1 shows the pre-programmed commands your Xoom currently understands and obeys. Saying "Map of" followed by "gas stations," for example, fetches the map and shows you the gas stations closest to your current location. (I cover maps and navigation in Chapter 14.)

Table 4-1	Your Xoom's Voice Commands	
Say This Command	*Along with These Words*	*To Do This*
Listen to	[artist/song/album]	Find and play this artist, song, or album in a music app like Pandora, Last.fm, Rdio, mSpot, or on YouTube.
Send e-mail	to [contact] [message]	Create an e-mail addressed to a particular person and then enter your message.
Set alarm for	[time am/pm]	Set an alarm to go off at this time.
Go to	[website]	Start the web browser and visit this website.
Note to self	[note]	E-mail the recording of this message to yourself and include a written transcription.
Navigate to	[location/business name]	Fetch the Navigation program, and get directions to this place, complete with a map.
Map of	[type of business]	Call up the map program, and find the location of the closest type of business.
Directions to	[location/business name]	Show directions to this place on a map. (Press the Navigate button to hear the Xoom guide you there, turn-by-turn.)
Map of	[location]	Fetch a map of this place.

After you give a voice command, you tap the OK button to approve the command. That rules out the chance that a pesky stranger will tell your Xoom, "Set alarm for 3 a.m." Until you touch the OK button, the alarm won't be waking you up.

Part II
Staying Connected

The 5th Wave   By Rich Tennant

"He saw your Xoom and wants to know if he can check his Gmail."

In this part . . .

*L*ike the most popular person at the party, your Xoom finds connections everywhere. It talks with your computer to swap files, and it grabs any Internet connection it can find.

This part of the book offers step-by-step instructions for connecting your Xoom to anything possible, from the web to your cellphone to your home stereo and TV set.

Also, it shows you how the Xoom can keep you connected through e-mail, updated contact information, neatly organized appointment calendars, and social networks such as Facebook and Twitter.

Contacts   Market

Gmail   Talk

Andy Rathbone's Blog   Dashboard - Google Anal

Twitter   Facebook

5

Connecting to the Internet, PCs, Cellphones, HDTVs, and More

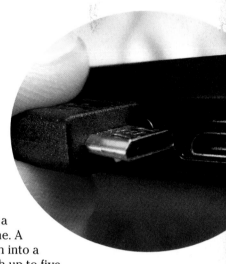

*T*he Internet surrounds us, yet we low-tech humans can't connect to it without mechanical help. Future generations may get Internet implants at birth, but today, humans remain stuck with the old standbys: computers, cables, Wi-Fi networks, and cellphone towers.

Luckily, the Motorola Xoom has proved to be quite versatile when it comes to sniffing out an Internet connection. It connects through a wireless network, a 3G or 4G cellular network, or even a nearby cellphone. A Motorola Xoom with cellular service can even morph into a Wi-Fi hotspot, letting you share your connection with up to five friends.

Your Xoom can hook up with more than just the Internet, however. If you're a heavy-duty typist, you can connect it to a keyboard. Connect it to a PC or Mac for quick file swaps. To watch your movies or play games on the big screen, connect your Xoom to your HDTV. While you're at it, connect your Xoom to your stereo for better sound.

This chapter explains nearly every connection your Xoom can handle. Eventually, you'll tire of making connections, so this chapter also explains the quickest ways to disconnect, thereby saving battery life and placating flight attendants worldwide.

Connecting to the Internet

Always eager for Internet action, your Xoom can latch on to the web any of three ways. I cover each method in its own section later in this chapter, but this short guide can help you narrow down the connection method that works best for you:

- **Cellular data plan:** Some Motorola Xoom models can connect to the Internet through a data plan offered by a cellphone service provider — if you pony up the monthly fee for always-on Internet access, of course. This type of plan puts the Internet at your disposal as soon as you activate your Xoom (a process that I cover in Chapter 2).

- **Wi-Fi:** Less-expensive Xoom models can't connect to the Internet through cellular data plans. But they can get online when they're within range of a *Wi-Fi network* — a wireless network commonly used in homes, coffee shops, and businesses. For more information, page ahead to this chapter's "Connecting to a wireless network" section.

- **Bluetooth:** All Xooms support *Bluetooth,* a short-range wireless technology for linking nearby gadgets. If your Android cellphone has both Bluetooth and a data plan, you may be able to ride the Internet through your phone's Internet connection. I cover Bluetooth/Internet sharing in "Tethering: Going online through a cellphone," later in this chapter.

Your versatile Xoom has one more trick up its sleeve. After it latches on to a cellular connection, your Xoom can create its own hotspot. That way, you can let your friends connect as well. I cover the whole thing in "Sharing Your Xoom's Internet Connection," later in this chapter.

Connecting to a wireless network

An always-on cellular data plan is a dream come true, giving you the power of the Internet anytime, anywhere — well, anywhere within range of a cellphone tower. That's all major cities in the United States and most points between them.

My data plan stopped working!

If your Xoom isn't connecting to the Internet through your monthly data plan, try these fixes:

✔ **Make sure that you've activated your Xoom.** I cover activation in Chapter 2. To try activating again, touch Apps⇨Settings⇨Wireless & Networks⇨Mobile Networks⇨Activate Device.

✔ **Make sure that you're not in airplane mode.** I cover airplane mode in this chapter's last section.

✔ **Make sure that your data plan is turned on.** Touch Apps⇨Settings⇨Wireless &

Networks⇨Mobile Networks, and make sure that the Data Enabled check box is checked.

✔ **Turn your Xoom off, then on again.** This trick has fixed countless electronic gadgets. Hold your Xoom's power button until your Xoom turns off. Wait a few seconds, then hold the power button again to turn the Xoom back on.

If those steps fail, take your Xoom to your cellphone provider's nearest store. You may have a billing problem.

Still, most people prefer to connect with a wireless network whenever possible. Wi-Fi connections are faster than cellular-data-plan service, and no hidden meter racks up charges without letting you know how much your bill will be at month's end.

This section describes how to turn on Wi-Fi on your Xoom and then connect with open and password-protected networks.

Toggling Wi-Fi on or off

When you don't need Internet access, or you'll be out of range of your Wi-Fi signal, you don't need to leave your Xoom's Wi-Fi radio turned on. Leaving it turned on constantly simply drains your Xoom's battery a little more quickly.

With Wi-Fi turned off, you can still connect to the Internet through a cellular data plan, if you have one. If you want your data plan turned off, as well, put your Xoom in airplane mode, covered in this chapter's last section.

To toggle your Xoom's Wi-Fi connection, follow these steps:

1. **On the home screen, touch the clock.**

   The notifications panel rises, as shown on the left side of Figure 5-1. It lists not only your notifications, but also your current battery power, Wi-Fi connection strength, battery level, and Bluetooth status (on or off).

2. **Touch the clock again.**

   The quick-settings panel appears, as shown on the right side of Figure 5-1.

Figure 5-1: Click the clock to fetch the notifications panel (left); click the clock again to bring up the quick-settings panel (right).

3. Tap Wi-Fi to bring up the Wi-Fi Settings page.

The Wi-Fi Settings page, shown in Figure 5-2, shows whether Wi-Fi is turned on, as well as whether you're connected to a Wi-Fi network and (if so) what the name of the network is.

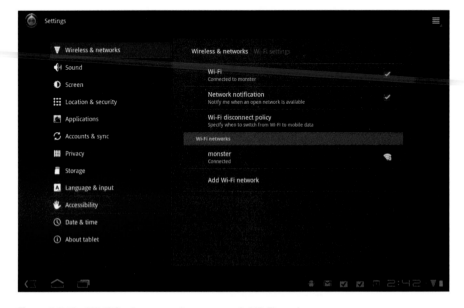

Figure 5-2: The Wi-Fi Settings page lets you toggle Wi-Fi service.

4. Toggle Wi-Fi on (check) or off (no check) by tapping it.

Turning Wi-Fi on is your first step in connecting. When you turn Wi-Fi on, your Xoom sniffs the air for any Wi-Fi networks you've used in the past. If it finds one, it connects to that network, automatically entering your previously entered password to save you time.

If no familiar network is nearby, connect with a new one — a task that I cover in the next section.

For quick access to your Wi-Fi settings, touch the clock on the screen's bottom, right corner. When the notification panel appears, touch the clock again, then touch Wi-Fi to see the settings page.

Finding and connecting to available Wi-Fi networks

When you need an Internet connection, but you're away from your usual gang of favorite hotspots, you need to see whether any new networks lie within range.

To see a list of nearby Wi-Fi networks and connect with one of them, follow these steps:

1. Touch the clock on the home screen to raise the notifications panel; then touch the clock again to see your quick-settings panel.

2. Tap Wi-Fi.

The Wi-Fi settings appear in the top portion of the window, as shown in Figure 5-3.

If you haven't turned on Wi-Fi (as described in the preceding section), tap Wi-Fi to turn it on and view any available networks.

The window's bottom half lists the names of any nearby Wi-Fi networks. Don't spot any? You need to move closer to a coffee shop, airport, or other business that offers Wi-Fi.

3. Find your desired Wi-Fi network.

Depending on your location, you may see several Wi-Fi networks. Scroll down the screen until you see the one you're seeking. There are two types of networks:

- *Open networks:* Networks without a padlock icon don't require any password. They're called open Wi-Fi networks, and they're free for anybody to use.

- *Secured networks:* Networks with a little padlock icon require a password for access. They're secured or locked-down Wi-Fi networks.

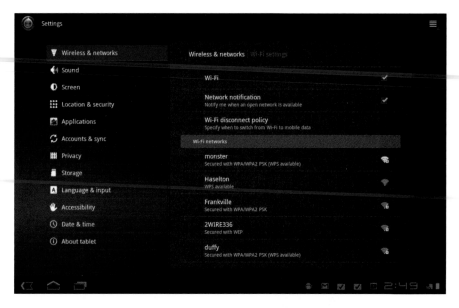

Figure 5-3: Available Wi-Fi networks appear in the Wi-Fi Networks section.

4. **Touch your desired Wi-Fi network to connect:**

• *For an open network:* The window shown at the top of Figure 5-4 pops up, listing Open in the Security line. Simply touch the Connect button, and your Xoom connects within a few seconds, giving you Internet access. You're through! (You'll spot a wireless signal strength icon, shown in the margin, near the clock. The taller the icon, the stronger the signal.)

• *For a secured network:* If the Security line lists WEP, WPA/WPA2, or PSK, as shown at the bottom of Figure 5-4, you must enter a password. Type the password and touch Connect. Your Xoom should be able to access the Internet with a few seconds.

If your Internet access still isn't working, or if you see the word *Disabled* below the network's name after you turn on Wi-Fi (Step 2), you've tried to connect with a password-protected network. Head to Step 5 to add one.

5. **To enter a password for an existing connection, hold your finger on the wireless network's name; choose Modify from the pop-up menu; type the wireless password in the Password line; and touch Save.**

Armed with the proper password, your Xoom should connect this time, and the Wi-Fi signal strength icon should appear in the screen's bottom corner, near the clock.

Where do you find the elusive password? Try asking the coffee shop's cashier, the hotel's front desk, the office manager, or the owner of the network. If nobody ponies up a password, the network may be private. Head back to Step 3, and try another network.

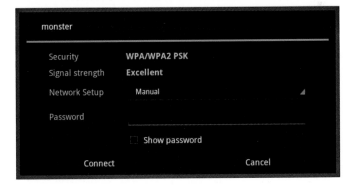

Figure 5-4: Touch Connect to enter an open Wi-Fi network (top). Enter the password and touch Connect to enter a password-protected Wi-Fi network (bottom).

✔ Before entering a password, touch the Show Password box. That option lets you see the characters as you type the password so that you can catch any typos.

✔ After you connect to a Wi-Fi network, your Xoom immediately switches away from your cellphone provider's data plan. As soon as you move out of range of that network, however, your data plan kicks back in — along with its charges.

✔ Because they lack passwords, open Wi-Fi networks make for easy connections. No security is involved, so dedicated thieves could be listening in on your entire session, grabbing your passwords on the fly. Think twice before entering any passwords on money-related websites.

✔ You only need to follow these cumbersome steps once for every new network you connect with. Whenever you move within range of that network again, your Xoom connects automatically, remembering your password from the last time it connected.

Deleting a saved network

Road warriors eventually accumulate a large list of Wi-Fi networks that they connected to in the past but no longer need. To update your list of networks, follow these steps:

1. **Tap the clock on the home screen to display the notifications panel; then tap the clock again to display the quick-settings panel.**

2. **Tap Wi-Fi.**

3. **Tap the network you want to delete.**

4. **Tap Forget.**

   The network disappears from the list.

If you ever want to connect with that network again, you'll have to enter any required password.

Tethering: Going online through a cellphone

Bluetooth lets you connect keyboards and wireless headphones to your Xoom, but it really shines in hooking up to a Android cellphone with a data plan — a technique called *tethering*. Tethering won't work with every Android phone, but at this writing, it works with a Droid X, Droid 2, and Droid Pro.

TECHNICAL STUFF

Adding a hidden Wi-Fi network

Some networks play hide and seek. They don't broadcast their names (known as SSIDs), so they don't show up on a list of available networks. If you know a hidden network's name, password, and type of security, however, you can still connect by following these steps:

1. **Turn on Wi-Fi, as described in "Toggling Wi-Fi on or off," earlier in this chapter.**

2. **Scroll to and tap Add Wi-Fi Network (refer to Figure 5-2, earlier in this chapter).**

3. **Type the hidden network's SSID, and tap Save.**

4. **Tap the Security field, and select the network's security option: WEP, WPA/WPA2 PSK.**

5. **Type the password.**

6. **Touch Connect.**

Follow these steps to link your Xoom to a Droid phone and kiss your data plan goodbye:

1. **Put your Xoom in airplane mode, as described in the last section of this chapter.**

   Airplane mode turns off all your Xoom's wireless connections: data plan, Wi-Fi, and Bluetooth.

2. **Turn on Bluetooth (refer to "Toggling Bluetooth on and off," later in this chapter).**

   You need to turn on Bluetooth; you don't need to turn on Wi-Fi or your data plan, if you have one.

3. **On your cellphone, turn on Bluetooth, and make it discoverable.**

   Head to Settings⇨Wireless & Networks, and turn on Bluetooth. Then touch Bluetooth Settings, and make your phone discoverable.

4. **On your Xoom, touch Apps⇨Settings⇨Wireless & Networks⇨ Bluetooth Settings⇨Find Nearby Devices.**

5. **Touch your cellphone's name when it appears as a found device, and choose Pair.**

6. **Confirm the pairing on your cellphone by choosing Pair.**

7. **On your Xoom, touch the wrench icon (shown in Figure 5-5; top) next to your cellphone; then touch Tethering (shown in Figure 5-5; bottom).**

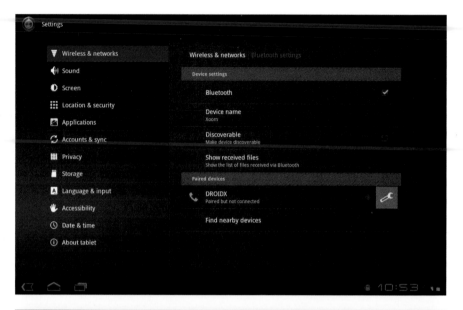

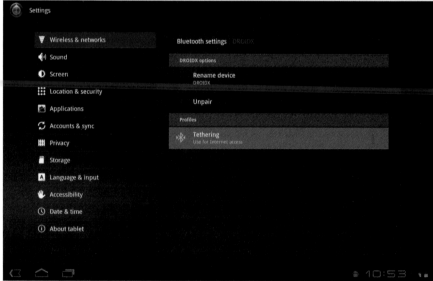

Figure 5-5: Touch the wrench icon (top); then touch Tethering (bottom).

 That's it. Your Xoom now has an Internet connection through your cell-phone's data plan. The Bluetooth Settings area says *Tethered,* and in the bottom-right corner of the screen, you see the regular Bluetooth icon and a larger blue Bluetooth tethering icon (see Figure 5-6).

Figure 5-6: Your Xoom shows you that it's tethered.

To turn off tethering from your Xoom, touch Apps➪Settings➪Wireless & Networks➪Bluetooth Settings. Touch the Wrench icon next to your phone's name, and touch Tethering to toggle tethering off.

Alternatively, you can just turn off Bluetooth on your phone or Xoom.

Sharing Your Xoom's Internet Connection

Unlike the cellphone companies, your Xoom's not greedy. Instead of charging for everything, it's eager to share. In fact, if your Xoom has a cellular data plan, it's willing to share that Internet connection with up to five other devices in the room.

That's right: The Xoom can create its own Wi-Fi network. This network shows up as AndroidAP on your friends' phones and computers, letting them connect and ride the Internet as well. The Xoom can also share its Internet connection with a PC through its USB cable.

Follow these steps to be the Internet-connected hero of the party:

   1. **Connect your Xoom to the Internet with its cellular connection.**

2. Tell your Xoom to share the connection.

Touch Apps⇨Settings⇨Wireless & Networks⇨Tethering and Portable Hotspot. In the resulting screen, your Xoom offers these three ways to share your connection:

- *USB Cable:* This method is the simplest one. Just connect your Xoom's Micro USB cable to a Windows Vista, Windows 7, or Linux computer; then select USB Tethering in the screen shown in Figure 5-7.

- *Portable Wi-Fi Hotspot:* Touch this option, and you instantly create an open Wi-Fi network, available for up to five devices around you to borrow for a quick Internet fix. (To add a password, touch Portable Wi-Fi Hotspot Settings and type the password.)

- *Bluetooth:* Tossed in as an eccentricity, this option does the opposite of piggybacking on your cellphone's connection. Choosing this option lets your PC, another Xoom, or another Bluetooth device (like your cellphone) grab your *Xoom's* Internet connection.

When you choose Portable Wi-Fi Hotspot, your Xoom can share its Internet connection with up to five of your friends in the room. Now, *that's* friendly.

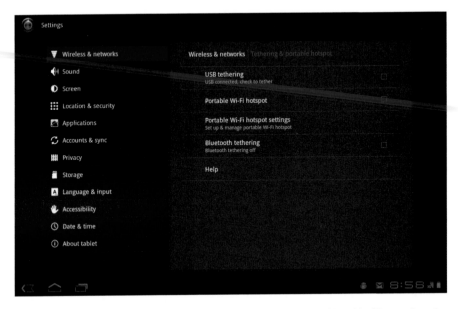

Figure 5-7: Your Xoom can share its cellular connection through a USB cable, Bluetooth, or by turning into a portable Wi-Fi hotspot.

Connecting to Your Desktop PC

You never *have* to connect your Xoom to a desktop computer. Your Xoom comes fully self-contained and doesn't need a PC hanging around. But if you own a PC, connecting it to your Xoom with a USB cable lets you transfer files quickly, as well as back up your Xoom.

Hooking up via USB

Follow these steps to connect your Xoom to your PC or laptop with a USB cable so you can begin swapping files or, in a pinch, share your Xoom's cellular Internet connection:

1. **Find your micro USB cable.**

   A micro USB cable came packaged with your Xoom. It looks like your average *mini* USB cable, but with a smaller end.

2. **Plug the small end of the cable into your Xoom's micro USB port.**

   The tiny plug fits into the black port on your Xoom's bottom edge, as shown at the top in Figure 5-8. Make sure that the flat end of the plug matches the flat end of the port.

   Don't force the plug, as you're dealing with small, delicate parts.

3. **Plug the cable's fat end into one of your computer's USB ports.**

   That rectangular plug fits into your PC as shown at the bottom in Figure 5-8.

As you plug the USB cable into your PC, your computer should beep in recognition. After a moment or two, your Xoom shows up as a new device in My Computer or Computer (depending on your version of Windows).

   ✔ If your PC doesn't recognize your Xoom, update your PC's USB drivers from Motorola's website (www.motorola.com), as described in Chapter 1, and restart your computer. (You can visit my website, www.andyrathbone.com, for clickable links to every website and web page mentioned in this book.)

   ✔ If you have trouble connecting, try unplugging your Xoom's USB cable, waiting a few seconds, then plugging it into a *different* USB port.

   ✔ If your Windows Vista or Windows 7 PC lacks Internet access, let it borrow your Xoom's cellular connection. Connect your PC to your Xoom through a USB cable, as described here; then head to "Sharing Your Xoom's Internet Connection," earlier in this chapter.

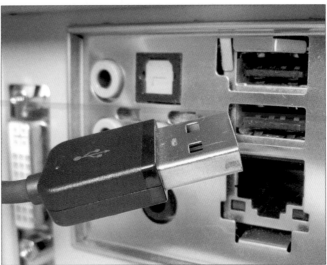

Figure 5-8: Push the small end of the micro USB cable into your Xoom (top). The large end plugs in to your computer's USB port (bottom).

✔ Having trouble connecting with Vista? On your Xoom, touch Apps↷Settings↷Applications↷Development and put a checkmark in USB Debugging. Unplug your Xoom from the USB port, wait five seconds, and plug it back in.

✔ When you're through connecting your Xoom and computer, simply unplug the cable from each of them, and save it for next time.

TIP

↳ Are you still running Windows XP? Nudge your computer a little closer to modern times by installing Windows Media Player 11 (available through Windows Update). That program comes with a driver that Windows XP needs to recognize the Xoom.

Transferring files through a USB cable

Nearly every owner wants to stuff the tablet with movies, photos, and music. Those large files flow most quickly through the bundled USB cable. After you've connected the cable between your Xoom and PC, as described in the preceding section, follow these steps to copy files between your Xoom and your desktop computer:

1. **On your Windows computer, open the folder containing the items you want to transfer.**

   When transferring files, you want *two* folders open on your desktop: the PC's folder containing the files to transfer, and the Xoom's folder where those files should go.

2. **Click your computer's Start button, and open My Computer (Windows XP) or Computer (Windows Vista and Windows 7).**

   When the window opens, you spot your Xoom in the Portable Devices section (see Figure 5-9).

Figure 5-9: Open the Xoom icon in the Portable Devices section to see its folders.

3. Double-click the Xoom icon.

An icon labeled Device Storage appears below the Xoom. This icon represents your Xoom's hard drive.

4. Double-click the Device Storage icon.

All your Xoom's folders appear on the right side of the screen. Table 5-1 lists the basic folders.

Table 5-1	Xoom Folders and Their Contents
Folder	*Contents*
Bluetooth	Any files you receive through Bluetooth from another Xoom, phone, or computer
Data	Rarely used programming information from downloaded apps
DCIM	Photos and movies taken with either of your Xoom's two cameras
Download	Files downloaded from the Internet with your web browser
Kindle	Books from the Amazon's Kindle app
Movies	Video files
Music	Music files
Pictures	Photos and pictures that weren't necessarily taken by your Xoom's camera
Podcasts	Talk and video shows downloaded from the Internet
Ringtones	Ringtones, either created or purchased

5. Drag and drop files and folders between your computer and your Xoom, as shown in Figure 5-10.

Click an icon or folder and then drag it either to your Xoom or to your PC. When you let go of the mouse button, a copy of that icon or folder appears wherever you dropped it, be it a folder on your Xoom or on your PC.

 ✔ To select several icons or folders quickly, hold down the Ctrl key while clicking them.

 ✔ Want to move *all* the files in a folder? Press Ctrl+A. That selects all the folder's files, making for an easy drag-and-drop transfer.

✔ Your Xoom doesn't care whether you place different types of files inside folders. It easily finds music files stashed in the movie folder, and vice versa. Keeping your files organized makes it easier for *you* to find them, however.

✔ To move files rather than copy them, hold down the right mouse button while dragging them. Then, when you let go of the mouse button, a menu pops up, letting you choose whether to copy or move the files.

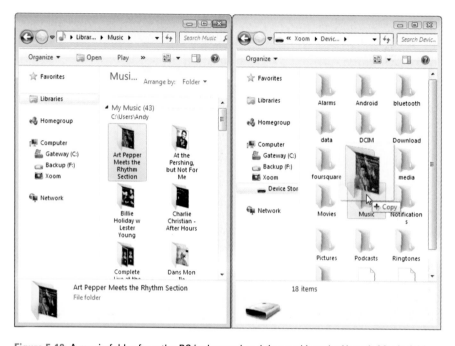

Figure 5-10: A music folder from the PC is dragged and dropped into the Xoom's Music folder.

Backing up your Xoom

Don't forget to back up your Xoom regularly, preferably before leaving on any trip.

Actually, backing it up is pretty easy, once you've connected it to your desktop computer. To back up your personal files on your Xoom, follow these steps:

1. **Link your PC and your Xoom with a micro USB cable, create a blank folder on your PC called Xoom Backup, and place the two windows side by side (refer to Figure 5-10).**

2. **On your PC, click anywhere inside your Xoom's folder and then press Ctrl+A to select all the files and folders on your Xoom.**

3. **Drag and drop all the selected folders and files from your Xoom to your PC's Xoom Backup folder.**

A complete backup takes anywhere from a few minutes to an hour or so, depending on the amount of files. You'll *definitely* want to back up your Xoom before sending it in for the 4G upgrade, described in Chapter 1.

To reinstall backed-up files, just drag the folders from your computer's Backup folder to the Xoom, clicking the OK button when you're asked whether you want to overwrite any existing folders.

Google automatically backs up contacts, e-mail, settings, and appointments if you approved Google's backups when you first set up your Xoom (see Chapter 2). Can't recall? Touch Apps⇨Settings⇨Accounts & Sync, and touch your Gmail address to see everything being backed up.

Google's Android Market backs up your paid apps, so you needn't worry about them.

Connecting through a cable to your Mac

Chances are that if you own a Mac, you have an iPad, not a Xoom. But on the odd chance you want to connect your Xoom to an Apple computer, here's the scoop: Unlike PCs, Macs don't recognize Xooms automatically. Therefore, you must follow these steps:

1. **Download Google's Android File Transfer program from www.android.com/filetransfer and install it on your Apple computer.**

2. **Use the micro USB cable that came with your Android device to connect it to your Mac.**

3. **Double-click the Android File Transfer icon to open the program for the first time.**

   Subsequently, it opens automatically.

4. **Browse your Xoom's files and folders, transferring, moving, or deleting files as you like.**

   Choose Help⇨Android File Transfer Help for more information.

Connecting to your Xoom's GPS

Like most smartphones these days, your Xoom supports GPS (Global Positioning System). GPS pinpoints your location to within 30 feet or so, which helps the Xoom guide you to addresses, locate nearby services, and tailor your searches to match your location. The Xoom turns on GPS automatically when it's needed and turns it off when it's not, thereby saving power.

GPS knows your exact coordinates, but if your Xoom doesn't have an Internet connection, that knowledge doesn't do you much good. The Xoom needs Internet access to fetch the appropriate map and display your location (which is why you need a cellular data plan for navigation).

Do you feel creeped out by the fact that your Xoom and Google can know your exact location? It's easy to turn off GPS by following these steps:

1. **Touch Apps⇨Settings⇨Location & Security.**

2. **Clear the Use GPS Satellites and Use Location for Google Search check boxes by touching them.**

   From now on, your Xoom knows your general neighborhood but not your actual street.

3. **If you don't want to share your current neighborhood's location, either, clear the Use Wireless Networks check box.**

   Now your Xoom knows only what city you're in.

Personally, I don't mind giving up my location in exchange for my Xoom's tailoring information to fit my surroundings.

Connecting via Bluetooth

Even if you haven't heard the term *Bluetooth,* you've encountered it. Remember that oddball talking to himself as he walked down the grocery-store aisle? Chances are that he was wearing a Bluetooth earpiece that connected wirelessly with the cellphone in his pocket.

Most people won't need an earpiece with their Xoom, as it can't make voice calls, but Bluetooth connects to more than just earpieces. Your Xoom's Bluetooth technology lets it connect with keyboards, headphones, watches, and even some cellphones for borrowing an Internet connection — all through the time-tested technology of Bluetooth radio.

No matter what you're hooking up, you must jump through the hoops described in this section to connect a Bluetooth gadget to your Xoom.

Toggling Bluetooth on and off

Like anything else on your Xoom, Bluetooth consumes battery power. Turn it on when necessary; then turn it off. These two steps show you how to do both:

1. **Touch Apps⇨Settings⇨Wireless & Networks.**

   Your Xoom shows all its wireless options.

2. **In the Bluetooth section, touch the box marked Turn on Bluetooth.**

   • Touching a blank box turns on Bluetooth, as shown in Figure 5-11, so that you can connect with other gadgets. When turned on, a gray Bluetooth icon appears in the screen's bottom-right corner.

   • Touching a checked box clears the check and turns off Bluetooth.

   To conserve battery power, turn off Bluetooth when you're through using your gadget. When turned off, the Bluetooth icon disappears from the screen's bottom-right corner.

Figure 5-11: Touch the empty Bluetooth check box to turn on Bluetooth.

Pairing with another Bluetooth device

Turning on the Bluetooth radio, as described in the preceding section, is like turning on any other radio: It picks up useless static until it's tuned to a station.

In the Bluetooth world, tuning to the right station is called *pairing*. After you've paired your Xoom with another Bluetooth device, the two can begin carrying on meaningful conversations.

To pair your Xoom with another Bluetooth device, follow these steps:

1. **Turn on Bluetooth, as described in the preceding section.**

2. **On your other device, turn on Bluetooth and make it discoverable.**

   Just about every Bluetooth gadget comes with its own obtuse command for making it discoverable. If you don't have the manual, look up the gadget's part number on Google for advice. You make the Motorola Bluetooth keyboard discoverable, for example, by holding down its On button until its green light flashes three times.

   If your Windows XP, Vista, or Windows 7 computer supports Bluetooth, or if you've plugged a Bluetooth dongle into one of its USB ports, make the computer discoverable by right-clicking the Bluetooth logo near the PC's clock. When the menu appears, choose Open Settings or Open Bluetooth Settings. Finally, on the Options tab, check the box labeled Allow Bluetooth Devices to Find This Computer, and click OK.

   Most devices stay discoverable for only about a minute or so; then they hide. If a device hides before your Xoom recognizes it, repeat the steps that make it discoverable.

3. **Touch Apps⇨Settings⇨Wireless & Networks⇨Bluetooth Settings⇨Find Nearby Devices to display the screen shown in Figure 5-12.**

   Your Xoom begins looking for any nearby device that you made discoverable in Step 2.

   Is nothing showing up? Make your device discoverable again, and touch Find Nearby Devices again.

4. **When the device's name appears on your Xoom, tap its name to pair (connect) with it.**

5. **If you're asked to do so, type the personal identification number (PIN), accept the pair on the other device, and type the same PIN for the other device.**

   If a gadget asks for a PIN or passcode without telling you what to enter, type **0000** or **1234**. Those ol' favorites work many times.

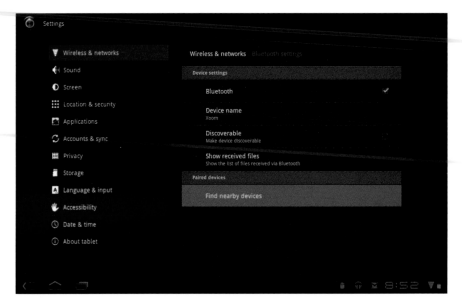

Figure 5-12: Touch Find Nearby Devices to search for Bluetooth gadgets.

Yes, this procedure is way too much work, and you may have to repeat it several times before pairing the devices successfully. After they're paired, though, they remember each other, so you never need to hassle with these bothersome steps again.

✔ Tired of the Xoom's soulless and silent onscreen keyboard? Use Bluetooth to connect a real keyboard, ready for hard-core word processing. Motorola's Bluetooth keyboard even has dedicated Home, Volume, Browser, Gmail, and music-player keys.

✔ If you have a Droid 2, Droid Pro, or Droid X smartphone, be sure to check out this chapter's tethering section. After you pair your phone with your Xoom through Bluetooth, the Xoom can borrow the Droid's Internet connection whenever you want (which keeps you from having to pay for a separate data plan for your Xoom).

✔ Right out of the box, the Xoom doesn't work with a Bluetooth mouse. That situation may change through an update or an app, though.

✔ There's not much use in pairing a cellphone's headset with your Xoom, because a Xoom can't make phone calls.

✔ If you no longer need a paired device, touch the wrench icon next to its name, and choose Unpair from the menu.

Whence Bluetooth?

An engineer who was obsessed with tenth-century Scandinavian history was fretting one day about all the cables covering his desktop. Recalling that King Harald I of Denmark united competing Danish tribes into a single kingdom, the obsessive engineer whipped together a single communications standard from several competing communication protocols. Then he named that standard Bluetooth as a tribute to the Scandinavian King Blåtand/Blåtann. (Presumably, the king's name sounds like *Bluetooth* in Danish.)

Sending files from your PC to Xoom with Bluetooth

Transferring files through Bluetooth is a slow and laborious process. If you're shuttling files to a computer, stick with the micro USB cable or use Gmail to e-mail the files.

If you're determined to send a small file or two from your PC to your Xoom through Bluetooth, follow these steps:

1. **Turn on Bluetooth, and pair your Xoom with your Windows computer, as described in the preceding two sections.**

2. **Right-click the Bluetooth logo on your Windows PC, and choose Send a File.**

   A window appears on your PC, asking where to send the file.

3. **Double-click your Xoom's icon in the window.**

4. **Click the Browse button, and browse to the file or files you want to send.**

   When the Browse window appears, choose your files. To choose several files, hold down the Ctrl key while clicking the filenames.

5. **Click the Browse window's Open button; then click Next.**

   Your PC begins sending the files to your Xoom. (Bluetooth can be very slow for large files.)

6. **On your Xoom, touch Show Received Files (refer to Figure 5-12 earlier in this chapter).**

Connecting to HDTV or a Video Projector

Connecting to a high-definition television set (HDTV) is pretty straightforward if you have an HDMI cable, and if you have an HDMI video projector, it connects just as easily as an HDTV.

Connecting to an older video projector is more difficult, though. You need not only that magic HDMI cable, but also a converter box — an expensive gadget that sits between the HDMI cable and the VGA connector on most video projectors.

To connect to an HDTV or digital projector, follow these steps:

1. **Buy an HDMI cable for your Xoom.**

   This cable doesn't come inside your Xoom's box, so you have to purchase it separately. It has a micro HDMI plug on one end and a regular HDMI plug on the other end. (The Droid X uses the same kind of cable, if you have that cellphone.)

2. **Plug the small end of the cable into the white port on the bottom edge of your Xoom, and plug the large end into the HDMI In port on your HDTV.**

   Plug the small end into your Xoom, shown in Figure 5-13, left; plug the large end into your HDTV, shown in Figure 5-13, right.

Figure 5-13: The small plug goes into your Xoom (left); the large plug goes into your HDTV (right).

3. Switch your TV's input to the HDMI In port with your Xoom.

The wildcard in the process, this step involves figuring out how to change inputs on your TV's remote or front panel. (Try pressing the Input button slowly, once every second or two, and see whether you eventually see your Xoom onscreen.)

When it's working, your HDTV should show everything you're seeing on your Xoom. To show off your photos, for example, choose Apps⇨Gallery⇨Camera.

Connecting to a Stereo System

If you've already connected your Xoom to your HDTV with an HDMI cable, you probably don't need this section. HDMI cables carry both sound and video to the TV set.

But if you just want to hear music — or you want to hear your movies with the best sound possible — read on.

To connect your Xoom to a home stereo system, you need only one thing: a cable with a ⅛-inch headphone jack on one end and two RCA connectors on the other (see Figure 5-14). You can find this type of cable at most office-supply and electronics stores.

When you have the cable, here's how to connect your Xoom to a stereo system for home-theater sound:

1. **Push the small, ⅛-inch plug into the headphone jack on the top edge of the Xoom.**

   Begin playing music through your Xoom by touching Apps ⌘ Music, then touching a song's name.

2. **Push the two RCA plugs into the analog input ports on the stereo system, then make sure your home stereo is turned on.**

   The white plug goes into the left port; the red plug goes into the right one. Take note of a number or label above the ports you've pushed the two plugs onto. It may say Tape Input, for example, or Line In.

3. **Switch the stereo to the correct input setting.**

   This is a tough one. Switch your home stereo through each of its inputs until you hear the music you started playing in Step 1.

4. **Adjust the volume levels on both your Xoom and your stereo to reach a comfortable level.**

   Your Xoom's volume switches are on its narrow side.

Figure 5-14: The small plug goes into your Xoom (top); the two RCA plugs push into your home stereo (bottom).

Taking the Xoom Offline While You Fly

An Internet connection is hard to live without, but the airlines prefer that you pay by the minute for their own in-flight Internet services, thank you. So when the flight attendants ask you to turn off all Internet-connected devices, switch your Xoom to airplane mode, which turns off all your Xoom's wireless connections (3G/4G, Wi-Fi, and Bluetooth).

Airplane mode leaves your Xoom turned on, however, so you can still watch movies, listen to music, play games, read e-books, and take awkward photos out of the airplane window.

Turning on airplane mode also stops some games from displaying their annoying ads.

To toggle airplane mode on and off, follow these steps:

1. **Touch the clock on the home screen to summon the notifications panel.**

2. **Touch the clock again to display the quick-settings panel.**

3. **In the Airplane Mode section, touch the On/Off toggle switch.**

   The switch normally reads Off; touching it switches it to On.

Even while you're in airplane mode, you can toggle both Wi-Fi and Bluetooth on while leaving your cellular connection turned off. To do that, just touch the Wi-Fi setting in Step 3, leaving airplane mode turned on.

That takes you to the Wi-Fi settings where you can re-enable Wi-Fi and Bluetooth. That lets you still listen to music through your Bluetooth headset, for example, but keep your data plan turned off during the flight.

Connecting a Keyboard, Mouse, or Camera through USB

Android 3.1 boosts the usefulness of your Xoom's USB port. But before you unleash that port's new powers, you need a special cable or adapter. (Verizon and Motorola sell one called a "Camera Connection Kit," shown in Figure 5-15.)

Figure 5-15: The Camera Connection Kit has a male micro-USB plug on one end, and a female USB "host" port on the other end.

The cable or adapter has a micro USB plug on one end that plugs into your Xoom's micro USB port. The cable/adapter's other end has a female USB port, where you plug in a standard USB cable like the one found on the end of a keyboard or mouse.

Plug in a USB keyboard, and you can type with that rather than the Xoom's glass keyboard. Plug in a USB mouse, and a pointer appears onscreen, letting you select, scroll, drag, and drop items, just as if you were using a finger.

Plug a digital camera into the USB adapter cable, and the Xoom's Gallery app appears, bearing a new stack of photos named after your camera. Touch the words "Touch Here to Import," and the Gallery displays thumbnails of your camera's photos, all selected. To copy all the camera's photos to your Xoom, touch Import. After a minute or two, the photos all appear in their own Gallery folder, named after your camera.

To view the photos rather than copy them, touch the Gallery's Done button. The photo thumbnails remain onscreen, letting you scroll through them, touching the ones you want to view.

Chapter 11 covers the Gallery in more detail.

Walkin' the Web

Something about carrying the web around in a paperback-size gadget makes you take the Internet for granted. Family squabble over a crossword puzzle? Head for the Internet. Need the closest deli in a hurry? Yep, Internet.

Before walking to the deli, let your fingers walk over the web, touching links, stretching sites to fit your screen, and double-tapping photos to shrink or enlarge them.

This chapter explains how to find the web page you need, view it, bookmark it, and juggle several open windows — ideally, not while driving.

Loading the Web Browser

After your Motorola Xoom has Internet access (see Chapter 5), it's easy to load the Browser app. Touch the Apps button in the top-right corner of any home screen and then touch the Browser App icon, shown in the margin. The browser opens to your home page, which begins its Xoom life as www.google.com.

That's it. It's rather anticlimactic, actually, as the browser looks and acts very similar to the browser on your desktop computer. Keep these things in mind, though:

✔ To search for a site, touch the magnifying-glass icon and type what you're seeking.

✔ Although you can view nearly any website, consider downloading apps for your favorite sites. *Apps* — mini programs that I cover in Chapter 9 — are designed specifically for smartphones and tablets, making them easier to navigate. You can find apps for Twitter, Facebook, foursquare, CNN, and others from the Android Market, covered in Chapter 9.

✔ Your Xoom already comes with apps for Gmail, Google Calendar, YouTube, Google Maps, and Google Places. You needn't bother visiting those sites on their *real* web pages.

✔ No Internet connection? Head to Chapter 5 for detailed instructions. Your trusty Xoom can connect with the Internet in any of three ways.

✔ To change your browser's *home page* — the page you see when your browser first opens — visit your desired home page. Then press your browser's Settings button (shown in the margin) and touch Settings⇨Set Home Page⇨Current Page⇨OK.

✔ If you use your browser a lot, put the Browser widget on the home screen. The Browser widget shows scrollable thumbnail views of your favorite websites, letting you jump to them with a single touch. I describe apps and widgets in Chapter 9, and describe how to customize the home screen in Chapter 17.

Viewing a web page

The large screen displays a web page much as though it were on your desktop computer. Many of the browser's buttons work the same way as those in your desktop browser as well. Figure 6-1 shows the browser's main buttons.

Here's how to use the touchable buttons along the browser's top, from left to right:

Left arrow: Revisit the last page you viewed.

Right arrow: After revisiting the last page you viewed, move back to where you were.

Refresh: When a page doesn't load all the way, or you want to see the latest version of that page, the Refresh button fetches a fresh copy.

Globe: Type (or speak) a term to search for or a new website address to visit.

Add Bookmark: Add the current page to your bookmarks list.

Magnifying glass: Search for a website using Google.

Bookmarks: View a list of bookmarks, as well as your history of visited sites.

Settings: Change your browser's settings (see this chapter's last section).

Tabs: Click tabs (described in the next section) to move from one open page to another.

After you've arrived at a web page, your Xoom automatically shrinks or enlarges it to fit the screen. (Try turning your Xoom sideways to compare the views.)

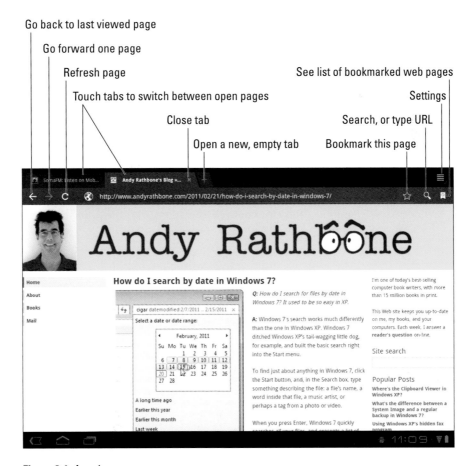

Figure 6-1: A web page.

The website thinks my Xoom is a cellphone!

Because the Xoom is the first Android product designed specifically for tablets, many websites still think you're visiting them from an Android cellphone, and naturally, they format the page for viewing on a tiny screen.

Until site owners tweak their sites to recognize your Xoom's larger screen, try this trick:

1. **Type** about:debug **in the browser's address bar and touch the Enter key.**

2. **Touch Settings; then choose Settings again from the drop-down menu.**

3. **Choose Debug⇨UAString⇨Desktop.**

   Now your browser will lie to websites, claiming to come from a desktop PC. The sites will stop thinking your Xoom is a cellphone and show their *real* formatting.

Because not all pages fit on the screen well, try these tricks while viewing a web page:

- ✔ Is the page too small or too large for easy reading? A quick double-tap either shrinks the page to fit the screen or shows it at full size.

- ✔ The finger gestures that I cover in Chapter 4 all work here. Enlarge a portion of the screen by stretching it between two fingertips, or shrink a portion of a large screen by pinching it between your fingers.

- ✔ To open a link, touch it. To enter text, touch where you want to type; a keyboard appears for you to type your words.

- ✔ Slide your finger up a page to see text farther down the page; similarly, slide your finger down to return to the top of the page.

- ✔ To speed online searching, search directly from your Xoom's home screen. Touch the Google search bar in the top-left corner, and enter your search by either typing or speaking. The Xoom opens a browser screen to the page that's it's found.

- ✔ If you're signing in to a favorite site with your username and password, take your browser up on its offer to remember that information, so that you don't have to enter it again.

Keeping tabs on open web pages

Sometimes, it's nice to switch between two open browser windows, to compare pages or gather information from each page.

Your Xoom can keep up to 16 sites open simultaneously — enough for all but the most obsessive web visitor. The tabs sit in a row along the browser's top edge (refer to Figure 6-1, earlier in this chapter).

To switch between open pages, just touch a page's tab. Your Xoom instantly switches to that page.

 To open a web page in its own tab, touch and hold the link. A menu appears, as shown in Figure 6-2. Or, you can open a blank new tab by touching the tab with the plus sign shown in the margin.

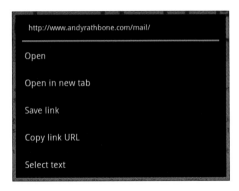

http://www.andyrathbone.com/mail/

Open

Open in new tab

Save link

Copy link URL

Select text

Figure 6-2: To open a link in its own tab, touch and hold it; then choose Open in New Tab.

That menu offers these options:

- **Open:** This option simply opens the page, replacing the page you're currently viewing.

- **Open in New Tab:** When you choose this option, the site opens in its own tab, which sits right next to the tab of the currently open page.

- **Save Link:** This option saves the current page in your Downloads folder for later offline viewing. (To see inside the Downloads folder, touch Settings⇨Downloads.)

✔ **Copy Link URL:** Choose this option to copy the link's web address to the clipboard for later pasting — perhaps in an e-mail to share with friends.

✔ **Select Text:** This option fetches the editing tools and lets you choose exactly which portions of the page you want to select for later copying and pasting. (I cover selecting text in Chapter 4.)

 To close a tab, tap the little X just to the right of its name. If you don't close tabs manually, they stay open until you turn off your Xoom by holding in its power button.

Bookmarking your favorite sites

When you spot an engaging site that you absolutely *must* revisit, bookmark it. That site is added to a list for one-touch access the next time you're browsing. (Sometimes, bookmarking a site is the only way you can remember that you were once excited about it.)

To bookmark a site for easy access, follow these steps:

1. **Visit a site that you'd like to revisit or remember.**

2. **Touch the Add Bookmark button.**

    This button, shown in the margin, looks like a little star.

3. **Change the bookmark's name, if you want, or just touch OK.**

   Your browser normally names the bookmark after the web page, but feel free to shorten it. (It looks nicer when it's short enough to fit on the browser's tab.) Touching OK adds it to your list of bookmarks.

 To see your list of bookmarks at any time, touch the Bookmarks icon, shown in the margin. The bookmarks appear (see Figure 6-3).

While viewing your bookmarks list, you can do any of the following things:

✔ Jump directly to a bookmarked site by touching its name in the list. To open a bookmarked site in its own tab, touch and hold its name; then choose Open in New Window.

✔ Delete an unloved (or accidentally added) bookmark by touching and holding its name, and then choosing Delete Bookmark.

✔ Edit a bookmark's name by touching and holding it, and then choosing Edit Bookmark.

 ✔ You can view your bookmarks either as thumbnails (refer to Figure 6-3) or as a text list — useful for viewing dozens of bookmarks. To toggle the view, touch the bookmark's Settings icon, shown in the margin.

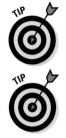

✔ Did you forget to bookmark a site that you want to revisit? Click the History tab (refer to Figure 6-3). There, you'll find a list of all the sites you've visited, sorted by date and visitation frequency.

✔ Touching and holding down the browser's Back button also fetches your history page, letting you see all the sites you've previously visited.

✔ For easy access to your bookmarked sites, add the Browser widget to one of your many home screens. The Browser widget lets you flip through little screens showing your favorite sites. When you spot the one you like, tap it, and it appears onscreen. (I cover widgets in Chapter 9.)

Filling out forms automatically

Although computers were supposed to free us from mundane tasks, they often do just the opposite. How often do you fill in the same online form with your name, address, phone number, or e-mail address?

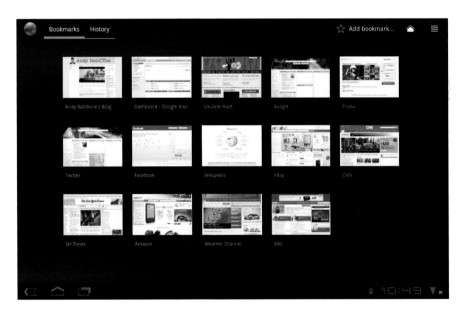

Figure 6-3: Find your bookmarks and history of visited sites.

Fortunately, the browser lets you automate that chore. By filling out that information once on a form within your Xoom, you can choose to enter it in any online form by touching a button. Here's how it works:

1. **Open your browser.**

2. **Touch the Settings icon, shown in the margin, and choose Settings from the drop-down menu.**

3. **Touch the box labeled Form AutoFill to put a check in it.**

4. **Touch AutoFill Settings.**

5. **Fill out the resulting form.**

   Add any information that you'll want to enter into online forms automatically, such as your name, company name, street address, city, state, zip code, country, phone number, or e-mail address.

6. **Touch Save Profile.**

The next time you visit a site and touch a form to fill out, the word *AutoFill* appears below the form's entry box. Touch AutoFill, and your Xoom fills in that part of the form with the information you've already entered. This feature is an incredible time-saver, especially when you're typing on glass.

If you don't want this information to be entered automatically, never touch the form's AutoFill drop-down menu, and it won't be entered.

The sneaky browse

Sometimes, you want to visit a website but don't want to leave any trace of your visit behind. You may be at a friend's computer and don't want to add your visited sites to his browser's history, for example. Or perhaps you're at work and don't want the boss to know how much time you spend playing Farmville on Facebook.

No matter what your motive, the surreptitious solution is to open an *Incognito window* — a window that leaves no trace in the Xoom's web history and accepts no *cookies* (little identifiers left by some websites).

To browse in Incognito mode, open your browser, touch the Settings icon, and choose New Incognito Tab from the drop-down menu. That's it. A blank web page appears in its own tab. Your browsing within that tabbed window leaves no trace on your Xoom.

Downloading from the Web

Few people can visit a website without seeing something that they can't leave behind. Perhaps you need to download a file for work, a menu from a restaurant, or a photo to use as wallpaper on your home page.

You won't be downloading *programs* to your Xoom, however, as you do on a desktop PC. Programs, known on mobile devices as *apps,* come from the Android Market, which I cover in Chapter 9. (Many apps for the Xoom are free.)

To download a file, touch and hold its link on the web page. When a menu pops up, as shown in Figure 6-4, choose Save Link.

To download an image, touch and hold it. When a menu appears, choose Save Image.

When you're downloading an item, the icon in the margin appears in your notifications panel, just below the clock in the bottom-right corner.

Just how do you find your downloaded treasures? They all live in your Downloads folder. To view them, connect your Xoom to a PC with a USB cable as I describe in Chapter 5. Alternatively, you can visit that folder on your Xoom. To do that, touch Apps⇨Downloads in the home screen or Settings⇨Downloads in the browser.

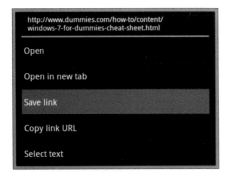

Figure 6-4: Touch and hold a file you want to download, and choose Save Link.

Downloaded photos will also appear within the Gallery app, which I cover in Chapter 11.

Changing Your Browser's Settings

The more often you browse the web on your Xoom, the more urges you'll have to tweak something. A joy to tweakers everywhere, the browser's Settings menu lets you customize your browser in a variety of ways.

Touching the Settings button, shown in the margin, fetches the menu shown in Figure 6-5.

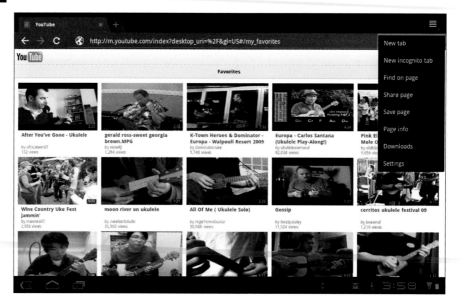

Figure 6-5: Your browser's Settings menu offers many handy tools and tweaks.

Many of these options are covered elsewhere in this chapter, but Table 6-1 offers the full rundown. You may never use them, but now you know why they're there.

Table 6-1	Your Browser's Settings Menu
This Option	*Lets You Do This*
New Tab	Open a new tab in your browser.
New Incognito Tab	Open a new blank tab that keeps the browser from remembering your session.
Find on Page	Find a term on the current page.
Share Page	Share the page's web address with friends through e-mail or a social-networking app like Facebook.
Save Page	Save the currently viewed page to your Xoom for reading offline.
Page Info	View the current page's web address.
Downloads	View and manage files that you've downloaded.
Settings	View and change your browser settings, including those involving privacy and security, as well as more advanced and experimental settings.

7

Endless E-Mail

In This Chapter

▶ Understanding e-mail on the Xoom

▶ Reading and sending mail

▶ Setting up e-mail

▶ Searching for e-mail messages

▶ Working with attachments

▶ Getting an e-mail account on your Xoom

Kids continually dash off rapid-fire text messages to their eager friends. Adults, by contrast, check *e-mail* — the old-school messaging system built more around the drudgery of work than around friendships. The Motorola Xoom comes with two e-mail apps, both of which are helpful for keeping work and friendship separate (if that's what you'd like to do).

The e-mail app of choice is Google's Gmail; it's free to anybody with a Google account. You're not limited to Gmail, though, as Xoom lets you check mail from several accounts.

This chapter explains how to set up your Xoom with your e-mail account information; how to send, receive, and forward e-mail; and how to find that darn message you received last week.

Bowling tonight

Tom Cruise
tomcruise@cox.net

To: me

Hey, did you get Barack's invite to g◌ there, and I'll give Charlie Sheen a c◌

See you at the La Mesa Bowl around

Finding Your E-Mail

Your Xoom comes with not one but two e-mail apps:

✔ **Gmail:** Your Xoom requested your Google account's username and password when it was first awakened from its box (see Chapter 2). That account grants you access to Gmail, and your free Gmail app awaits both on your home screen and in the Apps area. (I cover the Apps area in Chapter 9.)

Your Xoom's Gmail account works just like your Gmail account on the web. Both your Xoom and PC receive the same e-mails; when you delete an e-mail on one device, it disappears on the other as well.

✔ **Email:** This second app lets your Xoom handle e-mail accounts from providers other than Google. It's a handy way to keep your Gmail separate from your other e-mail, should you want to do that.

No matter whether you choose the Gmail app, the Email app, or both, e-mail on your Xoom works just like e-mail on your desktop PC or even your cellphone. You can send, receive, delete, and forward messages. You can even send or receive files attached through e-mail.

✔ To access your Gmail messages, touch Gmail on your Xoom's home screen, or touch Apps⇨Gmail.

✔ To access e-mail flowing through accounts other than Gmail, touch Apps⇨Email.

✔ The Gmail and Email apps look almost identical and behave almost identically. This chapter's instructions and figures apply to both apps.

✔ I explain how to set up both Gmail and Email app accounts in this chapter's last section.

✔ To remove an unwanted e-mail account, choose Apps⇨Settings⇨ Accounts & Sync. Touch the unwanted account's name; then touch the Remove Account option hidden in the screen's top-right corner.

Noticing and Reading New E-Mail

Like any other newsworthy bits of information, newly arrived e-mail first appears as a *notification,* which is a small blurb in your Xoom's bottom-right corner. The *blurb* — the sender's name and the Subject line — disappears after a few seconds, leaving an envelope icon sitting in the notifications panel below the clock.

If your Xoom's asleep, your notification light along the right edge will begin blinking, and you'll hear an alert sound; if your Xoom's turned off, you won't know of the incoming mail until you turn your Xoom back on.

To see which account delivered the e-mail, glance at the icon, shown in Figure 7-1. The Gmail app's icon (left) cleverly wears the letter *M*; the regular Email app's icon (right) looks like a regular envelope.

 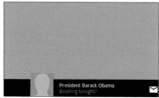

Figure 7-1: Newly received e-mails herald their arrival with a pop-up notice. The notice's icon reveals whether it came from Gmail (left) or another account (right).

Browsing e-mail

You can fetch your newly arrived e-mails for reading in any of several ways:

- ✔ **Touch the notification.** Should you spot an e-mail notification, like the ones in Figure 7-1, touch it. Your Xoom fetches the appropriate e-mail app, Gmail or Email, and opens it to display your newly arrived e-mail.

- ✔ **Touch the icon.** If the notification fades before your fingertip arrives, touch the tiny e-mail icon. The blurb reappears. Touch it to fetch your mail app and read your message.

    To delete any notification that's become old news, press the X next to it. (Your e-mail won't be deleted — just that little nagging icon and blurb in the notifications panel.)

- ✔ **Open your e-mail app.** Touch Apps, and then touch either the Gmail or Email app, depending on which one you've set up to collect your e-mail. (I explain how to set up either app or both apps in this chapter's last section.)

After you open the e-mail app, it fills the screen, as shown in Figure 7-2, ready for you to read and digest your newly arrived communiqués. Your newest unread e-mails sit atop the Inbox in boldface type. (Your other storage areas are listed below the Inbox in the left column.)

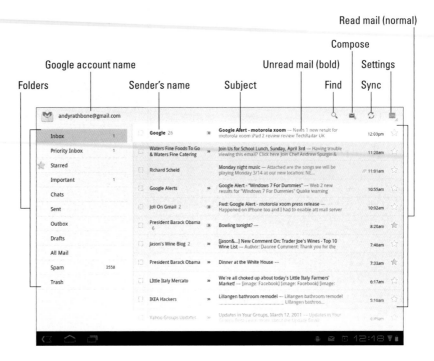

Read mail (normal)

Compose

Google account name   Unread mail (bold)   Settings

Folders   Sender's name   Subject   Find   Sync

Figure 7-2: Gmail displays your storage areas on the left and the selected area's contents on the right.

Reading an e-mail

To read an e-mail within your e-mail app, touch any part of it; the Subject line will do. Your e-mail app quickly shifts your view, spilling the e-mail's message to the right, as shown in Figure 7-3, and showing your Inbox's contents along the left.

After you've read your e-mail, you can take any of several actions:

- **Ignore it.** You needn't do anything. Flee back to your home screen with a touch of the home button, or stick around and browse other e-mails in your Inbox area. Alternatively, turn off your Xoom, and weed the parking strip.

- **Reply to it.** Touch the Reply button to tap a response to the e-mail, as discussed in the next section. (Touch the adjacent Reply All button to respond to everybody who received the e-mail.)

- **Forward it.** Punt the mail into somebody else's inbox by touching Forward and entering the new recipient's e-mail address.

- **Add a star to it.** Touch the star icon to mark the e-mail for later action. (All your starred e-mails live in your Star area for one-touch retrieval later.)

✔ **Delete it.** Touch the little trash-can icon to delete the mail. Deleted it by mistake? Head for the Trash area, and drag the e-mail back into your Inbox area.

✔ **Archive it.** Touch the file cabinet icon, shown in the margin, to *archive* a message that doesn't require further action. That keeps your Inbox tidy, yet your archived messages remain indexed and retrievable through Gmail's search feature, which I describe later in this chapter. If you need more organization than the archive's "big box of old e-mail" approach, use labels, described next.

✔ **Give it an existing label.** Unlike most e-mail programs, Gmail doesn't use folders. Instead, Gmail lets you add descriptive labels to e-mails that deal with a similar theme. You can't *create* labels with the Gmail app, but you can drag and drop messages onto any of your *existing* labels. They appear along the app's left edge, below the Trash label shown earlier in Figure 7-2. (You can create labels using your desktop computer, and they'll appear in your Gmail app.)

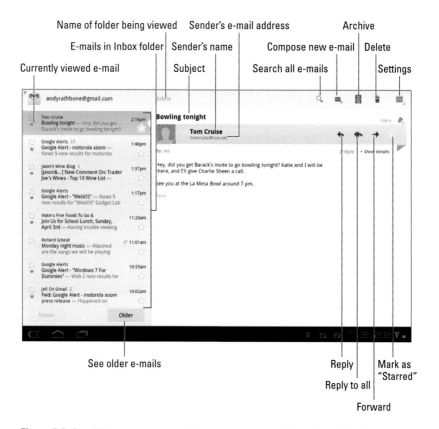

Figure 7-3: Gmail displays your e-mail's contents on the right and the Inbox's contents on the left.

Replying to a message

If you spot a reply-worthy e-mail in your e-mail app's inbox, touch the Reply button, shown in the margin. Your e-mail app changes yet again, as shown in Figure 7-4, giving you room to compose your missive.

Figure 7-4: The Gmail and Email apps devote the entire screen to your reply.

When the keyboard appears, enter your response in either of two ways:

✔ **Type it.** Touch the keys on the keyboard, just like you do in normal typing. To speed things up, check out all the typing tricks I describe in Chapter 4. (Tap the spacebar twice at a sentence's end, for example, to add a period, a space, and uppercase formatting to the next letter automatically.)

✔ **Dictate it.** Touch the keyboard's microphone key, and dictate your reply. Speak slowly and clearly, in one-sentence bursts. When your spoken words magically appear inside the e-mail, clean up any mistakes by using the keyboard. See Chapter 4 for more tips.

When you're done entering your response, press the Send button to send your response back through the Internet's pipes and into the recipient's inbox.

✔ Did you change your mind while you were still composing an e-mail? Touch the trash-can icon to delete it, touch OK to confirm, and then move on to something more productive.

✔ If you started to reply but want to finish later, touch Save Draft to stash your partial response in the Draft area for later retrieval.

✔ If you're responding to an e-mail sent to several people, touching Reply sends your response only to the message's originator. To reply to everybody who received the message, touch Reply All.

✔ Don't touch Reply All unless you're sure that everybody *really* needs to see your response. Everybody's inboxes are getting pretty crowded these days.

Forwarding an e-mail

Received an e-mail by mistake? Or do you just want to bring another person into the conversation? Either way, those are perfect times to *forward* an e-mail. When an e-mail arrives that must be seen by other eyes, follow these steps to share it:

1. **Open the e-mail you want to forward, and touch the Forward icon.**

   Shown in the margin, the Forward icon brings a standard Reply form to the screen, shown earlier in Figure 7-4. There's one big difference, though: This time, the Reply form contains the text of the e-mail you're forwarding.

2. **Enter the recipient's e-mail address in the To: area.**

   If you've corresponded with that person in the past, Gmail automatically fills in the e-mail address after you type the first few characters.

3. **Enter your own message if you have one.**

4. **Touch the Send button.**

   The forwarded e-mail heads for its new recipient.

✔ The person who sent you the original e-mail won't know you've sent it along to another party, a fact appreciated by whistle-blowers.

✔ If you *want* the original sender to know you're forwarding the e-mail, touch the words "+Cc/Bcc". That fetches two extra address lines — Cc and Bcc. Type the original sender's e-mail address into either of those two lines.

✔ What's the difference between the Cc and Bcc lines? Well, the *Cc (Carbon Copy)* line lets every recipient see every other recipient's address. E-mail addresses listed on the *Bcc (Blind Carbon Copy)* line remain secret to everybody but the original sender.

Creating and Sending E-Mail

Perhaps you're feeling sociable, or perhaps you just want the co-worker in the next cubicle to stop cooking fish in the office microwave. Either way, sending an e-mail lets you put your feelings on paper.

After you open your preferred app (Gmail or Email), you can create your own e-mail in either of two ways:

✔ **Touch the Compose button.** A blank message appears, ready for you to add the recipient's e-mail address and a message.

✔ **Touch a contact.** Touch Apps➪Contacts. The Contacts app appears, with all your contacts' names staring back at you. (I cover contacts in Chapter 8.) Touch the name of the contact worthy of receiving your mail; touch her e-mail address; and choose Compose, specifying whether the Gmail or Email app should handle the job.

No matter which of the two methods you use to start the e-mail, touching the Compose button fetches a blank e-mail. Follow these steps to fill it out and kick it into the appropriate party's electronic mailbox:

1. **Add the recipient's e-mail address, if necessary.**

   If you began composing your e-mail by touching a contact's name, your blank e-mail opens preaddressed — a nice timesaver.

   If you simply touched the Compose button, add the e-mail address by touching the To button, and entering characters (or speaking names). A drop-down menu lists all the potential matches in your contact list; when you spot the right recipient or e-mail address, touch it to add it to the To line.

   Alternatively, if the person isn't in your contact list, type the entire e-mail address.

2. **Touch the Subject line, and enter your subject.**

3. **Touch Compose Email, and begin typing or dictating your message.**

   I describe typing and dictating in Chapter 4.

4. **(Optional) Include an attachment.**

   Want to include a photo you've sent? Touch the paper-clip icon (refer to Figure 7-4, earlier in this chapter), choose Gallery, and touch the image you'd like to send. It's added as an attachment that rides along with your e-mail.

5. Touch Send.

If doubts nag you before you finish composing your message, touch Save As Draft to stuff your message into the Drafts area for later. Touch the Drafts area to retrieve it and continue your diatribe when you smell fish in the office microwave yet again.

Copies of all your sent e-mails live on in your Sent area for later reference.

I describe sending attachments in more detail later in this chapter.

Searching for Mail

Google works pretty well at finding things on the Internet. With Gmail, Google lets you use that search power on your own e-mail, enabling you to find e-mail containing a specific subject, contact name, or key words.

To search for an e-mail in your Gmail account, follow these steps:

1. Open your Gmail account, or touch Apps⇨Gmail.

2. Touch the Search button, and enter the text to find.

As you enter text, a drop-down menu lists the names of contacts. If you're looking for e-mail to or from a particular contact, touch that name in the drop-down menu. Gmail fetches all your correspondence with that person, sorted by date.

If you're more interested in the e-mail's content than in the sender/receiver, ignore the drop-down menu, and keep typing the search words.

3. Start the search by touching the keyboard's Enter key.

The search results, dubbed *conversations* by Gmail, appear onscreen, with your most recent correspondence at the top. Keep scrolling down to find the e-mail you seek.

Searches delving more than a few days into the past require a working Internet connection. Gmail keeps the bulk of your mail on Google's own computers, not on your Xoom.

Sending or Receiving an Attachment

Your Xoom can send and receive e-mail *attachments* — files embedded in the e-mail. When an e-mail arrives bearing an attachment, you'll spot a paper-clip icon both near the mail's subject and embedded in the e-mail.

When your Xoom recognizes the attachment, it places buttons next to the files. Depending on the attachment, you may spot buttons like Preview, View, Play, or Save (see Figure 7-5). Touch one of those buttons to see, play, or save your attached file.

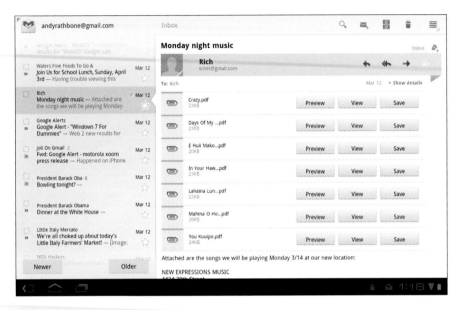

Figure 7-5: Buttons adjacent to the attached file show how your Xoom can handle the file.

If your Xoom doesn't recognize your attached file, though, it still offers a View button (but because the file's not recognized, the View button displays gibberish). When your Xoom can't handle an attached file, try logging in to your Gmail account on a desktop PC. Ideally, your PC has a program that recognizes the attached file.

- Out of the box, you can send photos that you've taken with your camera, as I describe in "Creating and Sending E-Mail," earlier in this chapter.

- You can also send any files stored in your Downloads folder. (Touch Apps⇨Downloads to view them.) To send a file within there, touch and hold its icon. When a menu appears, choose Share⇨Gmail.

- To send files deeper inside your Xoom's folders, download an app like ASTRO File Manager, covered in Chapter 18. Then, when you spot any file you want to send as an attachment, touch and hold it with your finger. Choose Send⇨Gmail. A blank message appears with the attachment, waiting only for an e-mail address and a touch of the Send button.

✔ The key to handling incoming attachments is installing some apps. For better handling of PDF files (Adobe Acrobat), for example, install the Adobe Reader app.

✔ You can *view* Microsoft Word and Excel documents, but not edit them. When you touch a Word or Excel document, an app called Quickoffice displays its contents.

Setting Up an E-Mail Account

Gmail accounts are by far the easiest accounts to set up. Not only that, your messages will be nearly spam-free, backed up automatically, easily searchable, and accessible from any computer.

If you prefer another e-mail account, though, your Xoom is graciously accommodating.

This section explains how to set up Gmail and other types of e-mail accounts on your Xoom.

Need to tweak the settings of an existing e-mail account? Choose Apps⇨ Settings⇨Accounts & Sync, touch your account's name, and choose Account Settings to change anything you've set up in this section.

Setting up a Gmail account

When you first turned on your Xoom and followed the steps detailed in Chapter 2, you either entered your Google account or touched Skip to enter it in later.

This section's for all the Skippers who now want to create a Gmail account, unlocking their free Gmail account, backups, and other Google-account-holder perks.

To create your own Gmail account, follow these steps:

1. On your home screen, touch the Gmail app.

   The screen asks you to sign in to your Google account.

TIP

If there's no Gmail account icon on your home screen, touch Apps↪Gmail.

2. **Touch the Create Account button.**

3. **Fill out the form with your desired username, password, and other information (see Figure 7-6).**

Figure 7-6: Fill out the forms to create your Google account for Gmail.

The onscreen keyboard appears, ready for you to type your information. When you choose your desired username, touch the Check Availability button. (All the good names are already taken, as John Smith discovered early on.)

4. **When the approval screen appears, touch to approve automatic backups for your Xoom, if you want, and touch Done.**

Automatic backups protect the Xoom's settings, mail, appointments, apps, items purchased from Google's online store, and similar Google-controlled ephemera.

5. **Accept any updates that arrive soon afterward.**

Google tries to prolong your Xoom's eventual free fall into obsolescence by continually updating its software over the Internet — for free. It's a nice touch.

Want to create a second Gmail account, perchance? Touch Apps↪Settings↪ Accounts & Sync↪Add Account (it's hiding in the top-right corner)↪ Google Accounts. That puts you at Step 2. (Within Gmail, you can switch between the two accounts by touching the account name at the top of the Gmail app's screen.)

Can't remember your Gmail password? Google jogs your memory at this site:

```
https://www.google.com/accounts/recovery
```

Setting up other e-mail accounts

Google welcomes you to create a Google account within seconds after you first turn on your Xoom. After you enter your Google name and password, Google automatically fills out the other bothersome forms. After all, Google knows its own e-mail settings.

Google doesn't know every e-mail provider's settings, however. It automatically fills out the right forms for big e-mail providers, but if you're not lucky, you must discover and enter those settings yourself.

To add a *non*-Gmail e-mail account to your Xoom, cross your fingers, and follow these steps:

1. **From the home screen, touch Apps⇨Settings⇨Accounts & Sync⇨ Add Account (hidden in the top-right corner)⇨Email.**

2. **Enter your full e-mail address like this, substituting your own username and e-mail provider:**

   johnsmith@e-mailprovider.com

3. **Enter your password, and touch Next.**

   If you're using an e-mail address from Windows Live, Mobile Me, Yahoo!, or a few other popular e-mail accounts, Google usually fills in the ugly server technicalities for you, letting you leapfrog to Step 8 to fill out a few brief formalities.

   If Google *doesn't* automatically fill out the details, it's your job. Trot onward to Step 4.

4. **Contact your e-mail provider for its e-mail server information; then, when you have it, touch the Manual Settings button, and repeat Steps 1–3 to return to this step if need be.**

   Specifically, you must request these two facts from your e-mail provider:

   • *Incoming server:* You need your incoming mail server's name and whether it supports POP3, IMAP, or HTTP. (When in doubt, choose POP3.)

   • *Outgoing server:* You need your outgoing mail server's name, which usually includes the acronym SMTP.

You can find this information on your e-mail company's website or in the materials mailed to you when you signed up. Alternatively, you can call the company's support phone number. The phone staff continually repeats this information to customers who are trying to set up their e-mail.

5. **Touch your type of account: POP3, IMAP, or Exchange.**

6. **Enter or confirm the following information, and touch Next.**

   - Your username and password are the same ones you use when you retrieve your e-mail elsewhere.

   - The server name comes from your e-mail provider. (It almost always contains the string *POP*.)

   - The Port is almost always 110.

   - *Don't* choose to delete e-mail from the server if you're also collecting this e-mail on another computer. If this mail goes *only* to your Xoom, choose Yes.

7. **Enter your outgoing server information, and touch Next.**

   Enter the SMTP server you pried out of your e-mail provider. (It usually contains the string *SMTP*.) The Port is usually 25.

8. **Choose your settings by touching the appropriate boxes, and touch Next.**

   - *Inbox Checking Frequency:* Normally, your Xoom checks for new e-mail every 15 minutes. Too desperate to wait? Don't want to be disturbed? Change the number of minutes so that it meshes with your lifestyle.

   - *Send Email from This Account by Default:* Choose this option if you send most of your e-mail from this e-mail address.

   - *Notify Me When Email Arrives:* When new mail arrives, your Xoom beeps, and a message appears in the notifications panel.

   - *Sync from This Account:* Depending on your account, you may be able to sync your e-mail, contacts, and calendar from this account automatically. If this option is offered, touch these check boxes.

   - *Automatically Download Attachments When Connected to Wi-Fi:* To keep you from plowing through your data-plan minutes, this option grabs attachments only when you're connected through Wi-Fi rather than your carrier's data plan.

   Note: These options vary from e-mail provider to e-mail provider.

9. **Name your account, add your real name, and touch Next.**

   This is an optional amenity for folks with several e-mail addresses. By giving your accounts different names, you can more easily distinguish between them.

   Enter the name you want to appear on your outgoing e-mail addresses. Choose your real name unless you're working undercover.

At this point, your account appears as Yet Another Account in your Xoom's master list. To see the list, choose Apps⇨Settings⇨Accounts & Sync. There, your new account takes its place along with any other accounts you may have, including Gmail, Facebook, Twitter, and other message-flinging services.

Your Xoom doesn't limit your number of e-mail accounts. Add as many — or as few — as you want.

Are you having trouble with the POP/SMTP settings? You may need to call your e-mail provider and have the support staff walk you through the process (which some companies make a lot more complicated than they should).

Setting up a corporate e-mail account

Corporate e-mail companies often play by a different set of rules. If you need to set up your Xoom to send and receive information from your company's server — something called an Exchange account — don't try to set it up yourself. Instead, hand your Xoom to the company's IT person, and tell him that your boss said you need access to the Exchange server. This isn't something you want to tackle yourself, even if you're up for challenges.

8

People and Appointments

In This Chapter

▶ Managing your contacts

▶ Putting new contacts on your Xoom

▶ Finding contacts

▶ Sending e-mail to contacts

▶ Picking a calendar view

▶ Checking your appointments

▶ Configuring calendars

*Y*ou probably won't be spending much time with the Contacts app on the Motorola Xoom. Sure, if the Xoom could make phone calls, a list of contacts would be nice. Still, unless you're looking for a friend's street address or a company's website, your Contacts app may be more a general reference than a "go-to" app.

Instead, the benefits of a well-stocked contacts list helps you mostly while in other apps. Start addressing an e-mail, for example, and the Motorola Xoom automatically fills in that person's e-mail address from your Contacts app faster than you can type it yourself.

Everybody needs a good Calendar app, though. Imagine being able to confirm your next doctor's appointment while you're still in the doctor's office. As another plus, you have your Xoom to read while you sit stuck in one of those uncomfortable office chairs, surrounded by germ-filled magazines.

But I digress. This chapter explains how to manage both your contacts and appointments on the Motorola Xoom.

Contacts

It's not as small as a phone, but your Xoom still lets you tote around your contact information. Although you can't phone your contacts, you can still look up their addresses, send them e-mail, and even delete them should they wrong you.

The next few sections explain how to do just that.

Viewing, editing, and deleting contacts

To see your list of friends, foes, and in-betweens, touch Apps⇨Contacts. Your Contacts app rises to the screen, as shown in Figure 8-1. However, it displays everybody your *Xoom* knows about. And unless you've let your Xoom know about your social circle, your Contacts app may be completely empty.

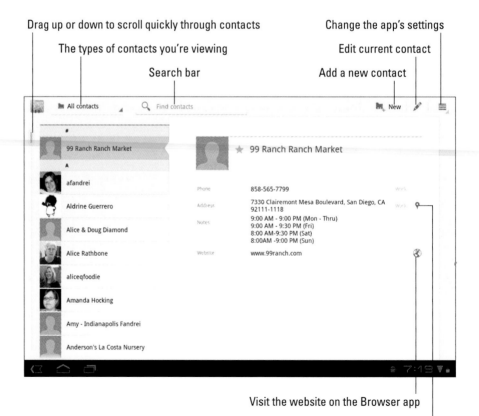

Drag up or down to scroll quickly through contacts
The types of contacts you're viewing
Search bar
Change the app's settings
Edit current contact
Add a new contact

Visit the website on the Browser app
See the location on the Maps app

Figure 8-1: The Contacts app stays up to date with your Google Contacts, as well as with some of your social-networking sites, such as Twitter.

You can fill it up several ways. If you entered your Google account information as I describe in Chapter 2, your contacts list may already be stocked. That's because your contacts always stay linked with your online Google Contacts.

The Contacts app lists your contacts' names in the left pane, sorted alphabetically by first name. Touch a name, and personal details spill across to the right pane.

To scroll quickly down your list of contacts, touch the slim blue bar on the far-left edge of the app's screen (refer to Figure 8-1). As you slide the bar up or down, a letter appears, letting you know your general location in your contacts list. Lift your finger when you've reached the desired letter — *R* for *Rebecca,* for example — and drag the list up or down to finish your search.

Because your Xoom can't make phone calls, your contacts' phone numbers probably won't interest you much, but keep an eye out for these nifty Contacts app features:

- ✔ To see a contact's address on a map, touch the adjacent pushpin icon, shown both in the margin and in Figure 8-1. The Maps app opens and pinpoints your contact's address with a little pop-up window that lists the address. Touch the address and touch the Navigate button, (which I cover in Chapter 15); your Xoom will guide you there.

- ✔ To look up a contact's website, perhaps to find an online menu for a restaurant, touch the web icon. The Browser app (see Chapter 6) rises and opens to the website, where you can check for extra-crispy fries.

- ✔ Do you spot a typo or need to change an address? Touch the Edit icon (shown in the margin) to edit any of the contact's details.

- ✔ Has a supposed friend violated your accepted social norms? Cross that person off your list by touching the Settings icon in the top-right corner, and choosing Delete Contact from the drop-down menu.

- ✔ For quick access to a few favorite contacts, add their names to your home screen as individual widgets. (I cover widgets in Chapter 9.) When you touch one of these names, a pop-up menu quickly lets you send that person an e-mail, navigate to his house, or nudge him through any social-media apps that you've added to your Xoom.

Adding contacts

Adding somebody's phone number is easy when she calls you on a cellphone. After all, she's left her phone number right on your phone's display for easy saving.

Because the Xoom can't send or receive phone calls, however, adding contacts on your tablet isn't as easy or natural as it is on a cellphone. The next two sections describe the two easiest ways to stock your contacts list.

Adding contacts automatically

You can add a whole mess o' contacts at the same time by syncing your Xoom with existing contacts you already have online. Your contacts from Twitter, Gmail, Skype, and possibly Facebook can pad your contacts list automatically.

To start gathering your online contacts and automatically stuffing them into your Xoom, follow these steps:

1. **Touch Apps➪Settings➪Accounts & Sync.**

   The Accounts & Sync screen appears (see Figure 8-2), showing the accounts your Xoom already uses to harvest your contact information.

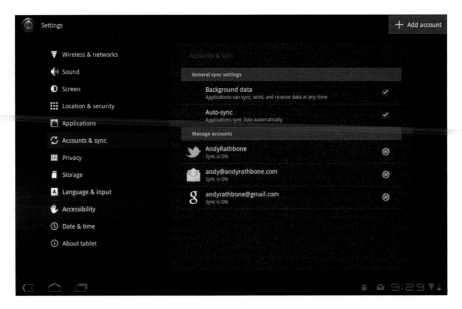

Figure 8-2: Your Xoom automatically grabs any contact information it finds from the accounts listed on this page.

2. **Touch Add Account in the top-right corner, and add your account information.**

   Out of the box, you can enter three types of accounts here, all from e-mail accounts I describe in Chapter 7:

   - *Corporate:* Meant for grabbing e-mail from corporate domains, this job is best handled in the presence of your office manager.

   - *Email:* Enter usernames and passwords for your e-mail addresses here to let your Email app fetch your mail. (Unfortunately, that app probably won't grab contact information from here.)

   - *Google:* Here's the mother lode: Signing up for a Google e-mail account automatically syncs your Google contacts as well. For the complete step-by-steps on creating a Gmail account, Chapter 7.

   Depending on the apps you've installed (see Chapter 9), you may find other accounts listed here, including Twitter, Skype, and Facebook. Downloading, installing, and signing in with Twitter's app, for example, adds *everybody* you follow to your Contacts app.

   Contacts added from third-parties like Twitter don't sync with your desktop computer's Google contacts list; they're limited to your Xoom.

3. **Make sure that the words *Sync Is ON* appear below the account name.**

   Those words mean that your Xoom actively exchanges information — be it new contact names, contact pictures, or status updates — with that account. When you look at a Twitter contact, for example, you can see her latest tweet.

   If an account isn't syncing correctly, touch that account's name. A page appears, listing all the information that account can exchange with your Xoom. Put a checkmark next to the items you want to stay in sync with your Xoom. Don't want items to sync? Then remove that item's checkmark.

Adding accounts and keeping them synced automatically is the easiest way to keep your contact list well stocked and up to date. Two other settings, also shown in Figure 8-2, also bear note:

- ✔ **Background Data:** When it's turned on, this option lets all your accounts stay updated in the background. When this option is turned off, you sync manually by touching the app's Refresh button. (If your battery power starts to drop at day's end, turn this option off to save power.)

- ✔ **Auto-Sync:** This toggle switch controls whether your accounts can grab data automatically. If you're traveling and don't care to waste your data-plan minutes on e-mail or status updates, tap the Auto-Sync check to remove it. (Turn the option on again when you have Wi-Fi to sync back up.)

Don't worry about fiddling with these two settings and then never finding them again when you need them. If an app needs one of these options turned on, the app tells you which setting to turn on and then drops you back at this screen.

If you follow 2,468 people on Twitter, you'll soon see your contacts list swell to unruly proportions. The solution lies in *filtering* your contacts, described later in this chapter's "Filtering contacts" section.

Adding contacts manually

Eventually, you'll run across somebody who's interesting enough to add to your contacts list. If you happen to be carrying your bulky tablet around at the party (and this person still wants to be your friend), follow these steps to add their essential details to your Xoom:

1. Touch Apps⇨Contacts.

The Contacts app opens (refer to Figure 8-1, earlier in this chapter).

2. Touch New at the top of the screen.

An empty contact sheet appears, as shown in Figure 8-3, ready for you to enter your newfound pal's details in the neatly labeled lines, called *fields*.

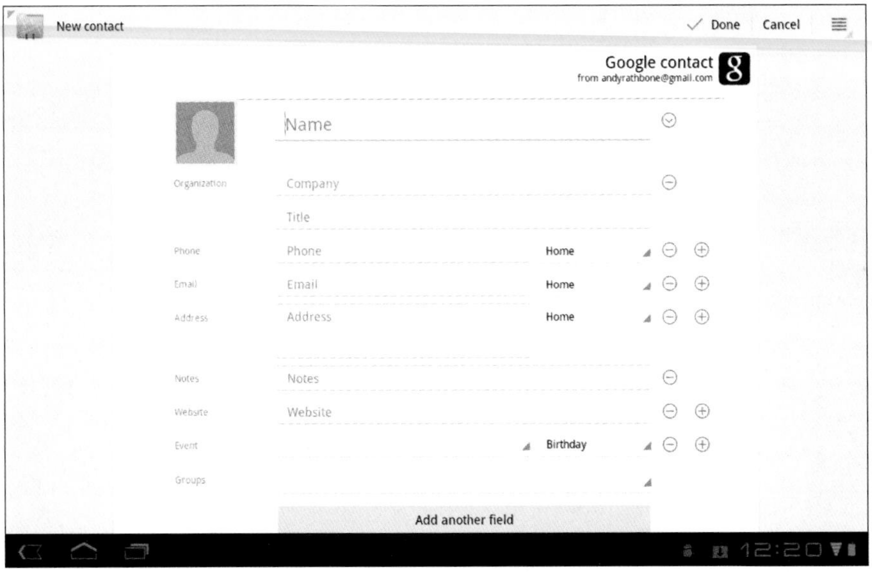

![Screenshot of the New contact screen showing fields for Name, Company, Title, Phone, Email, Address, Notes, Website, Event (Birthday), and Groups, with an "Add another field" button. The top shows "New contact", "Done", "Cancel", and "Google contact from andyrathbone@gmail.com". Time reads 12:20.]

Figure 8-3: Touch any field, and a keyboard appears for you to begin typing in information.

3. **Enter the person's contact information in the designated fields.**

   Touch a blank field, such as Name, and the keyboard rears its head, ready for you to tap in the correct information. (I cover both keyboard and voice entry in Chapter 4.)

   The little gray triangles, like the ones next to Phone and Email in Figure 8-3, fetch a drop-down menu for changing a field's name. When you're entering a work phone number, for example, touch the triangle to change the field's name from Home to Work.

   Need to add a second phone number or e-mail address? Touch the plus sign next to any field to create an extra field to handle the extra information.

4. **Touch Add Another Field to choose among more fields.**

   This button won't let you create your own fields (like Prefers Crispy Fries). Instead, the pop-up list that it displays lets you choose among a few popular fields, such as Relationship, Event, and IM.

   To add details like food preferences, touch the ever-expandable Notes line, and start typing anything you want.

5. **Add a photo, if desired.**

   Touch the currently empty face icon to get two options: snap and crop a quick photo with the built-in camera, or crop a mug shot from an existing photo. (I cover the two cameras and photo cropping in Chapter 11.)

6. **Touch Done in the screen's top-right corner.**

   Your Xoom saves your new contact, and syncs it with your Gmail account.

You can also add contacts directly from the Maps app (see Chapter 14). This feature is handy when you spot an interesting restaurant and want to save its information for later.

Copying contacts from desktop PC programs

The e-mail programs on your desktop PC probably brim with contacts. You can copy those contacts to your Xoom, but that process isn't particularly easy. In fact, it's much, *much* easier to import contacts from your desktop computer to the Gmail website (`https://mail.google.com`). Gmail pushes those updated contacts directly to your Xoom.

To add contacts from your desktop PC to Gmail, visit Gmail on your desktop PC. Choose Gmail's

Options menu and choose Mail Settings from the drop-down menu. Then, choose the Accounts and Import option, and click the Import Mail and Contacts button. Google walks you through the steps of importing both contacts and e-mail from Yahoo!, Hotmail, AOL, or other webmail or POP3 accounts.

Once those contacts arrive in your desktop computer's Gmail account, they automatically appear in your Xoom's contacts list, as well.

Filtering contacts

The only problem bigger than not having any contacts is having too many of them. After you add your Twitter and Facebook accounts to your Xoom, you could end up seeing thousands of extra contacts. How can you find anybody anymore?

The answer is by using *filters.* With filters, you can view only Gmail contacts, for example, or only your Twitter contacts. The secret lies in the drop-down menu in the Contacts app's top-left corner (see Figure 8-4).

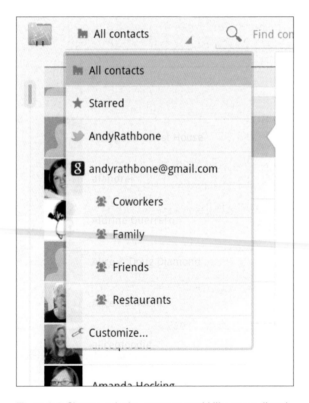

Figure 8-4: Choose only the contacts you'd like to see listed.

Choosing All Contacts lets you see everybody, which may be overload. To weed out everybody except your Gmail contacts, for example, touch your Gmail address listing from the drop-down menu. Similarly, see only your Twitter contacts by touching Twitter.

Searching for contacts

To search for a particular contact, begin entering his first name in the Find Contacts bar at the top of the Contact app's screen (refer to Figure 8-1, earlier in this chapter).

As soon as you begin entering letters, the Xoom's instant search kicks in, narrowing your visible contacts to names containing that letter. By the time you type your third or fourth letter, your long-lost contact's name will rise within view.

When you spot the name, touch it, and the details spill out into the right pane.

You can search for any word that appears in a contact's listing, as every word is fully indexed.

E-mailing contacts

This part is easy. Follow these steps to send an e-mail to somebody who's listed in your Contacts app:

1. **Open the Contacts app by touching Apps⇨Contacts.**

2. **Locate and touch the contact you want to e-mail.**

   I describe how to search for contacts in the preceding section.

3. **Touch the e-mail icon next to the contact's e-mail address.**

   If your contact has more than one e-mail address, touch the one you want to use.

   Your Gmail or Email app opens, displaying a preaddressed, blank e-mail form.

4. **Fill in the form, and touch Send.**

Not all contact listings contain e-mail addresses, however. If you've added Twitter contacts, for example, those contacts have no Email field. Pull up your Twitter app and send them tweets instead.

I cover all things e-mail in Chapter 7.

Consider adding the Email or Gmail widget to your home screen. It constantly updates to show the latest e-mails in your Inbox. I describe how to customize your home screen with widgets in Chapter 17.

Calendar

Your Google account comes with not only free e-mail (see Chapter 7) and a free contact manager (described earlier in this chapter), but a free calendar as well. All these features are available on your Xoom and on the web; update a calendar or contact list on your Xoom, and you've simultaneously updated your web versions, as well.

If you've never seen Google Calendar on your desktop PC, give it a visit here or on your Xoom:

```
https://www.google.com/calendar
```

In fact, if you plan to use your Xoom's calendar, spend a little time first with the web version on your desktop PC. The web version offers extra settings that aren't available in your Xoom's Calendar app.

 To see the Calendar app, fetch it from your home screen by touching Apps⇨ Calendar.

The rest of this section describes how to view the calendar in its many forms, as well as how to find, add, and delete appointments.

Choosing and understanding a calendar view

The calendar continually changes shape for your viewing pleasure. When it's first called up, it displays the current week (see Figure 8-5).

The current day is highlighted in blue, and a thin blue line highlights the current time. For example, the calendar in Figure 8-4 shows that it's 2:30 pm, Monday, March 14.

Switch to the current day's appointments by touching Day at the top of the screen. Again, your current appointment appears in blue, and a thin blue line highlights the current time. To see an appointment, touch it. A window pops up, providing more information.

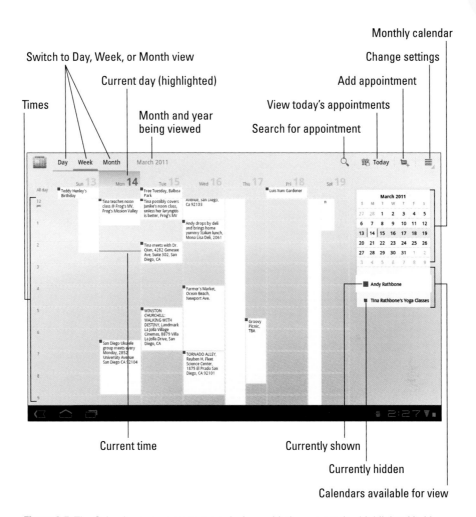

Figure 8-5: The Calendar app opens to a week view, with the current day highlighted in blue.

Touch Month at the top of the screen to see the current month's calendar, with the current day highlighted in blue.

> 🖙 To scroll through upcoming appointments in Day or Week view, drag your finger across the screen from right to left, just like you're paging through a book. Reverse the action to go back in time and see past dates.

✔ To scroll through upcoming appointments in Month view, drag your finger from *bottom to top.* (Yes, scrolling works differently in Month view.)

✔ Jump back to today's appointments by touching Today in the top-right corner of the calendar.

✔ See the monthly calendar on the right edge of the Day and Week views? (Figure 8-5 shows a Week view.) It's scrollable. Slide your finger up or down the dates to scroll ahead or in the past. The days on which you have appointments appear in bold.

✔ The Google Calendar program can overlay several calendars — a useful feature for tracking several people's appointments at a glance. To switch among calendars, choose from among the ones listed beneath the monthly calendar on the right. There, for example, I can choose between seeing my calendar, my wife Tina Rathbone's Yoga Classes calendar, or both.

✔ To overlay another person's calendar atop your own, use Google Calendar on your desktop computer. The Xoom's Calendar app doesn't offer that feature yet.

✔ Be sure to install the Calendar widget on your home screen. This widget (which I cover in Chapter 18) adds a small window that perpetually displays your next few appointments. Also, it's scrollable. A finger flick lets you see your upcoming appointments without opening the Calendar app.

Searching for appointments

To see any appointment — whether you're viewing your calendar in Day, Week, or Month view — just touch it onscreen. A window pops up, displaying more information.

If you can't see the appointment in your current view, search for it, as follows:

1. **Touch the magnifying-glass icon at the top of the calendar.**

   The Search line appears, and the keyboard arises, ready for you to describe your search. (If you have a hangnail, touch the keyboard's microphone icon to speak a keyword.)

2. **Enter a keyword, or even part of one; then touch the keyboard's Enter key (or touch the little gray triangle at the right end of the search bar).**

   The calendar shows both past and future dates that match your sought-after term (see Figure 8-6). Your next upcoming appointment that matches the search term appears in the middle.

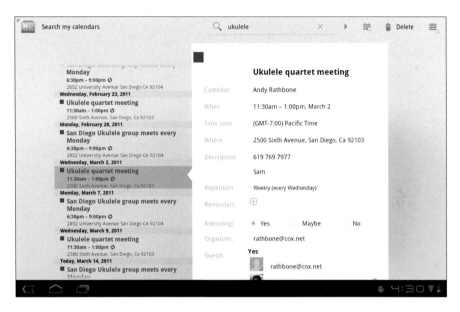

Figure 8-6: Searching for words, dates, or numbers brings up matching appointments.

The list of matching appointments along the left edge is scrollable; slide your finger up or down the list to see all the matches. Tap any one to view it in detail.

Adding, editing, and deleting appointments

By itself, the Calendar app is an empty canvas. To add some color and structure to your life, you want to add some appointments. You can add upcoming events while gazing at your calendar in any view, be it Day, Week, or Month.

Here's what to do:

1. **Move to a Week or Day view that shows your upcoming appointment's date.**

   To switch to the correct week quickly, touch the appropriate date listed on the monthly calendar (refer to Figure 8-5). If necessary, drag your finger up or down that little calendar to jump several months into the future.

2. **Find the day of the appointment and then touch the hour when the appointment begins.**

   (If your appointment doesn't start on the hour, you can easily edit it later.)

   A window appears, ready for you to fill in the blanks (see Figure 8-7).

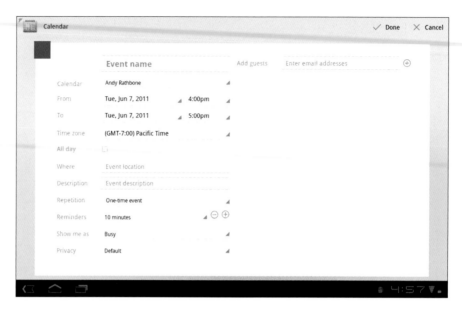

Figure 8-7: Enter the appointment's name, location, and description.

3. **Enter the appointment's name, location, and description in the proper fields, adjust the time, and add an alarm, if necessary.**

   The calendar lets you set many options, but the name, location, and description are the bare minimum you need to fill out.

   To adjust the appointment's starting or ending times, touch the little gray triangle next to the currently listed hour. A window appears, letting you choose the precise hour, minute, and time of day (a.m. or p.m.).

   Prefer to hear an alarm reminding you of an upcoming appointment? Choose the alarm's time by touching the Reminders drop-down menu and choosing a time from 10 minutes to 24 hours before the event. At the appointed time, your Xoom makes a sound and sends a notification to your Xoom's notification panel.

4. **After you add the details, touch Done in the top-right corner of the screen.**

You're not *done* done, though, as you can always go back and edit it for any changed details. Just touch your newly created appointment in the calendar, and the window shown in Figure 8-7 appears, ready for your updates.

✔ Your calendar calls upon your Maps app if you try to navigate to an address you've entered. To make the address easy for the Maps app to find, add it as clearly as possible (5555 Mayberry St., Falls Church, VA 22042, for example).

✔ To schedule regular events, touch Repetition. In the resulting screen, you can make the date recur daily, every weekday, weekly, monthly (by date or day of the week), or yearly. Here in Southern California, I can now remember which day is Trash Day and which day is Recycling Day.

9

All About Apps

In This Chapter

▶ Checking out your Xoom's bundled apps

▶ Getting your apps going

▶ Understanding the difference between apps and widgets

▶ Adding and deleting apps

▶ Getting new apps

▶ Keeping your apps updated

*A*pps — small programs made for mobile devices — really make the standard Xoom you got from Motorola your own. These mini programs, created by huge companies and hobbyist programmers alike, perform niche jobs that are tailored to specific lifestyles.

Big corporations typically create apps targeted after mainstream interests. You'll find apps promoting wares by major TV networks and movie studios, for example, as well as apps from big websites such as Yelp, Facebook, and YouTube.

Yet, you'll also find niche apps created by single programmers that cater to more esoteric needs. You'll find apps that teach you how to tie seafaring knots, turn on your Volvo's heater remotely, and track the latest grain prices in Iowa.

No matter who created the app, when it matches your own interest, it quickly becomes indispensable.

The Motorola Xoom runs Android apps written specifically for your tablet's large screen, as well as most apps written for Android mobile phones, giving you thousands of apps to meet almost every need. This chapter explains how to download and run them.

Viewing Your Apps

 The Apps icon (shown in the margin) lives in the top-right corner of the screen. Touch the word *Apps,* and your apps appear, as shown in Figure 9-1.

After you've owned your Xoom for a while, you'll collect more apps than can fit on one screen. When that happens, your Xoom adds the extra apps to a second screen off to the right. See the outlines of app icons on the right side of Figure 9-1? Touch an outlined app, or touch anywhere near the app screen's right edge, and the second page slides into view.

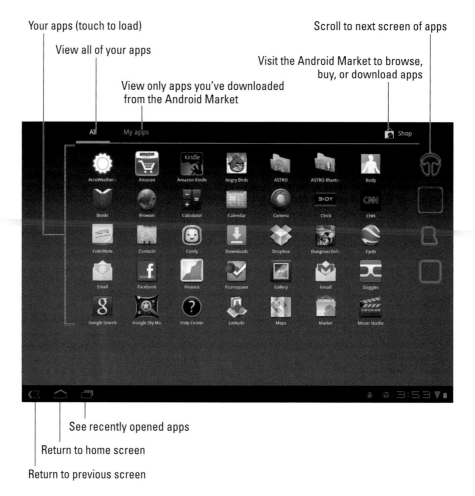

Your apps (touch to load)

View all of your apps

Scroll to next screen of apps

View only apps you've downloaded from the Android Market

Visit the Android Market to browse, buy, or download apps

See recently opened apps

Return to home screen

Return to previous screen

Figure 9-1: Touch any app's icon to launch it.

What's the difference between apps and widgets?

Widgets are specific types of apps that run constantly on your home screens, displaying new information as it's available. Widgets can display the current weather, for example, your latest piece of e-mail, the song you're currently playing, or your favorite contacts.

Apps, by contrast, usually wait in the background until you launch them.

Other than that, they're identical. Apps and widgets are downloaded, installed, uninstalled, and added to your home screen in the same way.

As you add more apps, your Xoom keeps growing more screens. It displays the apps alphabetically, stretching them off to the right, filling as many screens as needed to display them all.

To load an app, just touch it. The app loads immediately, usually filling the screen.

To close an open app, touch the Back button in your screen's bottom-left corner.

Exploring Your Xoom's Stock Apps

Your Xoom came stocked with a few apps when you bought it, as shown in Figure 9-2. Depending on your Xoom's model and data plan, you'll probably spot some or all of the apps in Figure 9-2 waiting for your touch.

Here's a quick explanation of what to expect from each app:

✔ **Books:** The Books app lets you view and read books from Google's bookstore, which was launched to compete with Amazon's Kindle and Apple's iBooks. (Check out the Free Books section for classics.) I go into detail about this app, as well as other e-reader apps, in Chapter 13.

✔ **Browser:** Your Xoom's web browser, launched from this button, works much like Internet Explorer, Mozilla Firefox, and similar web browsers. I cover it in Chapter 6.

✔ **Calculator:** A must for math students, this umpteen-digit calculator handles algebraic and trigonometric equations.

✔ **Calendar:** Covered in Chapter 8, this app keeps track of your appointments. It syncs automatically with Google Calendar on your desktop PC.

Figure 9-2: These apps come with nearly every Xoom.

✔ **Camera:** There are two cameras, as well as a video camera, all of which are launched from this app. (Cameras and video are covered in Chapter 11.)

✔ **Clock:** This snoozer simply turns your entire screen into a digital clock.

✔ **Contacts:** Touch this icon to see all your contacts. (I talk about contacts in Chapter 8.)

✔ **Cordy:** This graphics-rich adventure game keeps kids (and many adults) occupied for hours.

✔ **Downloads:** Did you download something from the Internet? Touch this app to find it waiting.

✔ **Dungeon Defenders:** When it's first launched, this huge role-playing– game downloads 600MB of data into your Xoom. Make sure that your Xoom is connected through Wi-Fi before you launch it.

✔ **Email:** Head here to send or receive e-mail through a service other than Google's Gmail. (I cover both the Email and Gmail apps in Chapter 7.)

✔ **Gallery:** This app lets you view all your Xoom's photos. I cover it in Chapter 11.

 ✔ **Gmail:** This app lets you read, browse, and send e-mail through Google's e-mail service, Gmail. (I cover both the Email and Gmail apps in Chapter 7.)

 ✔ **Google Search:** Meant as a way to add quick web searches to your home screen, this app simply places a Google search bar on the screen. (I describe in Chapter 17 how to customize your home screens with app shortcuts.)

 ✔ **Latitude:** This app allows you to see your friends' current location on a map — provided that they've opted in, that is.

 ✔ **Maps:** A stunning feature on the Xoom, maps and navigation get their due in Chapter 14.

 ✔ **Market:** Head here to download both free and paid apps from the Android Market, as described later in this chapter.

 ✔ **Movie Studio:** This app lets you edit the boring portions of videos that you shoot with your Xoom.

 ✔ **Music:** Covered in Chapter 12, this app lets you see and play all the music stored on your Xoom.

 ✔ **Navigation:** Thanks to this app, your Xoom can guide you verbally as you drive between addresses. (I cover navigation in Chapter 14.)

 ✔ **Places:** Looking for something nearby? Load Places to fetch a map showing nearby businesses.

 ✔ **Settings:** This huge control panel of settings, covered in Chapter 15, lets you change everything from the wireless networks your Xoom uses to how your keyboard sounds.

 ✔ **Talk:** Google Talk lets you hold video chats with other Google Talk users. (I cover video chats in Chapter 10.)

 ✔ **Voice Search:** Touching this app's icon is the same as touching the keyboard's microphone icon. It lets you dump the keyboard and simply dictate to your Xoom. (I cover voice search in Chapter 4.)

 ✔ **YouTube:** The TV of the Internet generation, YouTube lets anybody upload videos, ranging from Carnegie Hall performances to cats riding robotic vacuum cleaners.

Will phone apps work on my Xoom?

Your Xoom has a big screen. Your phone has a small screen. That difference inevitably leads to real estate issues. That said, most apps written for a phone work just as well on a Xoom. If you've enjoyed a free app on your Android phone, download it on your Xoom and give it a try.

Some apps make you hold your Xoom sideways, for example; others don't care. Apps that vibrate a cellphone won't work on a Xoom; neither will those that deal with phone calls.

Older Android phones sported a Menu button for accessing an app's options. When you run an app designed for a phone, you'll spot a Menu button sitting next to your regular suite of Home, Back, and Recent Apps buttons. The Menu button lets you control the app just as though it were running on your phone.

If you've already bought some apps for your phone, here's good news: Your paid apps are linked to your Google account, not to your phone. So if you sign in to the same Google account on your Xoom, your paid apps will be waiting for you, ready to be downloaded and installed onto your Xoom. You don't have to buy them again.

Also, note the menu option for My Apps in the Xoom's top-left corner, shown in Figure 9-2. Touching My Apps filters the apps to display only apps you've personally downloaded, handy when you're searching for a particular favorite among a sea of apps. To see all your apps, including the bundled ones, touch the All Apps option. Note: Installing the Android 3.1 update adds a Video app for renting and watching videos.

Launching Apps

You launch or start an app simply by touching it. There's no "double-touch" stuff, as you do with a mouse on a Windows PC (although you won't cause any harm if you try). A simple tap does the trick.

You'll find apps to launch in two main places on your Xoom:

- **App area:** This area (shown in Figures 9-1 and 9-2, earlier in this chapter) lists all the apps, including ones you've downloaded.
- **Your home screen:** The home screen comes stocked with a few apps when you first turn it on.

You may notice a few *widgets* on your home screen as well. Different from apps, widgets display constantly updating information, such as the temperature, your latest piece of e-mail, or a daily appointment agenda.

To close an open app, touch the Back button in your screen's bottom-left corner. That button doesn't really close it, though; the app keeps running in the background. It closes only when your memory runs low. That is, your Xoom closes your last-accessed app to make room for your newly opened app.

 To see your most recently accessed apps, touch the Recent Apps button in your Xoom's bottom-left corner. Those apps are still waiting for you in the background, and they'll jump to the screen almost instantly when you touch their icons.

Adding Apps to Your Home Screens

Whenever you turn on your Xoom, you end up at your home screen — the computer equivalent of your desktop. Just as you've rearranged your PC's desktop for easy use, you'll naturally want to organize your Xoom's workspace to meet your needs.

You can sprinkle your home screen with shortcuts to your favorite apps, keeping them a tap away. Your Xoom comes with *five* home screens, so you can customize each screen with apps gathered around a similar theme, if you want. Toss shortcuts to your travel apps on one screen, for example, and let your media apps live on another.

To add an app to your home screen, follow these steps:

1. **Visit the Apps screen by touching Apps on a home screen.**

    The Apps button, shown in the margin, lives in the top-right corner of all of your home screens.

2. **Touch and hold your desired app.**

   After a second, the screen changes, as shown in Figure 9-3. Thumbnails of your five home screens appear below your rows of apps.

3. **Without lifting your finger, drag your app to the home screen where you want it to live.**

   As your finger reaches one of the home screens, that home screen grows larger, as shown in Figure 9-4, letting you see exactly where to place your app's shortcut. Tiny-and-faint grid symbols, also shown in Figure 9-4, help you position it evenly.

4. **When you're happy with your app's new position, lift your finger.**

   The app stays in place on your chosen home screen, where you can gaze at it approvingly.

Your Xoom's five home screens appear as
you touch and hold an app icon.

Figure 9-3: Drag the app shortcut to any of the five home screens along the bottom.

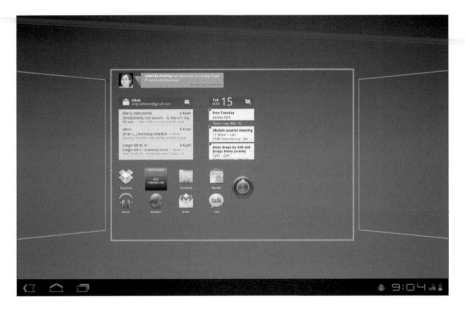

Figure 9-4: Lift your finger when you've placed the app in its new location.

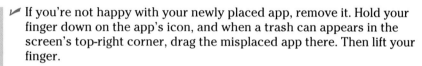
- ✔ If you're not happy with your newly placed app, remove it. Hold your finger down on the app's icon, and when a trash can appears in the screen's top-right corner, drag the misplaced app there. Then lift your finger.

- ✔ App icons placed on the home screen are only shortcuts — push buttons — that launch the real apps. Removing an app's icon from the home screen doesn't delete the app itself. The real app still lives safely in the Apps area.

- ✔ If your newly placed app's landing spot isn't quite right, move it over a tad. Touch it, keeping your finger pressed against the screen; then drag it to another spot on the screen. (You can even drag it to the screen's edges, leapfrogging it over to adjacent home screens.)

- ✔ Add a shortcut to your Settings button. You'll use that button a lot as you tell your Xoom how to adjust to your lifestyle and work habits.

- ✔ I describe how to add widgets, wallpaper, and more to your home screen in Chapter 17, but here's a spoiler: Touch the plus sign in the top-right corner of the home screen to fetch a similar screen where you can choose to add widgets, apps, or wallpaper by using the same touch-'n'-drag method.

Downloading New Apps

You can download and purchase apps from several online storefronts — Amazon's AppStore (www.amazon.com), Handango (www.handango.com), and GetJar (www.getjar.com) are just a few.

But most apps hail from Google's own Android Market (https://market.android.com), a virtual storefront that's accessible both from your Xoom and from a web browser on any desktop computer. Each access method has its advantages.

Feel free to download apps exclusively from your Xoom to get immediate gratification on a gadget that's almost always with you.

The Android Market website, though, lets you browse the apps from the comfort of any desktop computer, routing downloads to any Android devices you own, be they your Xoom, your phone, or another Android tablet.

The next two sections discuss how to handle both types of app downloads.

Viruses haven't infiltrated Android devices as much as they have desktop PCs. That said, stay protected by downloading an antivirus app for your Xoom. Just as important, however, is checking the permissions requested by any app you want to install. If an app requests permission to do something that's unrelated to its mission, don't install it.

From your Xoom

Your Xoom probably came with a shortcut to the Android Market (shown in the margin) already on your home screen. If that shortcut isn't there, touch Apps⇨Market to push open the virtual glass doors and stroll inside.

The Android Market (see Figure 9-5) lets you buy apps, books, or music; see your own installed apps; or download apps, either by searching for them directly or browsing the categories.

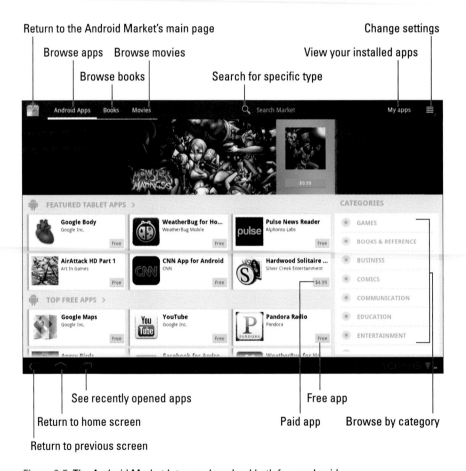

Return to the Android Market's main page   Change settings

Browse apps   Browse movies   View your installed apps

Browse books   Search for specific type

See recently opened apps   Free app

Return to home screen   Paid app   Browse by category

Return to previous screen

Figure 9-5: The Android Market lets you download both free and paid apps.

When you're visiting the Market, look for these things:

- ✔ **Search:** If you're looking for something specific, start with the Search Market box. Enter a few keywords, and let the Market show you its wares. Touch something that looks interesting; the Market usually shows you similar goods for browsing as well.

- ✔ **Categories:** Touch the categories on the right side of the screen to narrow down your search, which keeps you from wasting time in the Productivity section when you're interested in games.

- ✔ **My Apps:** This button lists your own apps and alerts you to any updates that may be available to add features or fix problems. (I cover updating apps later in this chapter.)

- ✔ **Price:** Many apps are free. Browse the free apps first to see whether one meets your needs. Many apps begin life as free apps; then, if you pony up some cash, they let you unlock extra features. Free apps are a nice way to test apps before throwing down cash.

- ✔ **Books and Video:** Google also sells books and rents videos through the Android Market. Click the Books or Video button at the top of the screen to visit those parts of the store. (Eventually, Music will appear here, too.)

DOWNLOAD When you spot an item that you'd like to download, touch its Download button (shown in the margin). In a few minutes, your new item appears in the appropriate area of your Xoom, be that area Apps, Books, or Music.

 Before an app downloads and installs itself, it *must* list the permissions it needs for every power it requests. Before downloading or installing an app, check those requested permissions *very carefully,* because even a virus must ask permission for everything it's allowed to do. If an app's permission requests don't match its mission, don't download it. A game, for example, shouldn't need permission to make phone calls, access your contacts list, or delete files on your device. If you're suspicious, wait. Most viruses are discovered within a few weeks of their release.

 The Android Market tosses in a home-screen shortcut for every app you download. To stop the Market from cluttering your home screen, touch My Apps; then touch the Settings icon in the top-right corner, and touch Add Shortcuts for New Apps to remove the check from the check box.

From a desktop PC

Although you can download apps directly onto your Xoom, a desktop PC can speed things up. Also, if you own more than one Android gadget, you can choose which gadget gets the goods.

To visit the web version of the Android Market, load any browser, go to `https://market.android.com` and sign in with your Google account.

As shown in Figure 9-6, the Android Market looks almost identical when viewed on your Xoom and when viewed on your PC.

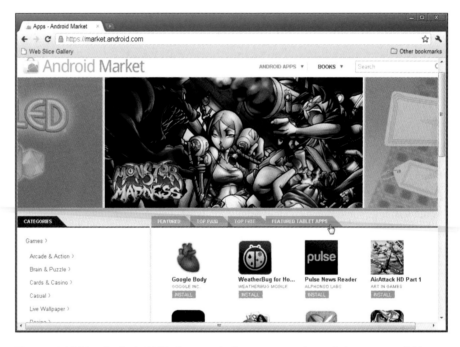

Figure 9-6: Visiting the Android Market on a desktop computer is much the same as visiting the Xoom version.

The biggest difference comes when you find an app you want. Choose Install, rather than Download, and a Checkout menu appears. Authorize the sale, if you're purchasing an app, then choose your Android device from a drop-down menu. (Do you own only a Xoom? Then your Xoom is automatically selected in the menu.)

Deciding which apps to download

With so many apps, how do you know which ones to download? Here are some guidelines:

- **Check the ratings.** Just as you do when you're shopping for restaurants, look at the reviews left by previous downloaders. Everybody rates apps on a scale from one to five stars. If an app has only one star, don't bother. Five stars means that the app has pleased a lot of people.

- **Check the reviews.** The rating system lets you weed out the stinkers and concentrate on the roses, but more details come from reviews: small write-ups left by other users. Remember, though, that if somebody says the app doesn't work on his particular phone, it may still work fine on your Xoom — and vice versa.

  After you've downloaded an app, give back by leaving a review saying what you liked or didn't like. (Click the website's Write a Review button to leave your rating and review.)

- **Check the developer's website.** Good app creators keep updating their apps by fixing bugs and adding features. Most also offer website support or offer a forum where app owners can compare notes. The developer's website address appears in the Developer section at the bottom of the app's page in the Market.

- **Check the permissions.** Be design, every app must ask your permission for things it can do to your Xoom, so make sure that the requests are reasonable. Social-networking apps need access to your contacts, for example. But if you download a screen-saver that wants permissions for things that don't pertain to your screen, you know that something's wrong. Avoid it.

In a few minutes, you've pushed the app off the Market's shelves and automatically placed it inside your Xoom, phone, or other bit of Android gadgetry.

- Your Xoom or other Android gadget needs a working Internet connection to receive the incoming app; if your Xoom is Wi-Fi only, make sure it's connected to a Wi-Fi network.

- Although most apps work on both Android tablets and phones, some are limited to one device or the other. If your Xoom isn't listed on the Checkout menu, then you're trying to download an app that isn't available for your Xoom.

Removing Unwanted Apps

Whether you hate an app or you're just housecleaning, you'll eventually want to remove some apps. Luckily, doing so is pretty easy.

To remove an app, visit your Apps area by touching Apps on your home screen. Touch and hold the unwanted app's icon; then drag it to the trash can labeled "Uninstall" that appears in your screen's top-right corner. The app disappears into the void.

You can also uninstall an app by visiting its page in the Android Market and touching the Uninstall button.

There's no way of deleting more than one app at a time.

Updating Your Apps

The best apps change all the time. Good developers listen to their customers and tweak things, fixing problems, adding new features, or smoothing rough edges.

Most of the apps you download will change eventually. You can make sure that your apps stay updated either automatically or manually:

Automatically: When you're downloading an app, touch the Update Automatically check box on the app's page in the Market. If you missed that one, touch Apps⇨Market⇨My Apps to bring your list of apps to the screen. Then, touch an app's icon, and touch the Allow Automatic Updating check box (see Figure 9-7). Repeat for all the apps you want to upgrade automatically.

Apps can only upgrade automatically when their permissions *haven't changed*. If an app suddenly requests a new permission, Google won't allow it to update automatically. Instead, you have to approve the new permission request by updating manually, described next.

Manually: You can easily tell which apps need updating by visiting the Android Market's My Apps area. There, at the top of the left column shown in Figure 9-7, the Market lists any of your apps that need updates. Touch the Update button to update them all.

There's no right or wrong way to update apps. Some prefer the convenience of automatically updating them. Others choose to manually update them, so they're more in control of the process.

I personally choose to update apps manually so that I can make sure I'm connected to a Wi-Fi network, thereby avoiding using my data-plan minutes. Also, I check the app's latest ratings to see if others report problems with the update.

✔ The My Apps section also lets you look over your app's permissions, making sure that it's not asking for more power than it needs.

✔ You can also uninstall an app from the My Apps area, as well as open it.

The Android Market's My Apps section

Touch to update all the apps needing updates   The app's required permissions

Your installed apps needing updates

Uninstall the app

Touch to allow the app to update itself automatically

Scrollable list of all your installed apps

Figure 9-7: The My Apps area of the Android Market lists your apps that need upgrades.

The Social

Combine your Motorola Xoom with Internet access, and your friends tag along wherever you go. Whether you're at home or traveling, sites like Facebook and Twitter can feel as though your friends are standing in your kitchen: Everybody chimes in. Sure, the responses may come within minutes, hours, or days, but the conversation never stops.

This chapter shows how to keep in touch with your friends, be it through social-networking apps like Facebook or Twitter or the more direct route: video chat. On the Motorola Xoom, it's all here.

Facebook

The most popular social-networking site today, Facebook attracts more than 600 million people for small talk, photo swapping, gaming, stalking old acquaintances, and finding new friends.

To get started, you need a Facebook username and password. Chances are that you already have them. If not, sign up for an account at www.facebook.com on either your Xoom or your desktop computer.

After you sign up, you can visit Facebook through your Xoom's browser or through the Facebook app (available from the Android Market). This section explains how to explore Facebook on your Xoom.

The Browser app provides the full Facebook experience. Try both the app and the browser to see which method you like better. You may prefer the app for quick status updates and the browser for more detailed browsing.

Setting up Facebook on your Xoom

For a quick-in-and-quick-out Facebook experience, download the Facebook app from the Android Market (see Chapter 9). Created by Facebook, this app is designed to help you get the most out of Facebook while you're logged on through an Android device.

Here's how to download and install the Facebook app:

1. **From your home screen, touch Apps⇨Market, and search for Facebook.**

   When the Android Market appears, you'll probably spot Facebook listed in the Top Free Apps section. If not, enter **Facebook** in the Search Market area, and touch the Enter button.

2. **Touch the Facebook for Android icon in the list of matching applications.**

   The Android Market shows you every app that works or exchanges messages with Facebook. (You'll see *many.*) When you touch the Facebook for Android icon (shown in the margin), the Facebook for Android page appears (see Figure 10-1).

3. **Touch the Install button and then touch OK to give Facebook permission to work on your Xoom.**

   After a few minutes, the Facebook app will float through the airwaves and nestle alongside your other installed apps.

4. **Load the app by touching Apps⇨Facebook; then touch the I Agree button to grant Facebook permission to run even more tasks on your Xoom.**

5. **Enter your Facebook username and password, and then touch Login.**

   Touch the username box, and enter your username; then touch the password box, and enter your password. (You won't be able to see what you type in the password line. Then again, neither will any people look-ing over your shoulder.)

When you touch Login, you're finally in. Facebook appears in all its Xoom-formatted glory.

Facebook continually tweaks its apps for mobile phones and tablets. Don't be surprised if your version looks or behaves a little differently from the version described here.

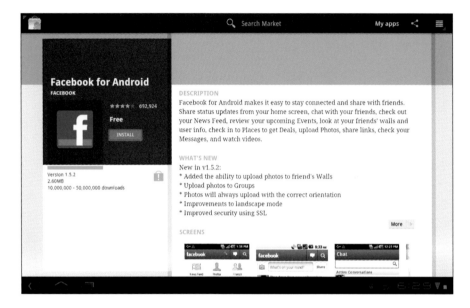

Figure 10-1: Touch the Install button to install the Facebook app.

Browsing Facebook

Stuck at the auto repair shop? Waiting at the post office? When you suspect that your friends and relatives may lead more interesting lives than you do, open your Facebook app to find out what they're up to.

Touch Apps➪Facebook, and Facebook rises to the screen (see Figure 10-2). It cuts to the chase by showing you the News Feed — status updates left by your friends, with the most recent update topping the list.

Touch to head to Facebook's main screen

Take a photo to post

Search a specific friend, or see a list of them all

A friend's photo

Touch to post your status update, so your friends see it.

Touch spot to enter your own status update

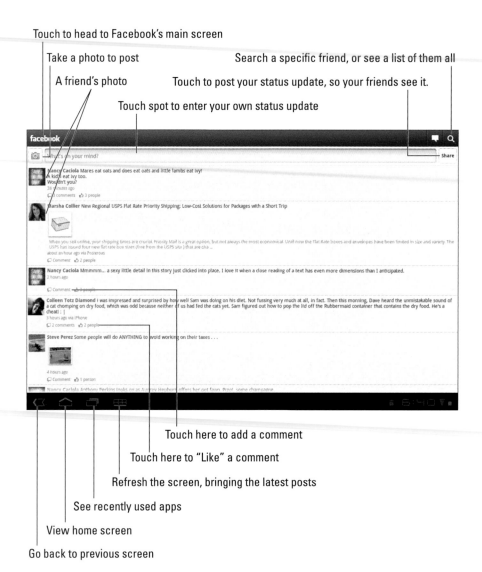

Touch here to add a comment

Touch here to "Like" a comment

Refresh the screen, bringing the latest posts

See recently used apps

View home screen

Go back to previous screen

Figure 10-2: Facebook shows a list of posts and photos, known as status updates, left by your friends.

To browse the News Feed, drag your finger up the screen. As your finger slides up the screen, older posts come into view. As you pore over your friends' posts, you can do two things:

✔ **Comment:** Whether somebody challenges you to a duel or simply says he's having a bad day, comment on the situation: Touch the post and then tap the Write a Comment line. Your trusty onscreen keyboard appears, ready to accept your message. When you're done typing, touch Comment again, and your words appear below your friend's comment.

Like

✔ **Like:** Can't think of anything witty to say about a friend's enthusiastic post? Pressed for time? Touch the post and tap the Like button, shown in the margin. The Like button isn't the same as a well-thought-out con-gratulatory message, but it works in a pinch. (Touch the post to see other friends who liked that post.)

facebook

Hard-core Facebookers won't be satisfied with the Facebook app's News Feed, although that's the real meat of Facebook. To see what else the Facebook app offers, touch the Facebook icon in the top-left corner. The app's main page opens, as shown in Figure 10-3.

Figure 10-3: Facebook's main page lists shortcuts to calendar items, upcoming events, private messages, and other Facebook amenities.

Facebook's main page lets you peruse Facebook's other popular areas:

- ✔ **News Feed:** Here's where you see your friends' posts, sorted chronologically.

- ✔ **Profile:** All about you, this self-centered area includes three sections: Wall, which lists messages involving you; Info, which lists your vital stats; and Photos, which lists any snapshots you've shared.

- ✔ **Friends:** Want to contact a particular friend? The whole gang is listed here.

- ✔ **Messages:** Head here for private, one-one-one exchanges with friends.

- ✔ **Places:** This area lists your friends' recent locations (if they've checked in with Facebook).

- ✔ **Groups:** Groups are pages built around common interests rather than people. Group members can convene for intellectual discourse on the previous evening's episode of *Dancing with the Stars,* for example.

- ✔ **Events:** A simple social calendar, this feature comes in handy for remembering your friends' birthdays.

- ✔ **Photos:** All the photos you've uploaded to Facebook appear here, whether you shot them with your Xoom or with other cameras. (I cover uploading photos later in this chapter.)

- ✔ **Chat:** If you happen to be on Facebook at the same time as a friend, her name appears here so that you're both ready to exchange private instant messages.

 As always, touching the Back button returns you to the previous page. Touching the Back button enough times eventually takes you out of Facebook and returns you to your home page.

- ✔ When somebody shows you a bit of attention on Facebook, either through a comment or a direct message, you'll see a notice in the notifications panel, directly below the clock. Touch the notice and then touch the resulting pop-up window to read the message.

- ✔ You'll see the same notifications if you touch the Notifications button at the bottom of the Facebook app's home screen (refer to Figure 10-3).

- ✔ To place a convenient shortcut to the Facebook app on your home screen, drop by Chapter 9. If you prefer Facebook's website over the app, Chapter 6 explains how to add bookmarks to your browser.

Updating your status

Are you standing in line at the Department of Motor Vehicles? Waiting for the grocery cashier? Ready to snowboard down the mountain? (If you *are* snowboarding with your Xoom, be sure to place it in a well-padded, gallon-size plastic bag with a zip closure.)

These situations are perfect Facebook moments. Whether the excitement level rises or wanes, Facebook's ready for you to share it with your friends.

To let your Facebook friends know that you're atop a ski slope, follow these steps:

1. **Visit Facebook's News Feed or Profile area.**

   The Facebook app automatically opens to the News Feed area.

   You can find shortcuts to both places in Facebook's main screen (refer to Figure 10-3, earlier in this chapter).

2. **Touch the What's on Your Mind? box, enter your comment, and then touch Share.**

   Facebook kicks your message to the top of the News Feed queue for your friends to ponder (see Figure 10-4).

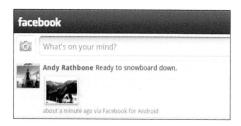

Figure 10-4: Your status report appears atop the News Feed, along with any photo you've uploaded to go with it.

The dictation feature, described in Chapter 4, works well for quick Facebook updates. You can speak your update, touch the Share button, and move on without fiddling with menus and keyboards.

Uploading a photo

For the easiest Facebook update, post 1,000 words in an instant by uploading a photo. Perhaps the best feature in Facebook's app, posting a photo automatically snaps your photo at the right resolution. You needn't bother with resizing or cropping: The image goes straight from the camera to the News Feed area.

Follow these steps to send a picture to Facebook:

1. **Visit Facebook's News Feed or Profile area, and touch the camera icon.**

   The camera icon, shown in the margin, sits to the left of the What's on Your Mind? bar, where you normally type updates.

2. **Choose Capture a Photo or Choose from Gallery.**

   • To send a photo that you've saved on your Xoom, touch Choose from Gallery, select a photo, and head to Step 4.

   • To snap a new shot, touch Capture a Photo. The camera appears (see Figure 10-5).

3. **Touch the camera's shutter button and then touch one of the onscreen icons to handle your photo.**

   After you've snapped a photo, the little icon in the photo's upper-top corner (shown in Figure 10-5) offers three options:

   • Touch OK to upload the photo to Facebook.

   • Touch the camera icon to delete the photo and try again.

   • Touch X to delete the photo and forget about the whole crazy photo-posting idea.

4. **Type a caption, if you want, and then touch the Upload button to send your photo off to Facebook.**

   Before sharing your newly uploaded photo, Facebook shows a thumbnail view, along with space to type a caption. Type the caption in the "Add a Caption Here" box, then touch Upload.

   Your photo appears on the Photos tab. If you snapped the photo through the Facebook app in Step 3, the photo also appears in the Gallery.

I cover the Gallery app — your Xoom's photo and movie viewer — in more detail in Chapter 11.

Delete the photo and exit

Delete and take a new, better photo

Upload the photo to Facebook

Snap the photo

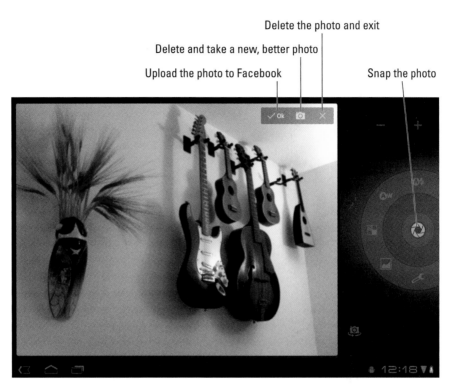

Figure 10-5: Facebook's app takes photos that you can post as updates.

Twitter

Whereas Facebook lets you share photos and hold conversations with your friends, Twitter (www.twitter.com) lets you hold conversations with the entire world. Unless you deliberately protect your messages, they're open for everybody to read.

Twitter works on a simple premise: You post messages, called *tweets,* up to 140 characters long. With millions of people tweeting all over the world, you can use that huge Twitter stream in many ways, including these:

- **Search:** Twitter offers up-to-the minute news. If you think you felt an earthquake, search Twitter for your city and the word *earthquake.* Instead of ducking and covering, most Twitterers tweet about their shaking walls, confirming your suspicion that you did indeed just feel an earthquake.

✓ **Follow:** Create a list of your favorite Twitter users, both friends and strangers. Those people appear in your Following list. Your Following list shows only tweets from those special people, filtering out every other tweet. Watching tweets by your list of followed friends works much like watching Facebook's News Feed.

✓ **Trends:** Set up a Twitter search for something you're interested in — the Motorola Xoom, for example. When anybody tweets about the Xoom, you'll read that post, which may tell you about recent updates, bug fixes, or policy changes.

Twitter's free. The only things you need to start tweeting are a username and password. Preferably, you also need something interesting to tweet about, but many people overlook that requirement.

You can access Twitter either through the Browser app, or you can download and install the Twitter app.

Setting up the Twitter app

Download the Twitter app from the Android Market, as described in Chapter 9, or just follow the steps for downloading the Facebook app, as described earlier in this chapter.

After you've installed Twitter, load it by touching Apps⇨Twitter. Then touch the Sign In button if you already have a username and password; otherwise, touch Sign Up to create a Twitter account.

When you're signed in, Twitter takes you to the main screen (see Figure 10-6), which shows the tweets of all the people you follow. If you're new to Twitter and aren't following anyone yet, this page is blank.

Touch the four buttons along the top to peruse Twitter's services:

✓ **Tweets:** This page lists tweets by everybody you follow. The newest tweets appear at the top; slide your finger up the screen to see them.

✓ **Mentions:** If somebody mentions your Twitter name, that tweet appears here.

✔ **Direct Messages:** You can exchange private messages with the people you follow, provided that they also follow you.

✔ **Lists:** Lists are collections of people who tweet around a certain theme. Head here to find people who tweet in your area of interest.

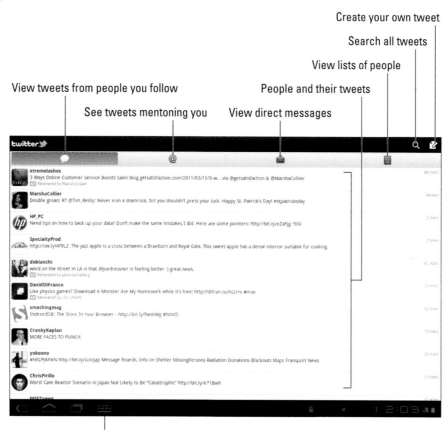

Create your own tweet

Search all tweets

View lists of people

People and their tweets

View tweets from people you follow

See tweets mentoning you

View direct messages

View your profile, settings, or log out

Figure 10-6: Twitter lets you view short messages posted by friends and strangers worldwide.

Need somebody to follow? Feel free to follow me (@andyrathbone) until you find somebody more interesting.

If you find yourself using Twitter a lot, check out some third-party apps for managing your tweets. Some of the popular ones include TweetDeck and TweetCaster for Twitter.

Sending a tweet

When you must shout something to the world in a tweet, touch the Compose button in the top-right corner of Twitter's main screen. A message window appears. Touch inside the window, and carefully craft your tweet, keeping it to 140 characters. (The character countdown appears in the top-right corner, letting you know how many characters you have left.)

Tweet To post your tweet, touch the Tweet button in the top-right corner.

Video Chat

When you and a friend fire up Google Talk, you can see and hear each other as you exchange small talk about how technology sure is changing things. Most people call it video chat, but Google calls it Google Talk.

This section shows you how to set up Google Talk on both your Xoom and a friend's Xoom or PC so that you can point your cameras at each other's cats.

Setting up Google Talk

Your Xoom comes full equipped with a front-facing camera and a video screen, so you have everything you need. If your friend has a Xoom or another brand of Android 3.0 or (higher tablet) with a front-facing camera, he's set too.

Lacking a Xoom, however, your friend needs a desktop PC, laptop, or Android tablet, and these things:

- ✔ **A front-facing video camera:** Some laptops include a built-in front-facing camera. If your friend's laptop or PC doesn't include one, he needs to pull out a credit card and head to an electronics store. (Front-facing cameras, often called *webcams,* plug in to a computer's USB port, as pictured in Chapter 1.)

✔ **Google Talk and its accompanying Video and Voice Plug-In software:**
The programs are available for free at this website:

```
www.google.com/talk
```

✔ **A Google account.** Google requires people to sign up for a Google
account for almost all of its services.

When the cameras are set up, the software is installed, and the Google
accounts are attained, you're ready to chat.

Starting a video chat through Google Talk

Video chatting between two Xooms is a breeze, because the devices know
each other like identical twins. Touch the Google Talk icon (shown in the
margin), touch a few buttons, and start chatting.

Starting a video chat between a Xoom and a PC takes a little more legwork.

Whether you're trying to video chat with another Xoom or a PC/laptop,
follow these steps:

1. **Open Google Talk on your Xoom by touching Apps➪Talk.**

   When Google Talk opens (see Figure 10-7), the left side of the screen
   lists the people who've already agreed to chat with you.

   To keep voyeurs at bay, Google Talk works on an invite-only basis. Only
   after you invite friends to chat — and they accept — do their names
   appear in the list.

2. **Do one of the following things:**

   - If you spot your friend's name, jump to Step 3.

   - If your friend isn't listed as a Google Talk contact, invite him to
     chat by touching the Invite button (shown in the margin) near the
     program's top-right corner. When the pop-up window appears,
     enter your friend's Gmail address, and touch Send Invitation. Then
     wait. Check for spinach between your teeth.

3. **If your friend uses a desktop PC, tell him to open Gmail (https://
   mail.google.com).**

   On a PC, video chats start and end with Gmail rather than Google Talk.

   Eventually, your friend will notice your invitation within Gmail. When he
   accepts, his name appears in the left pane of your Talk screen.

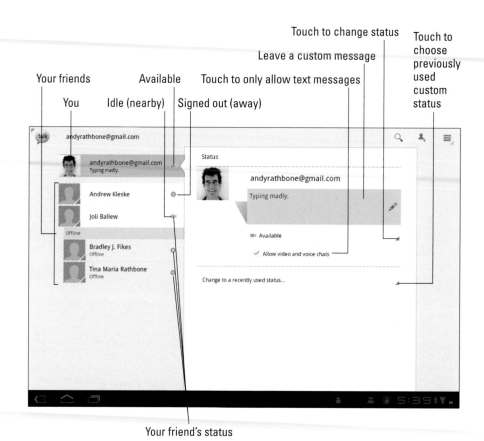

Touch to change status

Touch to choose previously used custom status

Leave a custom message

Your friends   Available   Touch to only allow text messages

You   Idle (nearby)   Signed out (away)

Your friend's status

Figure 10-7: Google Talk lists friends you can chat with.

4. **On your Xoom, touch your friend's name; then touch the video-camera icon on the far-left side of the screen.**

When you touch the video-camera icon, your Xoom makes a ringing sound, and your friend hears that same ringing sound on his computer.

5. **Wait for your friend to answer the call.**

If he's using a PC, shown in Figure 10-8, he answers by clicking the green Answer button in the bottom-right corner of the Gmail screen. If he's using a Xoom, he answers by touching the Accept button.

Figure 10-8: On a desktop PC shown here, your friend must click the Answer button to begin a video chat with you.

As soon as your friend answers, the video chat begins. On your Xoom (shown in Figure 10-9), you see a large video of the other person, with your own face in a tiny square in the video's bottom corner. Your friend sees the exact opposite.

6. To end the chat, close the program by touching or clicking the X in the chat window's top-right corner.

Don't see an X in your Xoom's top-right corner? Tap the screen to make it appear.

Figure 10-9: As you video chat on your Xoom, your friend's face appears on the big screen; your face appears on the small screen in the corner.

✔ Video chats can consume lots of bandwidth, so they're best done through a Wi-Fi connection. Otherwise, you may find an unwelcome surprise in your next cellphone bill.

✔ Just as you do with cellphones, take turns talking to each other. Talking simultaneously can keep the sound from coming through.

✔ Little icons next to your friends' names in Google Talk show their status. A green video-camera icon means that the person's available for a video chat. An orange icon means that she's around but not near her computer. Finally, an X means that she's offline and unavailable.

✔ To send a text message through Google Talk on your Xoom, click the recipient's name, and enter your message in the Type to Compose line at the bottom of the screen.

✔ If your friend responds, his message appears directly below yours. As you correspond, the screen slowly fills up, with the oldest messages scrolling off the screen's top.

✔ If you and your friend have trouble hearing each other, both of you should try wearing headphones. Headphones cut down on feedback problems caused when the microphones pick up too much sound.

Part III
Digesting Media

The 5th Wave By Rich Tennant

"I build bookshelves and Denise buys a Xoom."

In this part . . .

1 ndustry pundits say that tablets work best for "media consumption." The Xoom's generous screen certainly make vacation photos look great, and the tablet plays movies in stunning high definition. Electronic books include pages that flip like the real things. And it's easy to get lost — safely — in Google's fascinating digital maps, which let you walk through downtown Manhattan without stepping on something unfortunate.

Yet the Xoom's not just about consuming media. Its built-in cameras snap photos and shoot high-definition video. Music apps turn it into a four-track recording studio. Also, with the tablet by your side, you no longer have an excuse to put off writing your autobiography.

Whether you've created it or somebody else handled the production issues, this part of the book shows you how to enjoy media on your tablet.

tist   **Ahmad Jamal**   **The Allm**

a   **Bill Evans**   **Billie Ho**

Pics and Flicks

S ales of digital cameras began dropping soon after cell-phones began featuring built-in cameras. Why carry two gadgets instead of one?

With a Motorola Xoom in your backpack or suitcase, you can add two more cameras to your arsenal, because it sports digital cameras in both the front and the back.

The back camera shoots high-resolution video and photos — 5 megapixels worth — letting you video political protests while pretending to browse the web.

The front camera, by contrast, captures *you,* bringing yet another evolutional step in the art form known as cellphone self-portrait.

This chapter explains how to snap photos and movies with your Motorola Xoom's cameras, delete or crop the bad ones, and share the good ones with your friends or CNN.

Using Your Xoom's Cameras

To pull your cameras out of their digital bag, touch the Apps button and then touch the Camera icon. The Camera app opens (see Figure 11-1), turning your Xoom's screen into the world's largest viewfinder.

When it's first turned on, the Camera app assumes that you want to take a still photo, not a video, so it offers traditional digital camera settings as buttons on the round dial on the screen's right side. The settings let you tweak the camera settings manually when the automatic settings don't quite capture the moment.

Spoiler: To snap a photo, touch the camera's shutter button — the innermost round button on the round dial.

✔ If you plan to take lots of photos with your Xoom, drop that Camera app onto your home screen: Hold down your finger on a blank part of your home screen. When the Apps screen appears, touch the Camera app icon; the Camera app then appears on your Home screen. (I describe this in more detail in Chapter 17.)

✔ For the best photos, shoot outdoors. Like most cameras, the ones on your Xoom love natural light.

✔ Don't expect your Xoom to take shots with the same quality as those shot on a real digital camera. You won't find the same depth of focus or color. Still, when your digital camera's at home, your Xoom can quickly photograph Sasquatch as he visits the river.

✔ Many camera apps alter your Xoom photos to resemble vintage shots, masking the lower quality yet enhancing the photo's look and feel. Check out Retro Camera, for example, to take shots that look like they popped out of a Polaroid instant camera.

✔ For more camera applications, check out the camera-to-scanner apps, like Document Scanner, in the Android Market. Those apps let you take photos of documents — a restaurant menu, billing records, or an exam, for example — and convert them to PDFs for saving or mailing to other people.

Flash mode

Zoom in

Snap picture

White balance

Zoom out

Color effect

Scene mode

Your viewfinder Settings

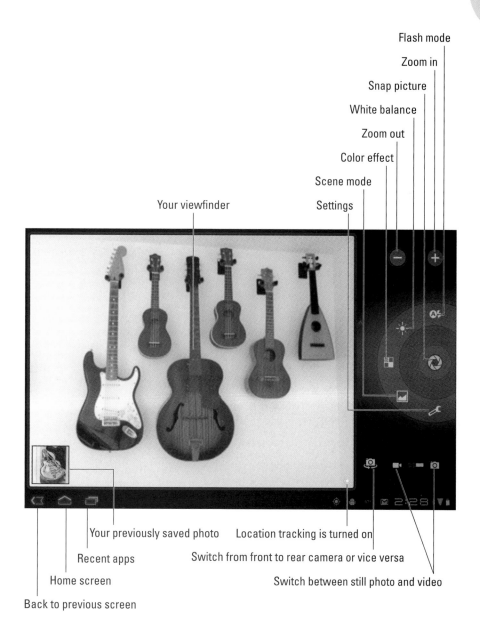

Your previously saved photo Location tracking is turned on

Recent apps Switch from front to rear camera or vice versa

Home screen Switch between still photo and video

Back to previous screen

Figure 11-1: The huge viewfinder places the controls along the right edge.

Snapping a photo

Your Xoom is missing a key component of nearly every camera ever made: a shutter button. There's no button on its case for snapping a quick photo. Instead, the shutter button lives onscreen.

To snap a photo, load the camera program by touching Apps⇨Camera.

Aim your camera at your subject, and touch the shutter button (shown in the margin) to snap a photo. Your camera takes a second to focus and gauge the light; then it snaps the shot, leaving a thumbnail of your work in the screen's bottom-left corner.

To view your just-snapped shot full screen in the Gallery app, touch the thumbnail image. (I cover the Gallery app later in this chapter.) To return to the camera for more photos, touch the Back button (shown in the margin).

- ✒ Your Xoom has two cameras, but the Camera app always starts by using the back camera, which takes better photos.

- ✒ If you want to shoot a self-portrait from the front camera, perhaps with a scenic vista behind you, click the Camera toggle button, shown in the margin. The front-facing camera can't take pictures nearly as well as the ones the back camera can, but it's fine for a quick "I'm here and you're not" Facebook shot.

- ✒ Unlike most apps, your Camera app stays on the screen in a fixed position: It doesn't change as you rotate the screen. If you want a portrait shot, perhaps of a tall tree, just turn your Xoom sideways and then touch the shutter button.

- ✒ If your photo doesn't quite meet your quality level, you probably need more light. If you're indoors, turn on some lights. If you're outdoors, wipe off the lens with a soft cloth. Still bad? Try turning on the flash or changing some of the other settings, as described in the next section.

- ✒ Your Xoom's size makes it an awkward handheld camera, but its huge viewfinder is a great asset: It looks just like a framed photo on your wall. So when you're taking a photo, pretend that you're creating something to hang in your living room. Keep changing your composition, subtly moving the Xoom until your scene is framed just right.

- ✒ Digital photos cost you only time and effort, so shoot with abandon, trying different angles and perspectives. Shoot group photos at least twice to reduce the chance that somebody blinked. It's easy to weed out any photo failures back home, but it's impossible to return and shoot more.

Stamping photos with your location

Unless you change the settings, your Xoom won't add Global Positioning System (GPS) coordinates to your photos or movies. The coordinates contain your exact position when you're snapping the photo, give or take 30 feet.

While you're on vacation or traveling, tell your camera to track your location. Then you can see your trip, photo by photo, in the Maps app.

When you're at somebody's house, though, your friend probably doesn't want her home's

address shared on Facebook or the Internet. Be wary of sharing photos taken with location tracking turned on.

You can toggle location tracking on or off within your Camera app by touching Camera Settings (the wrench icon)⇨Store Location.

The Camera app can't stamp videos with your location — only photos.

Changing your camera's settings

Unless you've deliberately fiddled with your camera's settings, it shoots on autopilot the entire time, and that's a good thing. Your camera's sensors are pretty good at choosing the right focus and exposure. When they're not doing the job correctly, however, or you want to experiment to see how new settings will change your shots, feel free to start tweaking.

Here's the rundown on the camera's controls (which are labeled in Figure 11-1, earlier in this chapter):

- ✔ **Viewfinder:** What you see framed here becomes your photo.

- ✔ **Previous Picture:** Embedded in the viewfinder's bottom-left corner is a thumbnail of the photo you last saved. Touch it to head to the Gallery app, which lets you show your photos to admiring friends.

- ✔ **Zoom In/Out:** The plus sign and minus sign let you zoom in or out, respectively. This action is *digital,* so the farther you zoom in, the blurrier your photo will become. Instead of zooming, walk up close to the flaming gas station to take your news photo.

- ✔ **Flash Mode:** Normally set to Auto, this setting also lets you switch to Always On, which removes shadows from day shots, or Always Off, which helps reduce shadows from low-light shots.

- ✔ **White Balance:** Different types of lighting change the coloring. Normally set to Auto, this setting also lets you choose among incandescent, daylight, or fluorescent for truer color.

✔ **Color Effect:** These gimmicky effects let you choose Mono (black and white) or Sepia (vintage photo color), or add trippy '60s effects.

✔ **Scene Mode:** Normally set to Auto, this setting lets you choose setups designed for specific settings: Action, Portrait, Landscape, Night, Night Portrait, Theatre, Beach, Snow, Sunset, Steady Photo, and Fireworks.

✔ **Camera Settings:** These settings, shown in Figure 11-2, let you tag photos with your GPS location, change the focus from Infinity to Macro (for close-ups), change the exposure for different light settings, set your photo size, and change your picture quality from Super Fine to Normal (which is something nobody would ever want to do).

✔ **Shutter:** Snap a photo by touching the round button in the ringed circle on the right side of the screen.

✔ **Camera toggle:** Switch from front to rear camera, or vice versa, by touching the little camera icon with the arrows. (Switching cameras while shooting a video will stop your movie at the point of the switch.)

✔ **Camera/Video toggle:** Switch from a still camera to a video camera, and vice versa. (The blue icon is the one that's currently active.) I describe shooting videos later in this section.

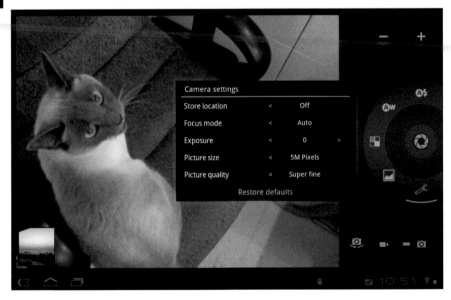

Figure 11-2: As you slide your finger around the circle, the drop-down menu changes for each type of setting.

Which camera settings should I care about?

Leave the camera set to automatic except for these specific situations:

- **Location tracking:** If you don't want people to know the exact address where you snapped the photo, choose Camera Settings⇨Store Location⇨Off.

- **Close-ups:** When you're shooting from less than a foot away, perhaps for close-ups of dinner plates or spring flowers, choose Camera Settings⇨Focus Mode⇨Macro.

- **Facebook:** Instead of shooting from the Camera app, use the Facebook app (see Chapter 10). It automatically takes a photo or video with the right settings for online shots.

- **Flash problems:** If the automatic flash washes out the details, choose Flash Mode⇨

Off and then hold the Xoom very steady, perhaps leaning one edge against a solid object.

- **Dramatic sunsets:** Choose Scene Mode⇨Sunset for deeper color.

- **Self-portraits:** Choose the Front/Back camera toggle to switch to the front camera.

When you're done tweaking your current shot, return your camera to automatic settings so that you'll be ready for impromptu shots. To do so, choose Camera Settings⇨Restore Defaults. Choosing Restore Defaults changes all your menu settings to automatic, even the options listed in the camera's other settings areas. It also turns off location tracking. Restore Default lets you experiment while shooting without having to remember which switches you flipped.

As always, the Back, Home, and Recent Apps buttons in your Xoom's bottom-left corner work within the Camera app. Touch any of them to leave the Camera app and do something else when the cat suddenly leaves the room.

To close an open menu, tap anywhere on your screen away from the menu.

Shooting Movies

Carrying around a large tablet is like toting a small high-definition TV set. It lets you watch high-definition movies, and the batteries may last longer than your flight, if you have it charged (see Chapter 1).

More than just a TV, though, you can make your *own* movies, whether you're filming ethereal clouds out the plane window or shooting exotic landmarks at your vacation spot.

No matter what your motive, this section shows how to make the most of the built-in high-definition camera. (For info on setting up video chats, drop by Chapter 10.)

Recording a video

When you open the Camera app by touching Apps⇨Camera, the app opens in camera mode, ready to snap a quick picture.

To switch to video mode, look for the Video/Camera toggle, which lives right above the clock. Touch the toggle's Video icon (shown in the margin), and the Camera app's controls change to video controls (see Figure 11-3).

Spoiler: To start recording a video, touch the Record button — the round red button on the round dial to the right.

✔ When you touch the Record button, it morphs into the Recording button, shown in the margin. Touch it to stop recording.

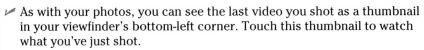
✔ When recording a video, keep your movements slow and steady. If possible, prop your Xoom against something to act as a makeshift tripod. The cameras used for professional movies capture most of their action while sitting on tripods.

✔ As with your photos, you can see the last video you shot as a thumbnail in your viewfinder's bottom-left corner. Touch this thumbnail to watch what you've just shot.

✔ You can shoot videos from either the front or back camera, but you can't switch between cameras while recording. To switch, stop your current recording; then touch the Camera toggle to switch to the other camera.

✔ The Camera toggle doesn't let you switch back and forth quickly. You may have to touch the button several times before it switches.

✔ As you record a video, a little clock ticks away in the viewfinder's top-right corner. For the best videos, let the clock run to at least the 30-second mark. Anything shorter than that makes the audience wonder why they're watching.

Changing the video camera's settings

When you're shooting video, the settings along the right edge look almost identical to the camera settings. Look closely, though, and you'll see a few differences.

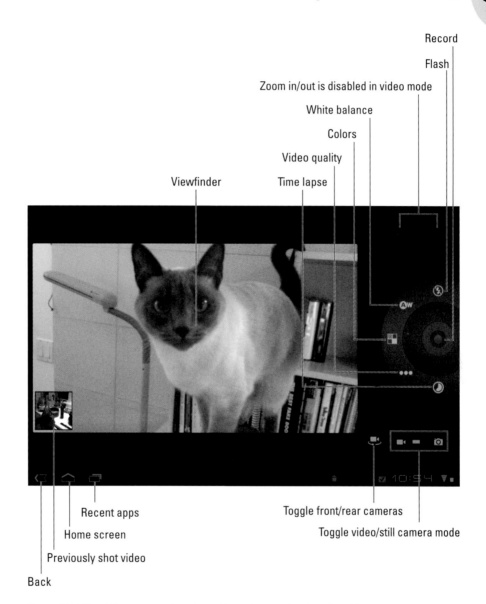

Record

Flash

Zoom in/out is disabled in video mode

White balance

Colors

Video quality

Viewfinder   Time lapse

Recent apps   Toggle front/rear cameras

Home screen   Toggle video/still camera mode

Previously shot video

Back

Figure 11-3: The video-camera icon turns blue when you're shooting videos.

The White Balance area still lets you choose your lighting, be it daylight, incandescent, or fluorescent.

The Color Effect area still lets you choose black and white (called Mono), sepia, negative, and all the other groovy effects.

But when you're shooting videos, the settings differ from the camera's settings in four major ways:

- ✔ **Zoom:** When you switch to video mode, you can't zoom in or out of a setting, as you can with the camera. Instead, walk a few steps closer to the growling tiger.

- ✔ **Scene Mode:** The Scene Mode settings are no longer available, which rules out shooting glowing orange sunset videos.

- ✔ **Main Settings:** Switching from camera to video nixes the main settings page, so you can no longer control focus and exposure.

- ✔ **Flash Mode:** When you're shooting videos, the flash no longer turns on or off automatically as needed. Take a short test video. If the test video is too dark, turn on the flash manually by touching the flash setting and choosing Flash On. Then the flash works like a floodlight, illuminating the area in front of you for clearer shots.

To make amends for video mode's missing settings, you have two handy video controls:

- ✔ **Video Quality:** High-definition videos are *huge,* which pretty much rules out sharing them through e-mail or on the web. This settings area lets you sacrifice high definition for ease of distribution. Choose Low for short videos meant for e-mail or the Internet; choose the YouTube setting for slightly higher-quality videos meant specifically for YouTube (www.youtube.com). Finally, use High for high-definition videos.

- ✔ **Time Lapse Interval:** Out of left field, this setting creates time-lapse videos. Prop up your Xoom so that it points at something ever-changing — a scenic vista, perhaps, or the cat's food bowl. Then choose your time-lapse interval, from 1 second to 10 seconds. Your Xoom snaps photos at the specified intervals and then stitches them together into a silent movie.

The key to making a good time-lapse video is stability. Prop your Xoom against something that doesn't move, and leave it there for a few minutes to a few hours, depending on your time-lapse interval. Try experimenting before you find the magic combination for the action you're trying to capture.

You can't adjust the video camera's settings controls while you're recording video. Set them *before* you shoot. If your video didn't turn out right, change the settings and then reshoot.

Converting videos

Most folks have some videos on their computers, shot either on their digital cameras or video cameras, or downloaded from the Internet. Some videos play fine when they're copied to the Xoom; others don't.

The problem is that videos come in a wide variety of packages, known as *codecs*. The Xoom prefers videos encoded with a codec called H.264 Baseline Profile. For the techies out there who care, a Baseline Profile means this:

✔ No CABAC entropy coding

✔ No B frames

✔ No 8x8 transforms (DCT)

✔ No weighted prediction

If you're the type who enjoys converting videos from one format to another with programs like HandBrake (`http://handbrake.fr`), heed those rules for success. Are you more into watching movies than encoding them? Stick with movies from Amazon's Video in Demand and other services that work on the Xoom.

Touring the Gallery

The Gallery serves as the digital equivalent of the old shoebox in the closet. It holds all your photos and movies. Unlike the tattered photos tossed in the shoebox, however, everything stored in the Gallery app stays neatly sorted.

To help you find your stuff, the Gallery app lets you sort everything quickly on the fly. Then it displays your sorting handiwork in stacks, just as though you'd stacked up all the matching photos in your shoebox.

Finding your photos and videos

Here's how to find your photos and movies as quickly and easily as possible:

1. **Open the Gallery app by touching Apps⇨Gallery.**

   The Gallery App appears, shown in Figure 11-4.

2. **From the Sort By drop-down menu at the top of the screen, choose how you want to sort your items: By Album, By Time, By Location, or By Tags.**

   Choose By Location from the menu, for example, and the Gallery places everything in different stacks, labeled by location.

3. **Touch an image or stack to view it.**

Settings or details about item

View information about selected item or items

Move back to top level

Show images, videos, or both

Sort by

Switch to camera

Stacks with lots of items

Stacks with few items

Stacks of videos

Stacks of photos

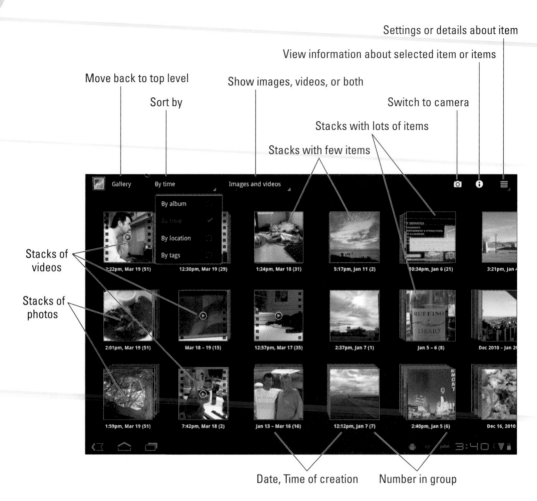

Date, Time of creation   Number in group

Figure 11-4: The Gallery app lets you view photos and movies by creation date, location, tags, or album.

Touch a stack to see all the photos and videos inside. To view a single photo or video in full screen, just touch it. (Touch the Back button in the bottom-left corner to return the Gallery.)

Touch the Paris stack, for example, to see all the photos from your trip to Paris.

While you're viewing the photos and videos in your Paris stack, feel free to sort them again by Time, as shown in Figure 11-4. The Gallery displays just the photos from your Paris trip, presented in chronological order.

4. **Back out of your stacks by touching the Gallery icon in the top-left corner.**

   Touch the Gallery icon enough times, and you end up back at the Gallery's top level.

Navigating the menus and icons

Here's the rundown on Gallery's menus and icons:

- **Gallery button:** As you navigate deeper into stacks of sorted photos, you can back out by touching the Gallery button in the top-left corner.

- **Sort By:** This drop-down menu lets you stack items four ways:

  - *By Album:* View the items according to the name of the folder containing them. Photos and videos taken by your Xoom appear in the Camera album, for example. If you downloaded a photo from the web, it's in the Gallery's Downloads album.

  - *By Time:* Your camera automatically stamps the time and date on every photo or movie you take. Sorting by time lets you view them in chronological order.

  - *By Location:* This option, available only when you turn on location tracking, covered earlier in this chapter, displays photos in stacks named after city or street names. If location tracking is turned off, your work appears in one group called No Location. (The Xoom doesn't stamp videos with their location.)

  - *By Tags:* Earlier versions of the Android operating system let you assign *tags* — descriptive words — to your photos. The Xoom doesn't come with that feature, but it may arrive in a future update.

- **Images and Videos:** This drop-down menu lets you view only photos, only videos, or a combination of both.

- **Camera icon:** This icon quickly puts the Gallery aside and fetches the camera for more pointing and shooting.

- **Details:** The little exclamation point in the white circle brings up information about the currently viewed or selected item. You can't edit the details, which include the image's size, camera settings, and location (provided that you've turned on location tracking, that is).

Sorting your Gallery images and movies in different ways and groupings cuts down on the time it takes to find your missing image.

Viewing Photos

Sooner or later, you'll want to impress your friends and family not only with your ample compositional skills, but also with your Xoom. The preceding section describes how to find images and movies; this one tells you how to show them off.

To view photos, follow these steps:

1. **Touch Apps⇨Gallery.**

   The Gallery app opens (refer to Figure 11-4, earlier in this chapter).

2. **Open the stack of photos containing your photos.**

   The preceding section explains how to find your photos.

   To view photos only, choose Images Only from the Images and Videos drop-down menu.

3. **Tap a photo to see it full screen, as shown in Figure 11-5.**

   Double-tap a photo to see it as large as possible; double-tap again to fit it inside the Xoom's screen. You can also pinch and expand photos with your fingertips, as I explain in Chapter 4.

4. **To close the current photo, touch the Gallery icon in the top-left corner.**

   When you're through viewing individual photos or movies, touch the screen to bring the menus back to life. Then touch the Gallery button in the screen's top-left corner to dig your way back out through the photo groups and return to the main screen.

While viewing individual photos, you can manipulate them in other ways:

✔ Touch the scrolling bar of miniature photos beneath your currently viewed photo to quickly find other photos. Tap a photo on the scroll bar to bring it up for full view.

✔ While you view a full-screen photo, the navigation buttons disappear along the bottom. To make them reappear, touch the screen, or touch where the button normally lives.

✔ Touch the Slideshow button any time it appears within the gallery to see a quick slideshow of all your sorted photos.

Settings drop-down menu ⎯

Settings

Delete photo

Tap to return to the other photos   Share photo

The photo's name   View slideshow

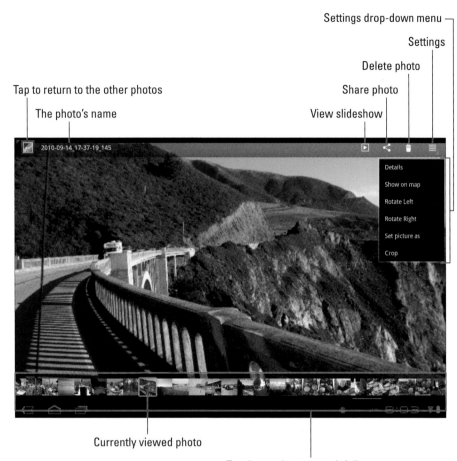

Currently viewed photo

Touch any photo to see it full screen.
Drag your finger along the strip to see other photos.

Figure 11-5: When you're viewing a photo, sliding your finger across the strip at the bottom brings other photos into view.

✔ Picked up an HDMI cable, as I recommend in Chapter 20? Then hook up your Xoom to your HDTV (described in Chapter 5) to show off your vacation photos to a room full of people.

✔ The settings menu in the upper-right corner, lets you see details about the photo, rotate it to the left or right, set the picture as wallpaper, or crop it — a task described later in this section.

Cropping Photos

Are you stuck with a group photo but only need a head shot of your friend in the middle row? Cropping is the answer. *Cropping* lets you trim away unwanted elements from a photo: the telephone pole growing out of somebody's head, for example, or the McDonald's logo poking up in the corner of your scenic vista.

You can crop any photo in the Gallery, whether you shot it yourself, downloaded it from the web, or received it through e-mail.

To crop a photo, follow these steps:

1. **Open the Gallery app by touching Apps⇨Gallery.**

2. **Touch the photo you want to crop.**

   You want the photo to be full screen for best results.

3. **Touch the Settings button, and choose Crop from the drop-down menu.**

   A box appears inside the photo, as shown in Figure 11-6.

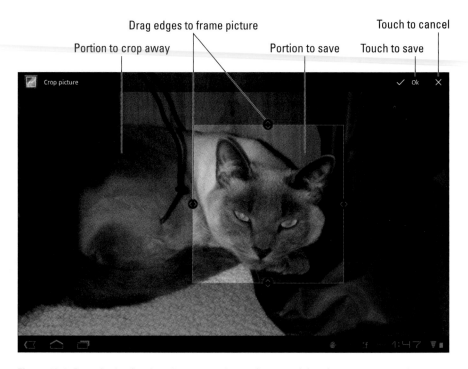

Drag edges to frame picture   Touch to cancel

Portion to crop away   Portion to save Touch to save

Figure 11-6: Drag the box's edges in or out to frame the part of the photo you want to keep.

4. **Drag the box's edges in or out until you've framed the portion of the photo you want to keep.**

   You can also move the entire box around by touching and holding it, and then moving your finger to the box's desired location.

5. **Touch the OK button in the top-right corner of the screen.**

   The Gallery app crops the photo and saves it under a new name, preserving your old photo.

Watching Movies

The "Finding your photos and movies" section, earlier in this chapter, describes how to find your images and movies. Here's how to watch movies you've taken with your Xoom, as well as movies that you've added to it:

1. **Touch Apps⇨Gallery.**

   The Gallery app opens (refer to Figure 11-4, earlier in this chapter).

2. **Open the stack of photos containing your movies.**

   To filter out photos and see just the movies, choose Videos Only from the Images and Videos drop-down menu.

3. **Tap a movie.**

   It begins to play, as shown in Figure 11-7, with a Play/Pause button and a scroll bar at the bottom of the screen.

   Soon after a movie begins playing, the controls disappear so that you can concentrate on the action rather than the mechanics. To make the controls reappear, touch the movie. The controls work as follows:

   • *Play/Pause:* Touch this button to stop the action.

   • *Scroll bar:* The scroll bar works like a timeline, and the dot represents your current spot. Touch the dot and drag it forward or backward along the bar to advance or rewind.

4. **Close the movie when you're done.**

   When you're through viewing your movie, touch the screen to bring the menus back to life. Then, to exit, touch the Back button in the screen's bottom-left corner to dig your way back to the Gallery. (You may have to touch the Back button a few times.)

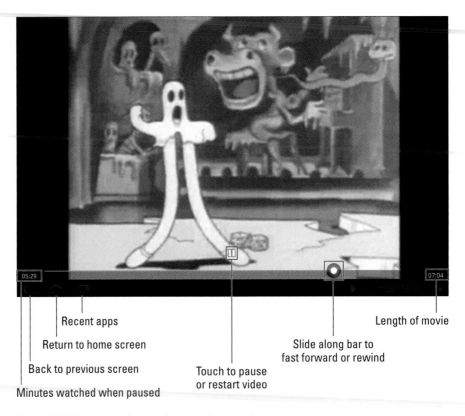

Recent apps

Return to home screen

Back to previous screen

Minutes watched when paused

Touch to pause or restart video

Slide along bar to fast forward or rewind

Length of movie

Figure 11-7: Touch a playing movie to see its controls.

Editing your movies with Movie Studio

The bundled Movie Studio app lets you trim the boring parts out of your vacation videos. To find it, touch Apps⇨Movie Studio. Using the program takes a little practice, but here are the basics:

1. **Touch New Project, type a name for your new movie-to-be, and click OK.**

2. **Add a movie or photos to your project by touching the Add Movie or Add Photo icon in the top-right corner and then selecting them from the Gallery.**

3. **When the movie appears in Movie Studio, touch it.**

The editing controls appear in the top-right corner, letting you change the colors, add titles, or choose fades between shots.

4. **Trim a clip's beginning or ending by touching it and then sliding the green bars inward.**

5. **To save your movie, touch the Settings button in the top-right corner, and choose Export Project from the drop-down menu.**

Movie Studio creates a new movie from your items, leaving your originals untouched.

Deleting or Sharing Media

Not every image you capture is worth saving forever. In fact, the best photographers delete far more images than they save. After you weed out the bad images, you're left with only the ones you want to share.

To weed out the stinkers and share the winners, follow these steps:

1. **Open the Gallery app by touching Apps⇨Gallery.**

2. **Select the photos or movies you want to delete.**

   Touch and hold the first ugly photo or movie. A green frame appears around the image's thumbnail, and the word *Done* appears in the screen's top-left corner (see Figure 11-8).

   Touch any other unwanted photos or movies; as you touch them, a green frame surrounds them.

   To select all the photos or movies shown, touch Select All.

Figure 11-8: Touch and hold an unwanted video or photo; repeat with others; and then touch the trash-can icon's Confirm Delete menu option to delete them all.

3. **Touch the trash-can icon in the top-right corner of the screen, and choose Confirm Delete from its drop-down menu.**

   When you touch Confirm Delete, the Gallery app deletes your photos or movies, and you have no chance of retrieving them. If you change your mind before touching Confirm Delete, press Cancel to keep your media from disappearing into the void.

4. **To share a winner, select the photos or movies that you want to share.**

   The steps are the same as in Step 2.

5. **Touch the Share button, and when the drop-down menu appears, choose the service to use for sharing your images.**

   The Share drop-down menu lists Gmail, along with some of your apps that can handle photos. You'll spot Facebook here, for example, if you've installed the Facebook app.

6. **Complete the sharing option within your chosen app.**

   This step differs according to the app you're using to share your image.

   If you choose Facebook, for example, the Facebook app appears with your photo already embedded in a blank post. Fill out the caption, if you want, and touch Upload to share your photo through your Facebook account.

   Your photo heads off to the service or program you've chosen.

12

And There Was Music

In This Chapter

▶ Adding music

▶ Browsing music by category

▶ Listening to your songs

▶ Making and editing playlists

▶ Deleting your songs

▶ Tuning in to Internet radio

*Y*our Motorola Xoom won't exactly fit in your shirt pocket, but it's still a portable music player. Call it a fashionably slim boom box that won't weigh down your shoulder.

Unlike a boom box, however, your Xoom can carry around thousands of songs. Add a free app, and it can tune in to thousands of radio stations as well.

For *really* good sound, connect your Xoom to a set of portable speakers, computer speakers, or — best yet — your home stereo, as I describe in Chapter 5.

No matter how you listen to your tunes, this chapter explains how to move music into your Motorola Xoom, browse your song stash, play music, and create playlists to match your mood.

Filling Your Xoom with Music

When you turn on your Xoom and touch Apps➪Music, you may see a well-stocked music library, full of your favorite tunes. The covers fly by as you scroll through them with a flip of a finger, as shown in Figure 12-1.

Figure 12-1: The Music app lets you scroll through music by browsing covers.

If your Xoom just came out of the box, though, the Music app greets you with a sad message: "You don't have any music in your library." You can stuff your music shelves any of three ways, all described in this section.

You can play music stored in any of these formats: AAC, AMR, MP3, WAV, AAC+, MIDI, and Ogg Vorbis. But it won't play WMA files (the type created by Windows Media Player; see "Syncing with Windows Media Player," later in this chapter), and it can't play any copy-protected music. Several music apps from the Android Market can play additional formats, including lossless formats like FLAC.

Copying your computer's music to your Xoom

The fastest way to copy music from your desktop computer to your Xoom is through a USB cable. (Check out the step-by-step instructions for connecting the cable and copying files to your Xoom in Chapter 5.)

After you've connected your Xoom and your desktop computer (PC or Mac), drag and drop the computer's music files or folders to the Xoom's Music folder.

Your Xoom comes with 32GB of memory, so feel free to move thousands of songs over. (Videos, which I cover in Chapter 11, are the *real* storage hogs.)

If you're using a Mac, download Android File Transfer, the program described in Chapter 5. From there, you can drag and drop music files from your Mac to your Xoom's Music folder.

Syncing with Windows Media Player

Windows Media Player can also send files to your Xoom. If you keep your music files organized in Windows Media Player, you can keep them synchronized with your Xoom. You can synchronize in either of two ways:

- **Manually:** Each time you plug in your Xoom, you tell Windows Media Player exactly which music files to transfer to your Xoom. The manual method works best when Media Player holds more music than can fit onto your Xoom. Transferring files manually lets you choose exactly which tunes to transfer, and which to leave behind.

- **Automatically:** By setting up a "sync partnership" between your Media Player and your Xoom, they'll automatically update each other whenever you plug in your Xoom. That keeps the same songs on both your Xoom and your PC. This works best when your Xoom has enough space to hold every song in your Media Player's library.

Here's how to sync your Xoom with Media Player manually:

1. **Plug the USB cable into the USB ports on your Xoom and on your PC.**

   I describe this process in detail in Chapter 5.

2. **On your PC, choose Start⇨All Programs⇨Windows Media Player.**

3. **Click the Sync tab on the right side of the Windows Media Player window.**

4. **Drag the music you want to sync from the Windows Music Player library over to the Sync tab.**

5. **Click the Start Sync button.**

   When you click the Start Sync button, shown in Figure 12-2, Media Player copies the music from the Sync tab to your Xoom.

Figure 12-2: Click the Sync button, and Windows Media Player copies the music to your Xoom.

To keep your Xoom *automatically* synced with Media Player's library, set up a sync partnership between them: Right-click your Xoom in Media Player's left pane, and choose Options⇨Set Up Sync.

After you set up that sync partnership, start Media Player before plugging in your Xoom. Then, when you plug in the USB cable, Media Player automatically synchronizes the two libraries.

For best results, don't keep anything in Windows Media Player that you don't want on your Xoom. Because Windows Media Player includes photos and videos, you may want to remove any unwanted items before syncing.

When you're copying to your Xoom through Windows Media Player, keep an eye out for the few things that may go wrong:

✔ If you ripped some of your CDs in WMA format rather than in MP3, Windows Media Player ignorantly copies those WMA files to your Xoom. The Music app can't play WMA files, but other music apps from the Android Market play them without problem. (If you need help navigating the Market for a music app, see Chapter 9.)

↙ You can delete unwanted WMA files from your Xoom by selecting the Xoom on the left side of the Windows Media Player window and choosing Music⇨Album. Take note of the albums that don't appear in your Xoom's Music app, and delete them from within Windows Media Player.

↙ To change the sync settings in Media Player, choose Tools⇨Options⇨ Devices tab, and double-click your Xoom's name from the list of devices.

↙ To stop the sync partnership, right-click your Xoom in the right-pane, and choose Options⇨End Sync Partnership.

↙ Windows Media Player plays TV shows recorded by Windows Media Center and even tries to sync them with your Xoom. The syncing will be cut short with an error message, though, because the Xoom can't play those shows.

↙ Microsoft and Google dislike each other, and Windows Media Player is a prime example of the tension. Your Xoom won't play WMA files, yet Media Player copies them anyway. And your Xoom won't play TV shows recorded by Windows Media Center, yet Windows tries to sync them anyway.

Buying music online

You can buy music on a CD, rip the songs to your computer by using your favorite media player, and then copy the MP3 files to your Xoom.

Alternatively, you can submit to immediate gratification by buying music online, which drops your purchased songs or albums directly into your Xoom.

The Xoom works with these online music stores:

↙ **Android Market (`https://market.android.com`):** Your Xoom's Market app lets you buy both apps and books. Google Music, available as an update, lets you buy music from the same store. The music you purchase here shows up in your Xoom's Music app.

↙ **Amazon (`www.amazon.com`):** If you've never bought music online before — or simply like to explore new artists — start thumbing through Amazon's extensive free section. Many exposure-seeking artists give away their tunes here, available both through Amazon's MP3 app and on the Amazon.com website, shown in Figure 12-3. (Exploring Amazon through the main browser shows a larger selection.) Like purchases from the Android Market, the songs you buy from Amazon turn up in the Music app on your Xoom.

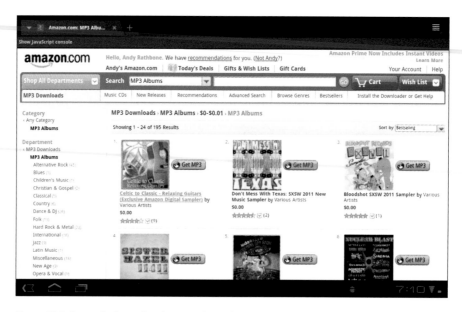

Figure 12-3: Instead of entering Amazon through its app, head there from your browser for a richer experience.

Be sure not to buy any copy-protected music files, as they won't play on your Xoom.

- ✔ Drop by the Android Market for free apps that let you shop at other online music stores, like Rhapsody and Walmart. You can also visit them directly in your Xoom's built-in browser.

- ✔ No, the Xoom doesn't work with Apple's iTunes. If you accidentally downloaded the iTunes program, get rid of it by touching Apps⇨ Downloads; touching the box next to the downloaded file; and then touching the Delete button at the bottom of the screen.

- ✔ Downloaded songs and albums almost always arrive with the correct artwork intact. By contrast, copying your computer's music onto your Xoom almost always brings artwork problems. (See this chapter's sidebar, "My album covers are messed up!")

- ✔ Most music stores sell songs in MP3 format these days, so you should be able to play them without problem. Your Xoom can't play copy-protected music, though, so keep an eye out for anything songs mentioning Digital Rights Management.

Browsing Your Music

No matter how your music enters your Xoom, either through a cable or from an online store, it ends up in your Music app. To see that music, touch Apps⇨Music.

When you first load the Music app, your music — if you have any on your Xoom — appears as a series of flying album covers (refer to Figure 12-1, earlier in this chapter). That view, called New and Recent, displays your most recently added music, as well as new purchases. It doesn't show all your music, though. To see the rest, touch the Browse drop-down menu, shown in Figure 12-4.

My album covers are messed up!

Fewer things are more frustrating than pouring your music into your Xoom and loading the cool 3D display of floating album covers only to find a sea of generic gray artwork. Where's the artwork? It's a long story, but here's how to fix it.

(First, a disclaimer: Following these steps deletes any playlists on your Xoom.)

1. **Head to the Android Market, and download Album Art Grabber Free, a free app by Tim Clark.**

2. **Start the program, and touch its Grab! button to fetch most of your artwork automatically.**

3. **Tap the covers that have missing artwork, and search for them manually, using the LastFM or MusicBrainz option.**

4. **Close the Album Art Grabber Free program.**

   Now you tell your Xoom to rebuild its album-cover database.

5. **Touch Apps⇨Settings⇨Applications⇨ Manage Applications.**

   The program opens to show your *downloaded* applications. Because the Music

app came bundled with your Xoom, you want to see the *All Applications* section, instead.

6. **Touch All Applications at the top of the column.**

7. **Scroll down the list to your Music app, and touch the Clear Data button.**

8. **Touch OK to approve clearing the data.**

   This step doesn't remove your music — only the Xoom's music database.

9. **Open your Music app again by touching Apps⇨Music.**

   Don't panic when the Music app says you don't have any music. It quickly begins rebuilding the database and displays your music once again. This time, though, your artwork should be correct.

If a few esoteric albums still need covers, find the artwork on the web, and save the files in your Xoom's Downloads folder. Fire up the Album Art Grabber Free app once more, but this time, tell it to search your SD card. Then choose the correct album art from your stash in the Downloads folder.

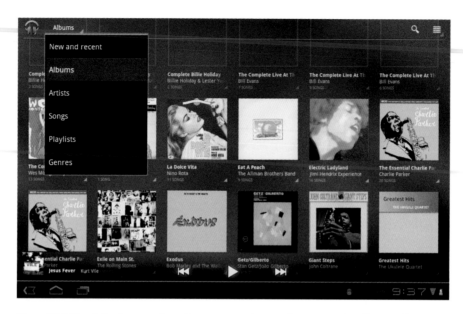

Figure 12-4: Touch the Browse drop-down menu to browse by new music, album, artist, song, playlist, or genre.

The Music app in Figure 12-4, for example, shows music displayed alphabetically by album. If you buy more single songs than you do albums, choose Songs from the drop-down menu, and the Music app shows all your songs (see Figure 12-5).

When you browse by artist or genre, the album covers line up in stacks organized by artist names, letting you burrow deep into music by a single artist.

✐ When you're viewing your music by song names, look for the words *Sort A-Z* at the very top of the list. Touching that phrase fetches a drop-down menu of options that can display your songs sorted alphabetically, by album, or by artist.

✐ The Music app always opens to the last view you used, letting you start where you left off. You'll also find your last-played song listed at the bottom of the screen, ready to play again when you touch the Play button.

Figure 12-5: Touch Songs from the Browse drop-down menu to see every song on your Xoom.

Listening to Music

It only takes a touch of a finger to begin playing a song after you've found the perfect tune for the moment. After you've browsed to the song, album, artist, or genre you want to hear, as described in the preceding section, touch one of the displayed songs. The Music app begins playing your selection and displaying the Play/Pause controls (see Figure 12-6).

Your Xoom varies a bit when it plays in different views. Here's the rundown:

- **Album view:** When you're viewing the contents of a single album, touch the first song. It begins to play, followed by the rest of the album.

- **Song-list view:** When you're viewing all the songs on your Xoom (refer to Figure 12-5, earlier in this chapter), touch any song to hear it. When it ends, your Xoom plays the rest of the songs in their listed order.

- **Artist or Genre:** Choose Artist or Genre from the Browse drop-down menu, as described in the preceding section; then touch the stack of covers that bear the name of the desired artist or genre. The name of the first listed album cover — the generic-looking one — bears the name All Songs; touch it to hear all the songs by that artist or in that musical genre.

Previous view

Song title

See all songs on album | Artist name

See more by artist | Album name

Touch to see drop-down menu

Artwork

Search for songs

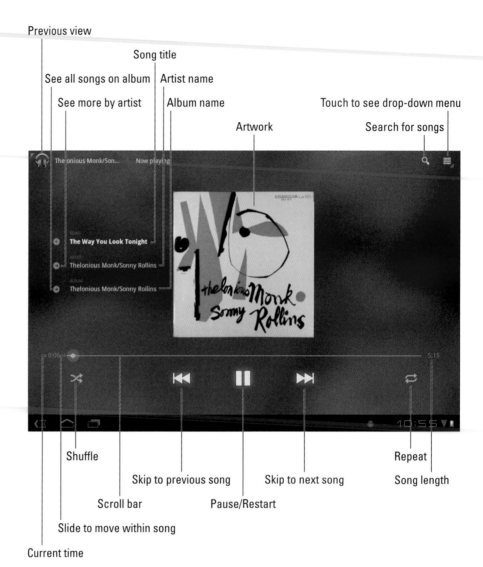

Shuffle

Skip to previous song

Skip to next song

Repeat

Song length

Scroll bar

Pause/Restart

Slide to move within song

Current time

Figure 12-6: When a song is playing, the Music app displays the album cover, song name, artist, and album name.

To create even more elaborate song arrangements than that, you need a *playlist* — a premade set of songs. I cover playlists in the next section.

To shuffle through your tracks randomly, touch the Shuffle button, shown in the margin. Shuffle play keeps things lively during a road trip or party.

To keep the same music playing constantly, touch the Repeat button, shown in the margin. Turn it off when the party lasts too long.

While you're listening to music, you can work on other tasks. Touch the home screen and start browsing the web, for example, and your music keeps playing in the background. To start or stop your music, touch the clock in the screen's bottom-right corner. The current song's name appears, along with buttons for skipping forward and backward or pausing.

When you choose New and Recent from the Browse drop-down menu, the first listed album song is called Shuffle. Touch it to shuffle through all your latest music.

To adjust the volume, touch one of the two volume buttons on the side of your Xoom. An onscreen volume control appears. Slide the control bar left or right to turn the music up or down; tap the speaker icon to mute the sound.

The Now Playing bar normally appears at the bottom of your Music app's screen (refer to Figures 12-4 and 12-5, earlier in this chapter). The bar lets you pause or skip tracks. If you don't like seeing it, touch the Settings icon in the top-right corner and choose Hide Now Playing Bar from the drop-down menu. (To bring back the bar, touch the Settings icon again and choose Show Now Playing Bar.)

Creating and Editing Playlists

Sometimes, playing albums and songs doesn't quite satisfy the mood. When you're looking to craft your musical experience, create your own mix with a playlist — your own take on the "Greatest Hits" package.

When you add certain songs to an ordered playlist, you can hear them any time you want, in the order you want, without hunting and pecking your way through the Music app.

Follow these steps to make a playlist:

1. **Navigate to the first song or album you want to add to your playlist.**

   I explain how to browse your music library earlier in this chapter.

2. **Touch the Settings menu in the top-right corner, and choose Add to Playlist from the drop-down menu.**

   The Music app sneaks the Add to Playlist menu into quite a few places, as shown in Figure 12-7. It appears when you touch the little triangle next to a song or album title, for example. It also appears in Artists view when you touch an artist's name. (Notice the generic artwork above the artist's name on the right side of Figure 12-7. This artwork signifies a collection of songs.)

   Did you spot the plus sign next to the playing song's name in Figure 12-6, earlier in this chapter? Touching that plus sign also fetches the Add to Playlist menu.

3. **Choose an existing playlist's name, or choose New Playlist and enter a new name.**

   When the Add to Playlist window appears, you can add your new music to the end of an existing playlist by touching that playlist's name.

   Alternatively, add your incoming item to the top of a new playlist by touching New Playlist and entering a new name.

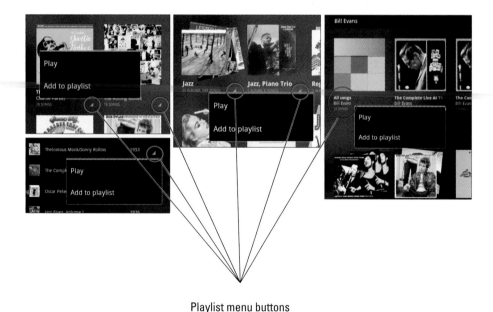

Playlist menu buttons

Figure 12-7: Touch the little triangles (or, in Artists view, the artist's name) to see the Add to Playlist menu.

4. Touch your newly created playlist's name to make any final changes.

To see your playlists, choose Playlists from the Browse menu in the top-left corner of the screen. Then touch the name of the playlist you want to edit, and it opens (see Figure 12-8).

To remove a song from the list, touch the little triangle at the far-right end of its row. When the drop-down menu appears, choose Remove from List.

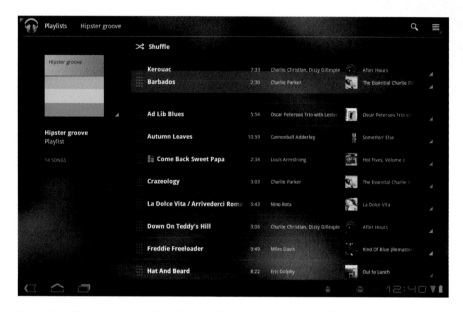

Figure 12-8: To change a song's order, drag its name up or down the list.

As always, you can touch a song to hear it while you're crafting your playlist. When you're done, move on to something else; your playlist is saved automatically.

- To shuffle your playlist, touch Settings⇨Shuffle All.
- To delete a playlist, choose Browse⇨Playlists; touch the playlist's name below the artwork; and choose Delete.

Deleting Music

You can't delete your music — not from within your Xoom, that is. To delete your music files, you must connect your Xoom to your computer with a USB cable, find the offending piece of music in your Xoom's Music folder, and delete it.

Alternatively, if you're automatically syncing your songs through Windows Media Player, remove the unloved album from Windows Media Library; then sync your Xoom with Media Player again.

Ideally, a future software fix will let you delete music directly from your Xoom. In the meantime, you can delete music with a file-manager app like Metago's ASTRO File Manager, available from Android Market as a free download. (I list ten essential free apps in Chapter 18.)

Listening to Internet Radio

Straight out of the box, the Xoom can't tune in to radio, so once again, apps come to the rescue.

My favorite radio app — TuneIn Radio by Radio Time, Inc. (see Figure 12-9) — seems to have it all. This free app lets you choose among 40,000 radio stations, sorted several ways to make them easy to find:

- **Presets:** When you've found a station you like, add it to Presets for one-touch listening later.

- **Local Radio:** The app knows your current city automatically, so touching Local Radio presents a detailed list of live local radio stations. Touch a station's name to hear it. You'll usually see the name of the current song and artist as well. (You can even listen to your current city's police scanners.)

- **Music:** This option categorizes thousands of radio stations by genre, letting you match the music to your mood.

- **Talk:** This option categorizes talk shows by genre, letting you hear people yak it up on your topic of choice.

- **Sports:** The Sports option places a list of sports stations one touch away.

Figure 12-9: Download the TuneIn Radio app to hear Internet radio stations, including stations in your current location.

✔ **Location:** Do you like foreign music? Head here to see stations listed by country as well as continent. Don't be surprised to hear American pop coming from other exotic foreign countries, though. Justin Bieber is quite well traveled.

✔ **Language:** Homesick for your native tongue? This option lists stations whose announcers speak everything from aboriginal dialects to Welsh.

✔ **Podcasts:** All the major podcasts are here, letting you hear bloggers gab away about their niche markets.

If you still haven't found the right music, talk show, or podcast, head for the app's Search bar. Chances are that the app can find a match somewhere in its list of stations.

13

Books, Magazines, and Newspapers

In This Chapter

▶ Finding, buying, and reading books

▶ Finding, buying, and reading magazines

▶ Finding, buying, and reading newspapers

▶ Browsing favorite sites with newsreaders

*M*usic, movies, maps, and photos began appearing on computers years ago. Now the digital shelves are slowly beginning to sag with books, magazines, and newspapers as well. Amazon already sells more digital books than paperbacks these days.

This chapter walks you through four digital book reader apps: the Amazon Kindle, Google's Books, Barnes and Noble's Nook, and the Aldiko eBook Reader. It explains how to buy books, turn their pages, scrawl in the margins, and sniff their electronic pages.

This chapter also describes how to subscribe to magazines and newspapers by downloading apps, or visiting their sites on your browser. Also, while you're waiting for more magazines and newspapers to tread the digital waters, you can install a newsreader to simplify your travels through your favorite websites.

As a bonus, you'll find the secret of how to put your favorite free classics on your e-book readers. The world's library has never been so portable — a fortunate technological feat when you're stuck in a doctor's office full of well-thumbed old magazines.

Reading E-Books

Buying digital books, magazines, and newspapers has never been easier. Instead of prowling bookstore aisles, you let your fingers walk across the Xoom's screen, browsing categories, authors, and titles, and then reading samples of the books that interest you.

Like the sample? Click the embedded Buy button, and when the full book arrives in digital form, the benefits come to life. You can change the text size to whatever seems most comfortable to your own eyes and lighting. Look up esoteric words when a pretentious author tosses you a stumper. Turn pages just like you learned in grade school: Flick the page with your finger, and the next one appears. Or flick backward if you can't believe what you just read.

How do the four main e-book reader apps compare? See for yourself in this section, which details the features of e-book reader apps from Amazon, Google, Barnes and Noble, and Aldiko. You can download any or all of the apps from the Android Market, covered in Chapter 9. When downloaded, they await in your Apps area.

Your Xoom automatically shifts the screen whether you're holding it in portrait or landscape mode. Feel free to hold it the way you feel most comfortable when reading.

Different e-book readers often support different *file formats* — the storage container they use for holding a book. If you already own e-books but need to convert them to a format that your current reader accepts, download calibre (http://calibre-ebook.com). This program converts just about any format, provided that the book isn't copy-protected.

Amazon Kindle

After neatly wrapping up the online-book-sales niche, Amazon cast its net over the e-book market by designing and selling its own e-book reader, the Amazon Kindle.

The Kindle grew in popularity, and Amazon quickly released Kindle programs for Windows and Macintosh computers; for Apple's iOS devices; and for BlackBerry, Android (your Xoom's operating system), and Windows Phone 7 devices. That legwork ensures that an e-book purchased from Amazon remains readable on nearly *any* platform. Your books won't disappear if your Xoom breaks.

No matter which platform you use to read your book, the Kindle always remembers your last-read page, opening to that same page when you open the book on another reader.

In short, Amazon started early in the game, and its reader has a polish and depth that the competitors lack.

Touch Apps➪Kindle to see the books in your Kindle library (see Figure 13-1).

Figure 13-1: The Kindle library lists only books currently stored on your Xoom; others remain on Amazon to be downloaded when you want.

Touch an e-book to see a page layout like the one in Figure 13-2.

Here's how the Amazon Kindle app handles the basics:

- ✔ **Page turning:** Pages scroll by sliding across the screen, replacing the existing page. You can drag a page with your finger or simply tap the edge of the page to make it turn forward or back.

- ✔ **Shopping:** You can shop within the app by touching Settings➪Kindle Store. You can also shop at Amazon's website (www.amazon.com), where books can be routed straight to your Kindle for immediate reading.

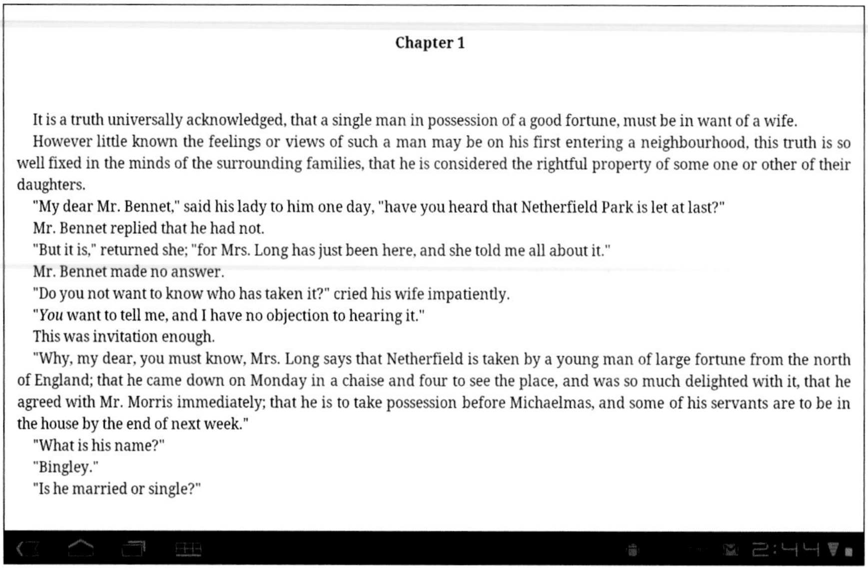

Chapter 1

It is a truth universally acknowledged, that a single man in possession of a good fortune, must be in want of a wife.

However little known the feelings or views of such a man may be on his first entering a neighbourhood, this truth is so well fixed in the minds of the surrounding families, that he is considered the rightful property of some one or other of their daughters.

"My dear Mr. Bennet," said his lady to him one day, "have you heard that Netherfield Park is let at last?"

Mr. Bennet replied that he had not.

"But it is," returned she; "for Mrs. Long has just been here, and she told me all about it."

Mr. Bennet made no answer.

"Do you not want to know who has taken it?" cried his wife impatiently.

"*You* want to tell me, and I have no objection to hearing it."

This was invitation enough.

"Why, my dear, you must know, Mrs. Long says that Netherfield is taken by a young man of large fortune from the north of England; that he came down on Monday in a chaise and four to see the place, and was so much delighted with it, that he agreed with Mr. Morris immediately; that he is to take possession before Michaelmas, and some of his servants are to be in the house by the end of next week."

"What is his name?"

"Bingley."

"Is he married or single?"

Figure 13-2: To flip a page, swipe your finger from right to left, and the next page slides into view.

🖉 **Making margin notes:** Touch and hold a word; then drag your finger around the area you want to annotate. Lift your finger, choose Note from the pop-up menu, and enter your scribbling. Touch Save, and your annotation appears as a colored footnote number. Touch it to reread your note.

🖉 **Managing formats:** The Kindle app supports Amazon's own e-book formats (AZW and AZW1), plain-text files (TXT), and unprotected Mobipocket files (MOBI and PRC). Amazon's Whispernet lets you e-mail files to Amazon, which will return them to your Kindle app in a supported format. Whispernet can translate Microsoft Word files (DOC and DOCX), web pages (HTML and HTM), Rich Text Format files (RTF), images (JPEG, JPG, GIF, PNG, and BMP), and Adobe Reader files (PDF).

🖉 **Adding books:** After connecting your Xoom to your computer with a USB cable, you can drop compatible book files into your Xoom's Kindle folder. If the files are truly compatible, they show up on your Kindle app's shelves. You can also e-mail supported documents to the Whispernet service, and those documents automatically appear in your Kindle app.

Amazon is the easy choice for reading books on your Xoom. With its low prices, huge inventory, and easy access to your digital library from nearly any platform, Amazon's hard to beat.

Google Books

Your Xoom comes with the Google Books app included. As a bonus, your Google Books library is already stocked with the four public-domain books shown in Figure 13-3.

Figure 13-3: The Google Books app presents your books much the way that it presents albums or photos.

Although the app is a little late to the e-book reader game, Google Books looks extraordinary on the Xoom's big screen. Pages look smooth, with crisp text, and the page turning is fancy (see Figure 13-4).

Google offers millions of books through the Android Market, including free classics. Like Amazon, it stores your books in the cloud, letting you download the ones you want to read as needed. When you finish a book, you can even delete it, which saves space for more music or movies. (Even when deleted from your Xoom, your books live on in the cloud, waiting for you to download them again for a reread.)

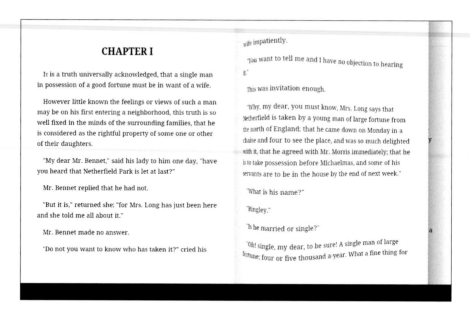

Figure 13-4: Google Books offers realistic page turning.

The Google Books app handles some of the following basics better than others:

✔ **Page turning:** Pages turn with a flick of a finger. As you slide your finger across the page, the sheet of "paper" follows along with a smooth rolling motion (refer to Figure 13-4).

✔ **Shopping:** Google sells books through the Books section of the Android Market (which you open by touching Apps➪Android Market). I cover the Market in Chapter 9. Unlike Amazon's store, you can't sort books by price.

✔ **Making margin notes:** Unlike most e-book reader apps, Google Books doesn't offer you any way to add your own notes.

✔ **Managing formats:** The app supports Adobe PDF and ePub formats.

✔ **Adding books:** Unfortunately, you have no way to stock the Google Books app with digital books you already own. Everything must be downloaded through the Android Market Books section.

Books that you buy through Google are also readable on the Nook and Sony e-book readers.

Barnes and Noble Nook

Clearly built for a smartphone rather than a tablet computer, Barnes and Noble's Nook app (see Figure 13-5) offers more problems than solutions. As you move through its menus, the reader jumps continually from landscape to portrait mode, and it crashes a few times as well. I hope that the rough edges will be smoothed when the company finally releases a tablet version.

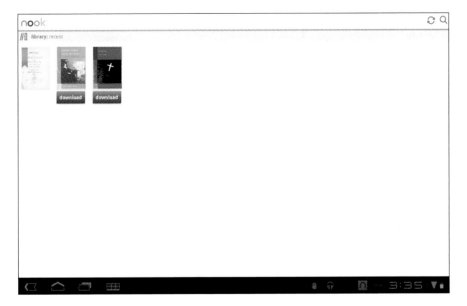

Figure 13-5: Designed for a smartphone's screen, the Nook app displays tiny covers in a sea of white.

The free-books section hasn't been culled very well. Amazon and Google wisely know that people will always want to download free classics, even if just for the purpose of lining their digital shelves. But my first download of *Pride and Prejudice* from the Nook store gave me an e-book that started with Chapter 6. A different version, shown in Figure 13-6, looks like it was scanned by a computer but never proofread.

Here's how the Nook reader fares on the basics:

- **Page turning:** Of all the apps, the Nook app features the most realistic page scrolling. It turns the page just as though you're turning the pages of a physical book. You can even hold a page partially turned while you finish the last sentence of the preceding page.

- **Shopping:** The app's bookstore offers only a few popular categories for shopping. Instead, shop directly from the browser for the best experience and to send books directly to the Nook app.

- **Making margin notes:** Touch and hold a word; then drag your finger around the area you want to annotate. Lift your finger, choose Add Note from the pop-up menu, and enter your scribbling. Touch Save, and your annotation appears as a footnote icon. Touch it to reread your note.

- **Managing formats:** The Nook supports ePub, PDB, PDF, and MP3 formats, as well as image files in formats such as JPG, GIF, PNG, and BMP.

- **Adding books:** Connect your computer to your desktop through a USB cable; then drag and drop compatible files into the Xoom's Nook/Content folder. (Mac owners need to download the Android File Transfer program, described in Chapter 5.)

Given time, the Nook app may catch up to the competition, but it needs to run pretty quickly, given the head starts of Amazon and Google.

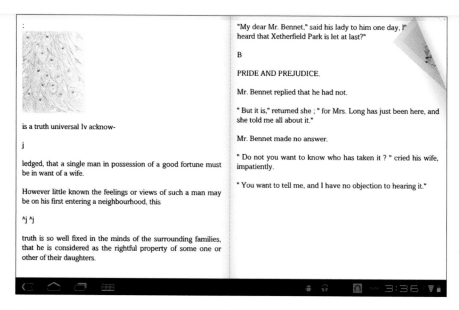

Figure 13-6: The pages of some public-domain classics may be gibberish, but the Nook app's page-turning animation shines.

Aldiko Book Reader

Aldiko Book Reader (www.aldiko.com) differs from the Kindle and the Nook apps in that it's not supported by a publisher. Instead, it works with a variety of digital publishers, including Feedbooks (www.feedbooks.com), All Romance Ebooks (www.allromanceebooks.com), Smashwords (www.smashwords.com), and O'Reilly Media (http://oreilly.com/ebooks).

The reader is ad-supported, so don't be surprised to see a few ads slide by as you browse the bookstore. (Ads don't appear while you're reading, thank goodness.)

The program opens to show wooden library shelves stocked with your books, as shown in Figure 13-7.

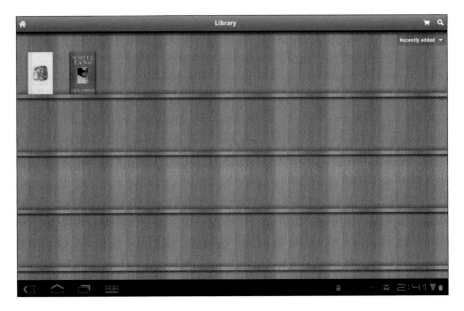

Figure 13-7: Aldiko presents your books shelved in an old-school, wood-panel library.

The reader is a fine way to explore works from smaller publishers, yet because it supports Adobe's ePub format, you can still buy the copy-protected *New York Times* bestsellers.

Here's how Aldiko handles the basics:

- ✏ **Page turning:** One page slides into another as you slide your finger or tap a page's edge, shown in Figure 13-8. There's no fancy animation, but the reader works without distraction.

- ✏ **Shopping:** The app lets you purchase e-books from several publishers and small distribution companies rather than large chains. Helpful categories not available in other e-book reader stores include "High School Reading: Free books commonly found on reading lists for U.S. high school English classes."

- ✏ **Making margin notes:** You can't add your own margin notes to books.

- ✏ **Managing formats:** Like the Google Books app, Aldiko supports ePub and PDF formats.

- ✏ **Adding books:** Copy e-books in ePub or PDF format to any folder on your Xoom. Then touch SD card in Aldiko's home screen, touch your added book file, and touch Open.

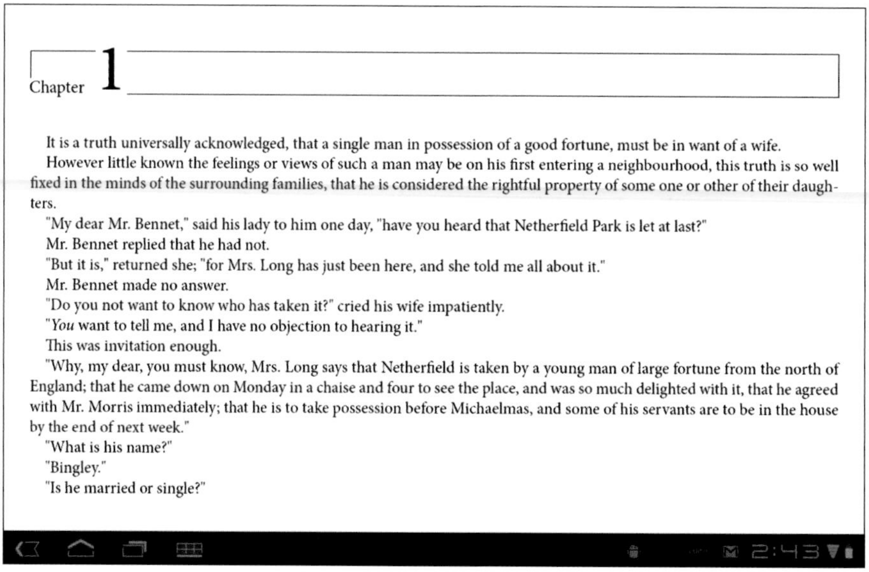

Chapter 1

It is a truth universally acknowledged, that a single man in possession of a good fortune, must be in want of a wife.

However little known the feelings or views of such a man may be on his first entering a neighbourhood, this truth is so well fixed in the minds of the surrounding families, that he is considered the rightful property of some one or other of their daughters.

"My dear Mr. Bennet," said his lady to him one day, "have you heard that Netherfield Park is let at last?"

Mr. Bennet replied that he had not.

"But it is," returned she; "for Mrs. Long has just been here, and she told me all about it."

Mr. Bennet made no answer.

"Do you not want to know who has taken it?" cried his wife impatiently.

"*You* want to tell me, and I have no objection to hearing it."

This was invitation enough.

"Why, my dear, you must know, Mrs. Long says that Netherfield is taken by a young man of large fortune from the north of England; that he came down on Monday in a chaise and four to see the place, and was so much delighted with it, that he agreed with Mr. Morris immediately; that he is to take possession before Michaelmas, and some of his servants are to be in the house by the end of next week."

"What is his name?"

"Bingley."

"Is he married or single?"

Figure 13-8: Aldiko's pages slide into view, pushing aside the old pages.

Finding free e-books

The e-book reader companies clearly want you to buy the latest bestsellers, but most of them make at least a token effort to offer some free books as well. After all, when they're faced with a new gadget, most people prefer to test a freebie on it rather than buy a ten-volume set.

Some publishers also offer free books for a limited time period, usually for promotional purposes. If you log on at the right time, you may get lucky.

With few exceptions, books published in the United States before 1923 now live in the public domain. Some book sellers may still charge you for them, but just as many let you download free digital versions as well:

- ✔ **Kindle:** From within the Kindle app, visit the Kindle Store, and enter the Free Popular Classics section, which carries well-formatted versions of the public-domain classics.

- ✔ **Google Books:** Head for the Google Books app's Top Free Books section, listed clearly in the menu. This section sorts free books by popularity, making it easy to spot the winners.

- ✔ **Nook:** You can find free books on Barnes and Noble's website and send them to your Nook app. But the Nook app itself only lets you purchase books, not browse or download free ones.

- ✔ **Aldiko:** Visit the Aldiko bookstore and touch Free Books to see the classics.

You can also find a wide variety of free public-domain books at Project Gutenberg (`www.gutenberg.org`), which is just a browser visit away. After you install Aldiko, you can touch a book listed in Project Gutenberg, then answer Yes when asked if Aldiko should open it.

If your stash of e-books and digital publications contains a variety of formats, download calibre (`http://calibre-ebook.com`). The free program lets you convert files from one program's preferred format to another's, as long as the files aren't copy-protected.

Aldiko Book Reader is the dark-horse candidate. Its main appeal — and greatest weakness — is its lack of ties to major publishers. Although you gain greater access to niche markets, that access comes at the expense of breadth of material.

Magazines and Newspapers

Most magazines and newspapers offer websites that you can visit directly from the Browser app. As smartphones and tablets have grown in popularity, more publishing houses have released apps that make it easier to touch your way through their products' pages.

Some publishers charge for their apps; others give them away free. To find them all, touch Apps⇨Market, and begin browsing the News and Magazines section (see Figure 13-9).

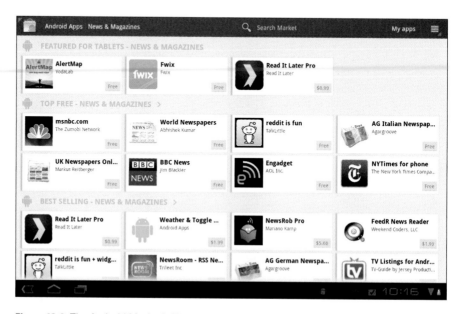

Figure 13-9: The Android Market's News and Magazines section lists apps from specific publishers.

As you can see by the lack of big names in Figure 13-9, newspapers and magazines haven't yet begun their digital migration. As tablets grow in popularity, expect to see more newspapers and magazines, as well.

- You'll find apps for *Time* and *Sports Illustrated* (including a Swimsuit Edition app), as well as *The New York Times* and *USA Today.* Drop by the News and Magazines section every so often to look for the latest newcomer.

- When you visit the websites of your favorite magazines and newspapers, keep an eye out for announcements of apps. When a publisher finally creates an app, its publications usually include a link directly to the app in the Android Market.

- Dale Jefferson's Newspapers app offers links to the websites of newspapers around the world — handy if you travel a lot.

Read me a story!

Sometimes, it's too much effort to turn a digital page. You don't want to flip pages while you're driving, for example. Or perhaps you're browsing in the craft shop or gardening but still want the pleasure of a good book. That's where *audiobooks* — recordings of people reading books chapter by chapter — come in.

The most popular audiobook app is Audible for Android. It offers a wide selection of bestsellers, read by the authors or professional narrators.

When you're in the mood for a good story but don't have your hands free, audiobooks are the ticket.

Newsreaders

Many web-savvy folk skip their daily newspapers and magazines, preferring to hit the blogs for their news. Blogs and websites provide up-to-the-minute news and niche coverage that's lacking in mainstream magazines.

It takes a lot of legwork to point and click your way through the blogs each morning, however. A newsreader program speeds your reading by gathering your favorite information and presenting it on one plate.

Alphonso Labs' Pulse newsreader app (see Figure 13-10), for example, grabs articles from your favorite sites and presents them as a unified web page, transforming your daily blog rounds into more of a makeshift magazine. Pulse presents a personalized magazine of content you used to gather manually.

Pulse arrives on the screen with some popular blogs and websites already listed, but feel free to add your own by following these steps:

1. **Touch the Settings button and then touch the plus sign.**

   (The Settings button is a gear icon in the top-left corner of the screen; the plus sign lives directly opposite in the top-right corner.) A list of suggested sites appears.

2. **Touch the Search icon (a magnifying glass), and type your favorite site's name.**

   Pulse turns up a list of matches. Alternatively, you can touch the Browse button to look through sites by category.

3. **Touch the plus sign next to your favorite site's name.**

   Pulse adds it to your list of subscribed sites.

Pulse serves as a great go-between, helping you fill the time while mainstream media gets its act together.

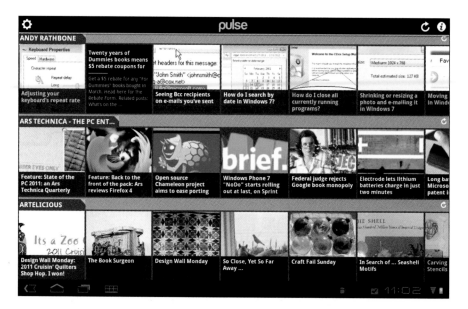

Figure 13-10: The Pulse newsreader collects articles from your favorite sites and presents them like a magazine.

Maps and Navigation

In This Chapter

▶ Opening the Maps app

▶ Viewing a map in different ways

▶ Adding informational layers

▶ Finding your location

▶ Finding other locations

▶ Navigating between locations

*T*reasured for centuries by emperors and explorers alike, maps once lived inside protective leather pouches to shield their delicate brushwork and parchment. A mere five years ago, maps lay clumsily folded in your car's door compartment, next to the soda-straw wrappers.

Today, maps live inside your Motorola Xoom. And they're alive, constantly updating themselves with your current location, the newest roads, the latest construction sites, and the heaviest traffic on your route.

Your Xoom boasts Google's latest twist: 3D maps. Instead of downloading bulky satellite photos, Google shows you 3D outlines of the building's shapes, letting you see your position quickly and easily while navigating unknown territory. The building's perspective changes along with your location, letting you see around tall buildings to orient yourself.

If you own a Wi-Fi–only Xoom, you're not left out. Plot your trips when you're connected to a Wi-Fi network, and your Xoom stashes away a copy of your trip plans, letting you navigate without an active Internet connection.

This chapter explains the wonder of Google Maps and the Navigation app, which gently directs you through whichever empire you care to travel through.

Unfurling the Xoom's Maps

If you're familiar with the Google Maps website, you'll rejoice when you see the Maps app on your tablet. It's better than the desktop version, with more features.

This section describes how to open a map, explore its many locations, and overlay its sections with features you need.

GPS must be turned on for a map to find your exact location. If it's not turned on, the Map app will ask if you'd like to turn it on, then open the appropriate Settings page for you to enable the Use GPS Satellites option.

Opening the Maps app

To unfurl the Maps app, touch App➪Maps. A map rolls out across your screen, as shown in Figure 14-1.

The first map that you see shows your location. As you examine the map, you can change your view with these finger tricks:

- **Scroll:** Drag your finger across the glass screen, and the map follows along, letting you pull the edges into view. You can also flick your finger across the map, quickly sliding more information onscreen.

- **Zoom in:** Two quick taps on the screen zoom in to that particular map area. Alternatively, place two fingers on the portion you want to see in detail. As you spread your fingers, the map expands.

- **Zoom out:** Pinch a spot on the map with two fingers; as your fingertips move closer together, the area you've pinched shrinks, bringing neighboring areas into view.

- **Rotate:** Place two fingers on the screen and turn your hand, just as though you were rotating a paper map sitting on a tabletop.

- **3D view:** Place two fingers on the screen near the top, and drag them both down. As you drag, you see a tilted view, as though you're viewing at an angle from a plane. Drag two fingers back up the screen to return to a direct overhead view.

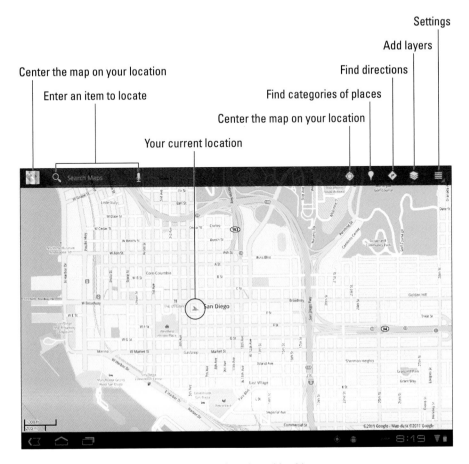

Settings

Add layers

Center the map on your location

Find directions

Enter an item to locate

Find categories of places

Center the map on your location

Your current location

Figure 14-1: Google's Maps app shows your location with a blue arrow.

The map's view changes constantly as you zoom in, adding more and more detail until you're looking at a boring map of property lots. (Spoiler: Touch and hold one of the lots to see its street address.)

- If you're indoors, or if your Xoom hasn't yet grabbed its GPS signal, your mapped location may differ quite a bit from your physical location. Lacking a GPS signal, Google Maps relies on cellphone towers for positioning. When the GPS signal arrives, the map updates to within 30 feet of your location.

- Still can't get a GPS signal? Touch Apps⊏>Settings⊏>Location & Security⊏> Use GPS Satellites. While you're there, turn on Use Wireless Networks as well. Google knows the names and locations of many Wi-Fi networks, so it can estimate your location based on the one you're using.

✔ Spot the Directions icon (shown in the margin) among the map's top row of icons? Touch it and enter your destination, and the Navigation app guides you there, turn by turn. (I cover the Navigation app in this chapter's last section.)

Adding layers of detail

When it first loads, Google Maps resembles a paper map, displaying drawings of roads, highways, lakes, and rivers. That's enough information to get you oriented, but for extra detail, add a few more layers.

Start by touching the Layers button, shown in the margin, and the Layers menu appears (see Figure 14-2).

Figure 14-2: Touch the Layers button, and choose new bits of information to place over your map.

Choose a layer from the menu — Traffic, for example — and the map updates itself to show traffic flow (see Figure 14-3). The red lanes have stop-and-go traffic, yellow lanes are slow, and green lanes flow at normal speed.

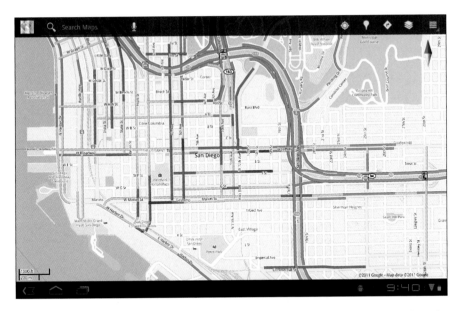

Figure 14-3: Choose the Traffic layer to see current traffic conditions on the map's roads and freeways.

Here's what each layer places on the map:

- **Traffic:** Traffic (refer to Figure 14-3) overlays colors on the roads to show their traffic speeds.

- **Satellite:** This layer overlays satellite photos of the area — handy for exploring cities or, in a pinch, finding an emergency heliport on a nearby skyscraper. (The Satellite layer disappears when you choose Terrain, described next.)

- **Terrain:** A boon for outdoors enthusiasts, this layer adds topographical information, letting you see changes in altitude among valleys, mountains, and deserts. To see exact altitude levels, zoom in as close as possible, and you'll see them labeled by feet. (The Terrain layer disappears when you choose Satellite, described in the preceding paragraph.)

- **Buzz:** This layer adds small thought bubbles to the map, each bubble containing a message left by a recent visitor. If you're into online social networking, Buzz is sort of a Twitter meets foursquare and lands on Google Maps.

- **Latitude:** This layer lets you and your friends stalk one another, as the map automatically updates to show everybody's locations. (All the friends must agree to be stalked by signing up for this feature, of course.)

✔ **Recent Searches:** For your convenience, this layer lists the last few items you searched for on the map. If you searched for pizza places, for example, you'll find a Pizza entry that overlays the map with locations of pizza joints.

Have you added too many layers to your map? Touch the Clear Map button at the bottom of the menu (refer to Figure 14-2, earlier in this chapter) to wipe the map clean and start over.

If you need even more layers, touch the More Layers button at the bottom of the menu to see these bonus layers: My Maps, which lists maps you've saved in Google's My Maps; Bicycling, which adds bike paths; Wikipedia, which adds icons for Wikipedia-listed locales; Transit Lines, which shows mass-transit stops; and Favorite Places, which shows worldwide locales favored by people of influence.

Finding Your Current Location

Finding your current location is as easy as opening Google Maps (touch Apps⇨Maps). Your location appears as a blue arrow, usually sitting in the very center of the map. This blue arrow has a blue circle around it, and the circle grows more noticeable as you zoom in. That's because your Xoom can't pinpoint your location down to your footprints. Instead, GPS knows your location only to within 30 feet, so that blue circle means that you could be anywhere within the circled area.

If no GPS signal is available, the blue circle grows much larger, because your Xoom falls back on the less-accurate cellphone towers for location information.

If you can't see the blue arrow on the map, touch the Maps icon in the top-left corner of the screen, shown in the margin. Your location appears again at the map's center.

Google Maps offers one more trick for viewing your location: a row of icons in the top-right corner of the screen (see Figure 14-4).

Figure 14-4: The leftmost icon changes depending on how you turn the map.

The leftmost icon changes to any of three shapes, depending on how you use the map. Here's the rundown:

When the icon resembles the one in the margin, touch it to center the map on your current position. When your position is centered, the icon changes to one of the next two shapes.

This icon means that the map always shows north at the top of the screen, just like most paper maps do.

When you see this icon, your Xoom constantly rotates the map to show what's in front of you — a handy trick when you're driving or walking through unfamiliar territory, as it lets you compare your immediate surroundings with what you see on the map.

To cycle through those three changes, just touch the icon.

✔ Are you lost and need to know your street address? Touch and hold the blue-arrow icon, and a My Location bubble pops up. Touch the bubble's words, and a menu appears, with your estimated street address at the top. (Tell that to the tow-truck driver.)

✔ If you own a Wi-Fi Xoom, Maps' rules change somewhat, because your Xoom won't have always-on Internet access through a data plan. If you're in a city that you visit often, Maps will probably still know your address. I explain more in the sidebar "Can I use Navigation on a Wi-Fi–only Xoom?," later in this chapter.

Finding Another Location

After you've pinpointed your own location in the Maps app, you'll naturally want to find another place to visit. Your Xoom helps direct your urge to travel, letting you see the location of a specific address, a business name, the address of one of your contacts, or even a specific point on the map.

The next four sections explain how to make the map locate places besides the spot you're standing on.

Finding a specific address

If you know your destination's exact address, you're ahead of the game. Touch the Search bar in the map's top-left corner, and type the address — such as **633 Stag Trail Rd, N Caldwell, NJ** — on the keyboard.

Alternatively, you can touch the Search box's microphone icon and dictate the address.

Either way, the map jumps to your chosen spot, marking it with a little bubble that spells out the address.

✔ You needn't type with precision. Just as is the case when you're searching Google on your desktop computer, a number, street, and city usually do the trick. Google's even pretty good at correcting your spelling.

✔ If you see a spot on the map and want its address, touch and hold that spot. A bubble appears, listing its address.

✔ To find out even more information about that place, touch the bubble. A menu appears, displaying more informational options (see "Searching for places near another location," in this chapter).

✔ For turn-by-turn driving directions to that spot, touch its address bubble. When the menu appears, touch the Navigation icon, shown in the margin. (I cover navigation in this chapter's last section.)

Finding a specific place

When you're out on the town, you're usually looking for a place, not an address. After all, a restaurant's name is easier to remember than its address.

Because the Maps app knows your location, it can easily search your surroundings for whatever you tell it to find. If you're looking for a restaurant, for example, enter that in the Search box, being as specific or as general as you want — **Indian restaurant**, for example. The Maps app whispers in Google's ear. Google glances at your location, searches for nearby Indian restaurants, and shows you the closest ones on the map.

If you search for businesses instead — say, waste-management businesses on New Jersey's Eastern Shore — the map shows you information like that shown in Figure 14-5.

See the little pushpins bearing letters on the map in Figure 14-5? Those letters correspond to the entries in the scrollable menu on the left side of the screen. To see more information about a business, touch its name in the menu. Touch one of the lettered pushpins to see a business's name.

To speed searches around your general location, touch the Places icon in the map's top-right corner. That icon fetches the menu shown in Figure 14-6, letting you search quickly by category.

Figure 14-5: The Maps app lets you search for businesses as well as addresses.

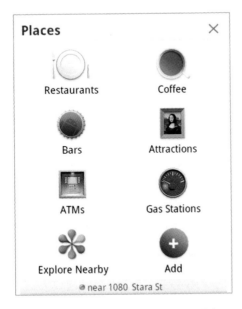

Figure 14-6: Touch the Places icon for quick searches of your immediate surroundings.

Touch Restaurants, for example, and the map drops lettered pushpins around your location, each pushpin listing a restaurant.

- ✔ If you find yourself searching for the same types of things over and over, touch the Add button in the Places menu. A window appears, letting you customize the Places menu with your own much-sought item, be it Trader Joe's or Walmart.

- ✔ You can launch Places directly from the Apps area. The menu shown in Figure 14-6 appears, tailored to your current location.

- ✔ If you've found just the right place, touch its bubble on the map and then touch the Navigate button, shown in the margin. In a moment or two, the Navigation app begins giving you turn-by-turn directions, as described in the last section of this chapter.

Finding a contact's address

Finding the location of somebody who's listed in your Contacts app (see Chapter 8) may be the easiest yet. Because you already have the person's address, call up the Contacts app (touch Apps⇨Contacts) and touch the address. The map appears, centered on that address, with a bubble listing the address.

Notice the pushpin icon next to your contacts' addresses. Any time you spot that symbol, you can touch it to see the address on a map.

Whenever the map sports a bubble listing an address, touch the address bubble. A menu appears, letting you touch the Navigate icon for turn-by-turn directions to that address, as described at the end of this chapter.

Searching for places near another location

Usually, you want to find places within walking or driving distance of your current location. When you're planning a trip, however, you may want to find restaurants or coffee shops near the hotel where you'll be staying in two weeks.

You can search when you arrive, of course, but here's how to search for places around that hotel before you set foot in the lobby:

1. **In the Maps app's Search box, enter the address you want to search around.**

   Alternatively, you can grab an address from your Contacts area.

   The map centers itself on that address, complete with a little white balloon listing that place's name and address.

2. Touch the balloon above the location.

A menu pops up to the left, as shown in Figure 14-7.

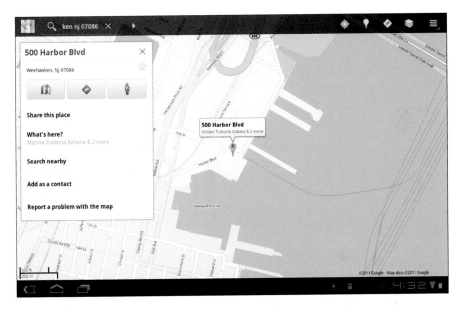

Figure 14-7: Touch an address, and a menu lets you explore nearby locations.

3. Touch a button on the menu to find what you're seeking.

Each button does something slightly different, so here's the rundown:

- *Star:* Touch the star, and it glows, marking it in your Maps app's memory. To find it again quickly, open the Maps app, touch Settings, and choose Starred Places. (Starred locales also appear as shortcut destinations in the Navigation app, which I cover at the end of this chapter.)

- *Show Location:* If you've been exploring around a found address, touch this button to return to the address you searched for.

- *Navigation:* Touch here to choose among hearing driving directions, walking directions, or seeing a list of turn-by-turn directions for either walking or driving. (I cover navigation in the next section.)

- *Street View:* This button brings up a photo of the address, just as though you were ogling it from the street.

- *Share This Place:* This button sends information about the place to one of your installed social-networking apps so you can brag that you've been there.

- *What's Here:* Touch this to see nearby businesses, including restaurants and shops.

- *Search Nearby:* Touch this button to see a list of other places at that address — perhaps different stores in a shopping mall or restaurants inside a hotel.

- *Add As a Contact:* One touch here, and the Maps app pours that place's contact information into your Contacts app (covered in Chapter 8) for later reference.

- *Report a Problem with the Map:* Nothing's perfect. If the map brings up the wrong property, or if something's mislabeled, let Google know by touching this button.

To close the menu, touch the X in its top-right corner.

✓ The menus change slightly, depending on whether you've searched for a business name or a specific address. If you've searched for a business name, the menu lists the first four buttons but fills the rest of the space with scrollable reviews. To see the other menu items, touch the drop-down menu button shown in the margin.

✓ After touching the Street View button, you can "walk" around the property by dragging the map with your fingers. It's a great way to become familiar with a place you're about to visit.

Navigating from Here to There

Your map not only shows detailed photos of places, but also comes with a backseat driver. When you're ready to head to a specific destination, the Maps app kicks the reins over to the Navigation app, which guides you on your trip, giving turn-by-turn directions.

Google's navigation program has two big advantages over the GPS navigation systems sold in stores:

✓ Google's navigator is free. The others cost $50 to several hundred dollars.

✓ Google's maps are free as well. The others come with a set of free maps for your continent, but after a year, most competing systems will ask you to purchase updated maps to stay current with new roads and changing businesses.

✓ Google always adds new features to its maps and navigation programs. The self-contained units are frozen in time.

Can I use Navigation on a Wi-Fi–only Xoom?

When you run Google's Navigation app, it locates your position, fetches the appropriate maps from the Internet, and then plots your trip. The app links its turn-by-turn navigation instructions with the proper GPS coordinates.

By gathering everything in advance, GPS can trigger the appropriate recording, letting you know which way to turn. The Navigation app even grabs some adjoining maps as a safety blanket in case you make a wrong turn. (It's probably already cached the entire map for your hometown.)

If you own a Wi-Fi–only Xoom, the Navigation app will still lead you from Point A to Point B, guiding you at each turn. Without the 3G connection, however, you miss out on these amenities:

✔ If you miss a turn, and your Xoom didn't cache that portion of your route, you're lost unless you can return to your botched intersection.

✔ You sometimes can't search for things along the way, like the nearest gas station, restroom, or coffee shop.

✔ You won't receive automatic rerouting to avoid heavily trafficked areas.

For driving through your hometown, your Wi-Fi–only Xoom's Navigation app will probably work fine. If you miss a turn on a long road trip between cities, however, you may need to find a coffee shop with Wi-Fi access so that the Navigation app can update its maps.

The next sections describe how to load the Navigation app and let it guide you down Route 66.

Whenever you're browsing the Maps app, as described in the preceding sections, look for the navigation icons shown in the margin. They both fetch the Navigation app to give you turn-by-turn instructions to your destination.

Loading the Navigation app from the Maps app

Your Xoom's omniscient backseat driver is the Navigation app, a good pal of the Maps app. After you've found your destination in the Maps app, touch the Navigation button and listen for turn-by-turn directions, always relayed in a calm, detached, and ethereally robotic voice.

You can fetch the Navigation app in any of several ways:

✔ **Maps:** Whenever you find your destination on a map, as described earlier in this chapter, look for the Navigate icon, shown in the margin. Touch it to fetch the Navigation app.

Don't see the Navigate button? If you see a bubble on the map that lists a place name or address, touch it. A menu appears, showing the Navigate button and other options.

✔ **Contacts:** Your Contacts app already holds a stash of addresses. If you're visiting a contact, touch his address. When the Maps menu appears, with a bubble over the address, touch the bubble and then touch the Navigate button.

✔ **Browse:** When searching with your browser, you'll occasionally spot thumbnails of Google maps embedded in your searches. When you spot one (like the one shown in Figure 14-8), touch it to put the location on the map. Then touch the address bubble above the location, and touch the Navigate button.

Figure 14-8: When the Browser app shows a thumbnail map like this one, touch it to launch your Maps and Navigation apps.

You can also fetch the Navigation app at any time from the Maps app. Open the Maps app (touch Apps➪Maps), and your current location appears automatically. Then touch the Directions icon, shown in the margin, and the menu shown in Figure 14-9 appears.

Figure 14-9: Enter your destination to receive driving, public transportation, bicycling, or walking instructions.

Because the Xoom already knows your location, you need enter only the destination.

Touching the End Point box drops down a list of destinations that you've accessed before; choose one as a shortcut. Alternatively, enter your address by hand; touch the appropriate icon for driving, public transportation, bicycling, or walking instructions; and then touch Go. The Navigation app begins guiding you there.

Navigating directly from the Navigation app

Did you just jump behind the wheel and need to scoot from Point A to Point B? Don't bother with the maps. Just load the Navigation app (touch Apps⇨ Navigation), and plot your course from there.

The Navigation app isn't as visual as the Maps app, but it's a cut-to-the-chase timesaver. When it's launched, the app presents the dark screen shown in Figure 14-10.

Each menu offers a different way to move you toward your destination:

- ✔ **Speak Destination:** This method (the fastest one) lets you speak a business name, a city, or even an exact address. Based on what your Xoom thinks you said, it presents a list of possible matches. Touch the one that's correct, and the Navigation app begins guiding you there.

- ✔ **Type Destination:** If your spoken instructions sailed over your Xoom's head, this fallback method lets you type your destination with the onscreen keyboard.

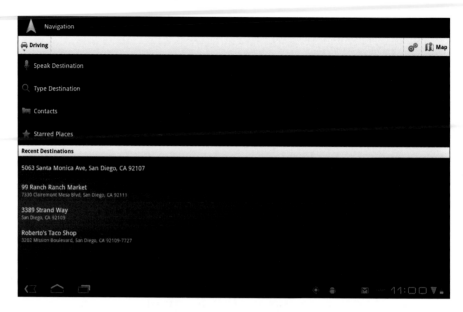

Figure 14-10: Enter your destination by speaking, typing, touching a contact, or accessing a place you've starred.

- ✔ **Contacts:** This option fetches your Contacts app. Touch the address of a contact, and the Navigation app guides you there.

- ✔ **Starred Places:** If you've added stars to favorite destinations, as in Figure 14-7, you'll find them listed here for quick reference.

- ✔ **Recent Destinations:** Being creatures of habit, we tend to revisit the same places. The destinations you searched for previously appear in this list for easy access.

If you're as eager to get on the road as a UPS driver, skip the maps, and head straight for the Navigation app. After you give it your destination, Navigation fetches the Maps app on its own, saving you a step.

Following the Navigation app's directions

No matter how you launch the Navigation app, two things happen:

- ✔ The screen changes to show your current location, with your route marked on the road ahead.

- ✔ The Navigation app's voice kicks in, telling you which way to go.

The Navigation app scouts out the best path to your destination and leaves you looking at a screen like the one shown in Figure 14-11.

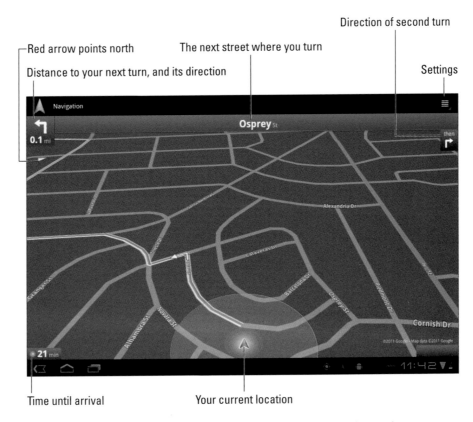

Figure 14-11: As you drive, the map changes to reflect your position and upcoming turns.

The voice tells you when you're about to make a turn within the next quarter mile. When the turn arrives, it tells you which direction to turn. You can drive the rest of the way without touching your Xoom — unless, of course, it's about to slide off your passenger seat during a turn. (See Chapter 20 for a fix.)

- ✔ The Navigation app keeps track of traffic, automatically routing you around the most congested freeways when possible.

- ✔ To stop the Navigation app, touch the Settings button (shown in the margin) and choose Exit Navigation.

- ✔ If you miss a turn, your Xoom doesn't say a word. It silently calculates rerouted instructions from your new direction and then tells you about your next turn. Ideally, that doesn't involve a U-turn in 60 miles.

- ✔ Because the Navigation app must converse constantly with satellites, it requires quite a bit of battery power. Invest in a charger that plugs in to your car's cigarette lighter.

- ✔ Touch the turn arrows at the top, left, and right for peeks at upcoming intersections.

- ✔ The Settings button lets you overlay the map with layers (refer to "Adding layers of detail," earlier in this chapter). Add the Traffic layer, for example, when you're moving through congested areas.

- ✔ To see your entire trip on the map, touch Settings⇨Route Info.

- ✔ Tired of the verbal instructions? Touch Settings⇨Mute. To make sure that you don't miss a turn, touch Settings⇨Directions List for a list of the intersections and the directions in which you must turn.

- ✔ For an extra kick, touch Settings⇨Layers⇨Satellite for a helicopter view of your route. (All those photos consume a lot of data from your data plan, however.)

Part IV
Tweaks

The 5th Wave — By Rich Tennant

"What I'm doing should clear your sinuses, take away your headache, and charge your Xoom."

Total
28.88GB

Media
15.82GB

Applications
518MB

Available
12.55GB

About tablet

15h 3m 11

Display

Android OS

Wi-Fi

In this part . . .

Some people are always straightening picture frames and rearranging pencils on their desktops until they're just so. Others limit their adjustment urges to shoveling aside that pile of dirty clothes when it blocks the doorway.

This part of the book tackles the digital equivalent of adjusting things until they're just right. Whether the sound's too loud, the wallpaper's boring, or the battery's not lasting long enough, this part of the book lets you tweak your Xoom to your satisfaction.

Toss in a few maintenance and troubleshooting tools, and this part is all you need to make your Xoom truly yours.

App shortcuts   Wallpapers

Settings

*L*ike cobweb-ridden circuit breakers hidden in a musty panel, your Motorola Xoom includes a huge number of hidden switches. When one needs to be flipped (to turn on GPS, for example), the Motorola Xoom usually drops you off at the proper switch, thoughtfully keeping the spider silk from staining your shoulders. Should you need to spelunk these dark corridors with your own candle, however, touch Apps⇨Settings to find the door.

This chapter describes the dozens of switches on the Settings page. If you've ever flipped one by mistake, or if you simply want to make sure that everything is set up correctly, this chapter can help. It points out the switches you must flip every so often, and why; which switches should stay flipped on or off; and which you can safely ignore.

Total
28.88GB

Media
15.82GB

Applications
518MB

Available
12.55GB

Wireless & Networks

This collection of switches that control networks lives atop the Settings page for a good reason: It's usually your number-one destination. Whenever your Xoom has problems connecting with either the Internet or your Bluetooth gadgets, these settings let you fix the problem.

TIP

To head here quickly, touch the clock in the bottom-right corner of the screen. When the notifications panel rises, touch the clock again. The panel suddenly unveils toggle switches for both airplane mode and Wi-Fi.

I cover these all settings in Chapter 5, but here's a quick rundown on the most oft-used settings in the Wireless & Networks area, shown in Figure 15-1:

Figure 15-1: Touch Apps➪Settings➪Wireless & Networks to change the connections to networks, the Internet, and Bluetooth accessories.

TECHNICAL STUFF

✔ **Airplane Mode:** Touch this option to turn on airplane mode, which satisfies flight attendants worldwide. Airplane mode turns off all your Xoom's data-transmitting radios, effectively killing any connection involving your cellular data plan, Wi-Fi, and Bluetooth. (The airplane crew worries only about your cellular radio being turned off.)

On many mobile phones, airplane mode turns off GPS, but your Xoom's GPS still works fine in airplane mode.

✔ **Wi-Fi:** This toggle turns Wi-Fi on or off, even when you're in airplane mode. That feature lets you take advantage of any in-flight Wi-Fi services yet comply with airplane mode by turning off your data-plan connection.

✔ **Wi-Fi Settings:** This option lets you pick and choose among available Wi-Fi networks, as well as delete any unneeded ones that you saved from previous hotel stays.

✔ **Bluetooth:** Touch this option to power on the Bluetooth radio; then touch the next setting, Bluetooth Connections, to connect with specific gadgets. (While you're in airplane mode, this setting also lets you turn Bluetooth back on so that you can reconnect with your wireless headphones, all the while complying with airplane mode.)

✔ **Bluetooth Settings:** This option lists every Bluetooth gadget you've connected with in the past, as well as options to connect with new ones. When you're trying to connect with a new Bluetooth item, be sure to turn on the Discoverable setting so that the Bluetooth gadget can find your Xoom.

✔ **Tethering & Portable Hotspot:** This option lets you connect to the Internet through a cellphone or share your Xoom's cellular Internet connection with up to five nearby PCs, cellphones, and other Internet-craving gadgets. Don't try this while flying, though, or risk the wrath of flight attendants.

✔ **VPN Settings:** These settings control Virtual Private Networks, something that nerds relish and others ignore.

✔ **Mobile Networks:** Xooms with a cellular data plan need to have Data Enabled turned on. All the other settings here should be turned off or left to automatic. (The exception would be Activate Device, an option chosen only if you're having trouble activating a newly purchased Xoom with your data plan provider.)

To restrict your Xoom to Wi-Fi Internet access, turn off Data Enabled. That saves a little battery life, as your Xoom will stop searching for nearby cellphone towers.

To activate your Xoom with your cellphone carrier for the first time, touch Activate Device in the Mobile Networks area.

I cover these settings in greater detail in Chapter 5.

Sound

Poking the cumbersome Up/Down volume buttons along the edge of your Xoom (near the Motorola logo) lets you change the volume.

Just pressing one of those buttons, however, brings a volume level control to the screen, letting you fine-tune the volume with a slide of your finger. That's much easier than fiddling with those hard-to-reach buttons.

The Sound settings (touch Apps⇨Settings⇨Sound to reach them) relate to your Xoom's sound. If you work in a TV or radio studio, you're probably going to turn them all off, lest your Xoom warble during a live broadcast.

You're probably in the Sound settings area to adjust one of these things:

- **Volume:** Unlike TVs and radios, your Xoom comes with three sources of volume: System (music and videos); Notifications (little noises that herald newly arrived e-mail); and Alarm, should you set a wake-up time through the Clock app (touch Apps⇨Clock).

  You can adjust the volume level for each noisemaker separately, keeping your alarm louder than your notifications, for example. To fiddle with your sound levels, touch the Sound setting's Volume button, and the panel shown in Figure 15-2 appears.

  As you slide the bars to the left and right with a finger, a sound plays, letting you hear its current level. Stop adjusting when the level meets your needs, be it max, mute, or somewhere in between.

- **Notification Ringtone:** Choose among the dozen or so sounds to alert you to each new e-mail or other noteworthy event. (The sounds are named after atoms, in case you're curious.)

- **Feedback:** Want to hear a little reassuring sound when you touch an onscreen button? Turn on Audible Selection. Similarly, toggle on Screen Lock Sounds to hear a robotic warble when you lock or unlock your screen.

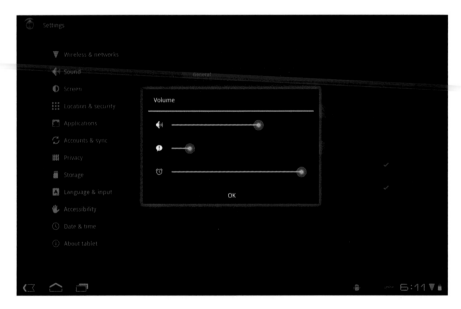

Figure 15-2: Touch Apps⇨Settings⇨Sound⇨Volume to adjust the volume levels of your music (top), notifications (middle), and alarms (bottom).

Screen

Three main Screen settings draw pilgrims to this page. Here, you can force the screen to remain in landscape or portrait mode to prevent those attention-jarring switches when you move your Xoom. Also, you can tweak screen brightness manually, should the default levels not meet your needs.

To find these switches, touch Apps⇨Settings⇨Screen, and check these settings:

- ✔ **Brightness:** Your Xoom normally reads the light around you and then brightens or dims the screen accordingly. For office rats or yachters who prefer a constant brightness level, touch Brightness, clear the Automatic Brightness check box, and then touch OK.

  You'll find a shortcut to the Brightness setting in the notifications panel. Touch the clock to open the notifications panel; then touch the clock again.

- ✔ **Auto-Rotate Screen:** Do you want the screen to stay in landscape mode or portrait mode all the time? This toggle switch lets you set your preference, forcing the screen to stop switching between display modes as you rotate your Xoom.

- ✔ **Timeout:** The screen normally dims after two minutes of inactivity to save batteries, forcing you to rummage for the back-mounted power button to wake up your Xoom yet again. Here, you can change the delay from the battery-preserving 15 seconds to the battery-draining 30 minutes.

If you don't ever want the screen to go dark when the Xoom is plugged in to a charger, touch Apps⇨Settings⇨Applications⇨Development, and check the Stay Awake box.

Location & Security

Many settings await in the Location & Security area, designed to placate both privacy cravers and those who feel that online privacy vanished long ago. No matter which camp you've staked your flag in, your privacy settings appear in this section, shown in Figure 15-3.

Personally, I willingly give up my location in exchange for more accurate information about the area around me.

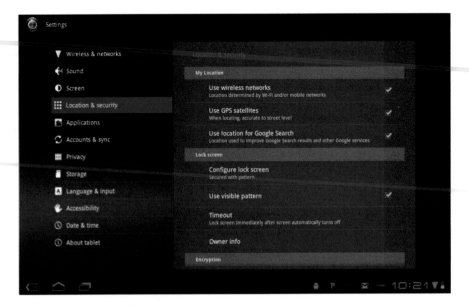

Figure 15-3: Touch Apps⇨Settings⇨Location & Security to balance your desire for privacy with your need for location-specific information.

The settings are the ones you use or ponder most often:

- ✔ **Use Wireless Networks:** Data-plan owners should select this option, which allows your Xoom to approximate your location based on the signal strength of nearby cellphone towers. Your cellphone company already knows where you are, so you may as well give your Xoom that information.

- ✔ **Use GPS Satellites:** When toggled on, this option lets your Xoom find your position on a map to within a block. It's a huge improvement in accuracy and a total defeat for those who crave privacy. (GPS requires a clear view of the sky, so it won't help you return to your car in the parking garage.)

- ✔ **Use Location for Google Search:** When turned on, this option sends your location to Google along with your web searches, making the results location-specific.

- ✔ **Configure Lock Screen:** Your Xoom comes without a lock, so you just push the On button to get inside. To safeguard your Xoom's information, head here (as described in Chapter 2), and choose a pattern, number sequence, or password.

✔ **Owner Info:** Here, enter your name, address, phone number, and the phrase *Reward if returned.* That information appears on your Xoom's locked screen so that kind strangers can return it.

✔ **Encrypt Tablet:** Described in Chapter 2, this option takes at least an hour to encrypt your Xoom's information. When it's encrypted, though, your information will remain more secure if your Xoom falls into the hands of thieves. (You need to scroll down the page to find this setting.)

Applications

Nearly everybody installs apps, and the Applications page lets you keep tabs on them. Most apps behave themselves, so you can usually ignore this page.

In fact, you can see your Apps by touching Apps on the home screen. You can uninstall unwanted apps directly from the Android Market's My Apps page.

Should you need more information about your apps, perhaps for trouble-shooting purposes, here's where to look:

✔ **Manage Applications:** This smorgasbord lists every app, its size, and ways to manage it, or even uninstall it. Come here only if an app acts up. Then touch your app's name, and touch the Clear Data and Clear Cache buttons. Ideally, your app's head will clear, and it will run without problems thereafter.

✔ **Storage Use:** If you're running out of storage space, this handy table lists all your apps and the amount of space they require. If you need more storage room, find the largest of your least-used apps, and uninstall them.

✔ **Battery Use:** Is the battery running down too quickly? This setting lists the biggest power suckers, and the display *always* tops the list, usually grabbing more than 80 percent of the power. (To prolong battery life, head to the Screen settings, listed earlier in this chapter, and switch Timeout back to dimming the screen every two minutes.)

✔ **Unknown Sources:** This toggle option lets you install apps from places other than the Android Market. Use it only temporarily, to install specific apps given you by trusted friends; then turn it back off. You don't want a virus in your Xoom.

✔ **Development:** This option is mostly for programmers who create apps. There's one user-friendly setting, though. If your Xoom stays plugged into the wall and you want the screen to be turned on constantly, choose Stay Awake. That ensures your plugged-in Xoom never sleeps.

Accounts & Sync

Three settings in the Accounts & Sync area, shown in Figure 15-4, can make all the difference. Usually, you set these options once and then forget them. But if you need to fiddle around, here's what these settings mean:

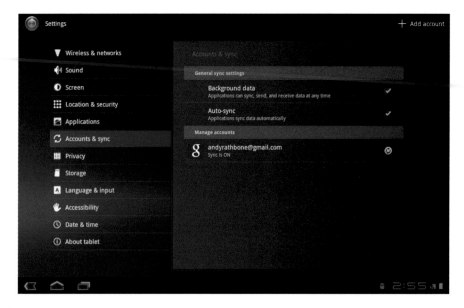

Figure 15-4: Touch Apps➪Settings➪Accounts & Sync to decide whether apps and e-mail should stay up to date automatically.

- ✔ **Background Data:** A one-touch battery saver, this toggle option specifies whether apps and accounts can update themselves in the background. Turning this option off saves battery power, but you'll see fewer notifications about incoming e-mail, Facebook updates, upcoming thunderstorms, and other information that normally flows into your Xoom.

  Turning off Background Data also turns off Auto-Sync, keeping your listed accounts from syncing automatically.

- ✔ **Auto-Sync:** Normally left on, this option lets your listed accounts grab information whenever they want. If this option is turned off, you must update information manually by touching the account's name and then touching Sync Now, or heading straight to your account's app and choosing Refresh from its menu.

- ✔ **Manage Accounts:** Unless you turn off Auto-Sync (see the preceding paragraph), accounts normally grab information when they want. You'll see your Gmail account listed in this section, as well as any accounts from Twitter and a few other social-networking apps.

At this writing, Google and Facebook were engaged in fisticuffs, and Google wouldn't let you enter your Facebook account settings in the Accounts & Sync section. Instead, head for Facebook from your Browser app or install the Facebook app, covered in Chapter 10.

Privacy

The Privacy settings determine how much of your information you're willing to share with Google. I turn both options on, as I enjoy the convenience of automatic backups.

If you're concerned about Google and your privacy, head for the Google Dashboard (`https://google.com/dashboard`). There, you can see, edit, and/or remove all the information associated with your Google account.

- **Back Up My Data:** When this option is turned on, your Xoom backs up some of your personal data to Google and ties it to your Google account. Should your Xoom die (or you perform a Factory Reset), just log in to your Google account with a replacement (or Factory Reset) Xoom. The Xoom loads all your Wi-Fi passwords, browser bookmarks, and installed apps; your custom dictionary; and most of the settings you've changed in the Settings area.

    When this option is turned off, Google deletes any existing backups and stops backing up your information.

- **Backup Account:** This option lists the account you need to access your backup. (It's usually the Google account you used when you first turned on your Xoom.)

- **Automatic Restore:** When turned on, this setting backs up settings you've made to apps. That way, when you install your favorite phone app onto your Xoom, the Xoom's app will have the same settings as your phone app.

- **Factory Data Reset:** Choosing this option and then touching the Reset Tablet button erases your Xoom. When it wakes up again, you're right back at the start, entering your Google account. (See Chapter 2 if you find yourself in this situation.)

    The Factory Data Reset option doesn't erase any Android updates that your Xoom may have downloaded. Also, unless you touch the SD Card check box, a factory reset won't erase anything from an SD card you may have inserted into your Xoom's SD card slot. (Presumably, the SD Card check box will appear in the menu when Google issues the update that gives life to your Xoom's SD card slot.)

Storage

The brightly colored charts in the Storage area (shown in Figure 15-5) merely tell you how much storage space remains in your Xoom. Unless your Xoom sends you anxious messages about low storage, you can safely ignore this section.

Figure 15-5: Touch Apps⇨Settings⇨Storage to see your biggest data hogs.

The red portion of the chart shows the amount of storage space consumed by your music and videos; the lime-green portion represents all your apps; and the gray matter represents available storage space.

If you're running out of space, deleting a video or two is the quickest and easiest way to free some room. You can delete videos easily by connecting your Xoom to your PC with a USB cable, as covered in Chapter 5, and deleting them with your desktop computer.

Language & Input

Chapter 4 explains the keyboard and voice commands, so head there before you change anything in the Language & Input area. If you just need a quick refresher, here's the rundown:

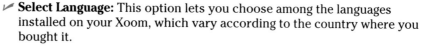

✔ **Select Language:** This option lets you choose among the languages installed on your Xoom, which vary according to the country where you bought it.

✔ **User Dictionary:** Drop by here occasionally to edit words or remove words from your custom dictionary — the master list of words that your Xoom never autocorrects as you type.

✔ **Voice-Recognizer Settings:** If you boss your Xoom around a lot with voice commands, head here, and choose Personalized Recognition. Google stores snippets of your speech, which helps your Xoom grow more accustomed to your voice and improves its accuracy over time.

✔ **Text-to-Speech Settings:** If your Xoom talks too slowly or quickly when giving navigation instructions, this option lets you change its pace.

Accessibility

The Accessibility area helps people with vision or hearing difficulties get the most out of the Xoom. Specifically, these two options may help:

✔ **TalkBack:** When this option is turned on, a speech synthesizer begins speaking the names of menu items you touch while navigating your Xoom.

✔ **SoundBack:** When this option is toggled on, the Xoom plays a confirming sound when you do certain things, such as fetch the notifications panel or touch a button.

If you prefer to use the accessibility options, be sure to turn on all the options in this section, including Download Accessibility Scripts, which allows apps to download voice and sound options that supplement your Xoom's own accessibility efforts.

Date & Time

Xooms with data plans automatically have their clocks set by their data providers. If you have a Wi-Fi–only Xoom, though, drop by the Date & Time settings every once in a while to make sure your clock is set to the correct time.

About Tablet

The items in the About Tablet area aren't settings so much as they're pure information. The equivalent of a medical patient's folder, this section lists your Xoom's vital statistics. Here are the highlights:

- **System Updates:** Google continually updates Android, your Xoom's operating system. When it issues improvements, it usually sends the updates right to your Xoom. This area lists when your Xoom last checked for updates. (It usually checks every day.)

  To install a waiting update, touch Install or Install Now. (You're best off waiting for a Wi-Fi connection, as those updates can be very large.)

- **Status:** If a tech-support person ever needs to know specifics like your Xoom's MDN, MIN, or MEID number, you'll find them listed in the Status area. In fact, you'll even see your Xoom's phone number listed.

  Your cellular carrier uses your Xoom's phone number only for billing purposes, because a Xoom can neither send nor receive phone calls or text messages. In fact, if you send a text message to your Xoom's phone number, your Xoom will never know. *You'll* know, though, when you see the text message appear as a charge on your Xoom's next Verizon bill.

- **Legal Information:** Are you feeling guilty about skipping the fine print and just clicking Accept whenever you're offered any of Google's services? Head to the Legal Information section, where all of Google's fine print awaits your scrutiny.

16

Maintenance and Troubleshooting

In This Chapter

▶ Keeping the battery alive longer

▶ Updating your Xoom and its apps

▶ Handling backups and restores

▶ Keeping the screen clean

▶ Running a 3G/4G Xoom without a data plan

▶ Drying out after a drenching

▶ Handling forced closes

▶ Rebooting and resetting

*K*eeping your Motorola Xoom running smoothly doesn't take much effort. None of the maintenance and troubleshooting tips described here requires any tools, potions, or incantations.

In fact, you'll spend most of your time *not* doing certain things. This chapter explains what not to do — and what to do if you accidentally did something you shouldn't.

If you drop by my website's *Motorola Xoom For Dummies* page (www.andyrathbone.com), you'll find direct links to every site mentioned in this book, including direct links to the Xoom's USB drivers, manual, and other handy items.

Sorry!

The application Facebook katana) has stopped unex

Force close

Prolonging Battery Life

Your Xoom enjoys remarkable battery life — up to 14 hours. That said, when your Xoom's turned on, it's natural to glance at the battery-level indicator in your screen's corner, because it's a ticking clock. When the countdown ends, your Xoom turns into a boring, empty picture frame.

That's why battery life quickly rises to the top of the importance stack when you think about Xoom maintenance. You need to keep watch as the battery drains, taking preventive steps to keep your battery running to day's end.

Monitoring your battery's life

Your Xoom displays its battery charge as a little green icon in the screen's bottom-right corner. Figure 16-1 shows how your battery charge drops continuously as your Xoom stays turned on.

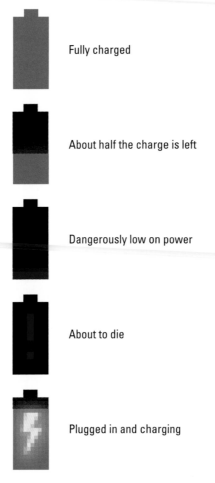

Fully charged

About half the charge is left

Dangerously low on power

About to die

Plugged in and charging

Figure 16-1: Your Xoom's battery icon changes as your battery drains.

The ever-changing icon gives you a general gauge of battery strength, but for more exact measurements, touch the clock in the screen's bottom-right corner. The top of the notifications panel appears (see Figure 16-2), showing the exact strength of both your battery and your current Wi-Fi signal, as well as the date and time.

Wi-Fi strength   Battery strength   Touch here to raise
the full notifications panel

Figure 16-2: Touch the clock in the bottom-right corner of the screen to see the percentage of power left.

When your battery level reaches a critically low level, your Xoom sends a worried message, as shown in Figure 16-3. That message means it's time to save your work frequently, all the while glancing over your shoulder for a nearby electrical outlet. (You *did* pack your charger, didn't you?)

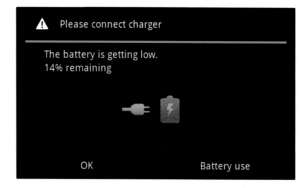

Figure 16-3: When your battery level reaches a critical level, your Xoom interrupts your work with this message.

Are you curious about what's hogging most of your battery? Touch the Battery Use button, shown in Figure 16-3. Surprise! Your Xoom's screen consumes at least 80 percent of your Xoom's power.

- ✔ When its battery finally loses power, your Xoom simply turns off, waiting for you to plug it in again.

- ✔ If you need to begin work immediately, plug your Xoom into its charger. You can work and charge at the same time, but your Xoom takes longer to reach a full charge if you use it while it's charging.

- ✔ When you're watching a movie, the icons in the bottom-right corner of the screen are replaced by tiny white dots. To check your battery life during the movie, touch the tiny white dots, and the notifications panel appears. (Touch your movie to close the panel and resume the show.)

- ✔ Some activities drain the battery more quickly than others do. Playing high-definition videogames with the screen brightness turned up, for example, consumes far more power than listening to music through headphones does. The point? Consider battery levels to be estimates rather than absolutes.

- ✔ You needn't charge the battery completely before unplugging it and rushing out the door. Fully charging a dead battery can take three hours. When you're on the road, plug in your Xoom when you can. An auto charger can be a lifesaver for heavy users.

Preserving battery life

Not using it? Turn it off. That's the mantra for preserving battery life. Toggle off the biggest charge-killers first; then move down the list.

These steps show you how to find out what's draining your power and adjust your display (the biggest battery hog of them all):

1. **Touch Apps⇨Settings⇨About Tablet⇨Battery Use.**

   The screen shown in Figure 16-4 appears, listing the biggest battery hog at the top. (It's always your display.)

   The battery shown in Figure 16-4 has been on for more than 15 hours, yet it still has about a third of its power left.

2. **Adjust your Xoom's Timeout settings.**

   To adjust the display settings, touch the word *Display,* listed atop Figure 16-4. When the menu appears, touch Display Settings.

   Adjust the amount of time before the screen dims by touching Timeout; then make sure that your screen dims after the default two minutes of inactivity. There's no sense draining your battery while you're away draining the water cooler.

Figure 16-4: Touch Apps➪Settings➪About Tablet➪Battery Use to see your biggest battery hogs and change their settings.

3. **Adjust your screen's brightness.**

The screen normally stays on autopilot, adjusting automatically as your ambient light changes. For extra battery life, turn off autobrightness and slide the bar to the dim end, making sure that you can still read the screen comfortably.

After you've adjusted your screen's timeout and brightness settings, you can subtly extend your battery life by turning these things on only when they're needed:

✔ **GPS:** The GPS system constantly listens to satellites, draining battery power in the process. When you're using GPS in a car for navigation, use an auto charger or count on having a big battery drain. To toggle GPS on or off, touch Apps➪Settings➪Location & Security➪Use GPS Satellites.

✔ **Wi-Fi:** Turn this option on when you're within range of a Wi-Fi network so that you can access the Internet. Turn it off when you'll be out of range for a while or don't need the Internet. To toggle Wi-Fi on or off, touch Apps➪Settings➪Wireless & Networks➪Wi-Fi.

✔ **Bluetooth:** Turn this option on only when you need it (for printing to a Bluetooth printer, talking through a headset, or tethering through your cellphone). As soon as you're done, flick it off. To toggle Bluetooth on or off, touch Apps➪Settings➪Wireless & Networks➪Bluetooth.

For even more battery statistics, touch the battery chart shown in Figure 16-4, earlier in this section. A new chart appears, showing the times when different items started and stopped draining your battery. This feature is useful for finding things that drain your battery, such as accidentally leaving Wi-Fi turned on.

Adding System Updates to Your Xoom

When it was first sold in late February 2011, the Xoom lacked several features. Motorola promised to add those features with updates sent through the airwaves to your Xoom. To check your Xoom's update status, touch Apps➪Settings➪About Tablet➪System Updates. To install any updates you find waiting, touch Install or Install Now.

Updates come one-by-one, so visit here often. And you'll still have to send your Xoom to Motorola for the upgrade to 4G data plan service, as covered in the next section.

You're best off waiting for a Wi-Fi connection to update, as those updates can be very large. (Some countries won't even send them through mobile networks.)

Not sure whether you have the latest update? On your desktop computer, visit www.motorola.com/myxoom, and check the Software Updates and Drivers section. If an update is available, you may find it waiting, along with installation instructions.

Updating Your Xoom to 4G

One of the perks of owning a Xoom comes from the free upgrade to 4G, meaning that your Xoom will be able to access the latest, fastest breed of cellphone towers. That simple upgrade keeps your Xoom up to date with many gadgets to be released in the months ahead.

To sign up for the 4G upgrade, fill out the form at this page on Verizon's website: www.verizonwireless.com/xoom4glteupgrade.

When you receive notice that Motorola's ready to upgrade your Xoom, follow these steps:

1. **Back up your Xoom (recommended).**

   Connect your Xoom to a desktop computer with a USB cable; then copy all your Xoom's available folders into a new folder called Backup on your computer. (I provide more detailed instructions on backing up your Xoom to a PC or Mac in Chapter 5.)

2. **Encrypt your Xoom, or perform a factory reset (optional).**

   Are you worried about another person accessing your Xoom's files? Then encrypt your Xoom, as described in Chapter 2, or perform a factory reset, as described at the end of this chapter. Neither option is mandatory, but either will keep your Xoom's information secure.

3. **Ship your Xoom to Motorola.**

   Motorola sends you a postage-paid shipping envelope that you can use to send in your Xoom. The update takes less than 30 minutes, but shipping takes time. Allow about a week for your Xoom to return from Motorola.

If your upgraded Xoom returns without any of your data on it, restore it from your backup. To do that, open the Backup folder on your computer, and copy your backed-up folders to your Xoom to retrieve your information. (I explain how to start a Xoom for the first time in Chapter 2.)

✒ Only Step 3 is mandatory. You can skip the first two steps if your Xoom doesn't have any information you'd miss and you don't care whether the repair folks at Motorola can see your data.

✒ You don't even have to upgrade your Xoom to 4G, but because the upgrade is free, adding 4G capability also adds to the Xoom's resale value.

✒ For more information about your Xoom's free 4G upgrade, visit Verizon's website at `http://support.vzw.com/faqs/Equipment/xoom_upgrade.html`.

Backing Up and Restoring Your Xoom

I describe how to back up your Xoom in Chapter 5. That backs up the items that *you've* put on your Xoom: music, movies, documents, and similar files. I explain in Chapter 15 how to let Google back up the rest: your apps, settings, bookmarks, and Wi-Fi passwords.

Google's backups have one odd side effect: Although Google backs up most of your settings, it doesn't back up your customized home screens. If you perform a factory reset, you'll still need to rehang your customized wallpaper, as well as drag your app shortcuts and widgets to the appropriate screens. (I explain how to customize the home screens with wallpaper, widgets, and app shortcuts in Chapter 17.)

To restore your Xoom from the files you've backed up, connect your Xoom with a USB cable to your desktop computer. Then copy all the files from your desktop computer's Backup folder back to your Xoom.

Cleaning the Screen

Breathing on a mobile phone and wiping it on your shirtsleeve works well, but a Xoom is a little large for most shirtsleeves. A better tool is a microfiber cloth, sold in most auto shops and hardware stores. This type of cloth doesn't scratch, and it won't leave lint on the screen.

Don't moisten your cleaning cloth with cleaning agents that contain ammonia or alcohol, as they can damage the screen. In fact, don't use *any* cleaning agents.

Just rub the screen with the dry cloth. If you encounter stubborn bits of crud, moisten the cloth very lightly with warm water. Then rub gently until the goo moves from the screen to your cloth.

Running a 3G/4G Xoom as Wi-Fi only

If you bought a Xoom with a cellphone data plan but don't want to *pay* for the cellphone plan, call your cellphone provider and discontinue it.

Even if you cut your data plan, your Xoom can still connect with the Internet in two ways:

- ✔ **Wi-Fi:** When a Xoom sniffs out a Wi-Fi connection, it offers to connect. You may have Wi-Fi around your home or office. If not, you'll find Wi-Fi in coffee shops and airports, or perhaps even drifting over from the home of a friendly neighbor.

- ✔ **Cellphone:** If you're already paying for a data plan on your Android cellphone, your Xoom can grab the Internet from that device. (See Chapter 5's section on tethering for more details about piggybacking on your cellphone's data plan.)

There's one drawback, though: Without a data plan, your 3G/4G Xoom will search constantly for available cellphone towers, just in case you've reactivated your plan. To save your battery life, turn off your Xoom's built-in 3G/4G radio by following these steps:

1. **Touch Apps⇨Settings.**

   The Settings page opens to its main section, Wireless & Networks.

2. **Touch Mobile Networks.**

3. **Touch Data Enabled to remove the check.**

   In fact, you don't want any checks on the Mobile Networks Settings page, as shown in Figure 16-5.

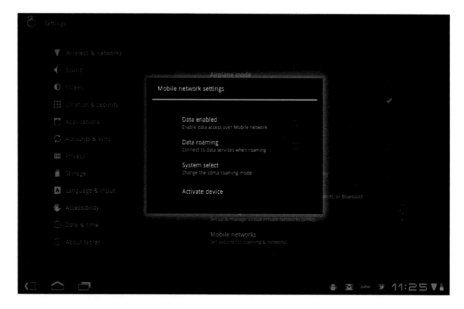

Figure 16-5: Touch Apps⇨Settings⇨Wireless & Networks⇨Mobile Networks, and turn off all the options to live a Wi-Fi–only lifestyle.

Discontinuing your data plan gives you the best of both worlds: You can live on Wi-Fi alone or piggyback on your cellphone's data plan.

If you ever want the data plan back, call your carrier, and ask to reactivate your device. Then follow the preceding steps again, but put the check back in Step 3 and then touch Activate Device (shown at the bottom of Figure 16-5).

When you turn your data plan back on, most carriers charge an activation fee, unfortunately. But paying an occasional activation fee is far less expensive than staying with a month-to-month plan that you don't really want or need.

Don't show this section of the book to anybody behind the desk of your carrier.

Surviving Water Damage

Tablets are much less likely to end up in a washing machine than cellphones are. But if your Xoom falls into water, turn it off as quickly as possible by pressing its Power button. Wipe off all the water you can find. Then leave your Xoom buried in a box of uncooked rice for a day and a half.

If you're lucky, the rice will pull the water out of the Xoom's circuits. Turn it back on and hope that luck is on your side.

Updating Your Apps

Your apps aren't alive, but they're growing all the time. Their creators almost always tinker with them, fixing old problems and adding new features.

It's up to you, though, to keep your apps up to date. To make sure that you're running the latest versions of your apps, follow these steps:

1. **Open the Android Market by touching Apps⇨Market.**

   The Market appears, ready to hawk its wares.

2. **Touch the My Apps button in the top-right corner.**

   This button switches the market's focus from all apps to just the ones installed on your Xoom and displays the My Apps page (see Figure 16-6), which lists all your installed apps on the left and any apps that need updates at the top.

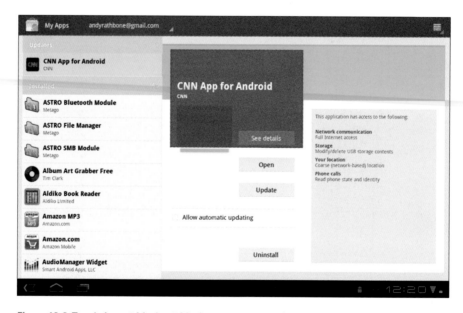

Figure 16-6: Touch Apps⇨Market⇨My Apps to see apps that need updating.

3. Touch the Update or Update All button.

To update them all, touch the Update All button. Your Xoom updates all your apps, one after another. (Some apps are large, so it's best to do this with a Wi-Fi connection.)

To update apps one by one, touch the app you want to update and then touch the Update button.

If an app changes its permissions, it won't update automatically. Instead, you must touch its Update button, and then read and accept the new list of permissions.

✔ Want your apps to update automatically? Touch the Allow Automatic Updating button. (Automatic updating may get expensive if you use a data plan and have lots of apps, however.)

✔ When apps update themselves, they replace their old versions but save your settings, high scores, and other things you've created with them.

Dealing with Force Close Messages

Occasionally, an app gets on its horse and heads for the mountains, leaving you staring at the apologetic message shown in Figure 16-7. This message means that the app has stopped responding to your Xoom's calls for attention.

Figure 16-7: Touch Force Close to stop the app; then try loading it again.

When you're presented with a Force Close screen, there's not much you can do besides touch Force Close. Your Xoom closes the app and leaves you wondering what went wrong. Sometimes, you can restart the app from the Apps section, and all will be well. At other times, restarting the app simply generates the Force Close message once again.

✔ If you like the app and hope that its developer will fix it, touch Report to send diagnostic information to the app's creator. Ideally, he or she will figure out the problem and tweak the app, and you'll find an update waiting at the Android Market (refer to "Updating Your Apps," earlier in this chapter).

✔ Some apps that work fine on cellphones cough up a Force Close message only on your Xoom. That situation means that the developer needs to tweak the app to work on a larger screen.

✔ Occasionally, you'll see a third option in the Force Close screen: Wait. If you see a Wait button, touch it. Sometimes, the app just needs more time to gather its information. If your patience wears thin, touch Force Close to move on.

✔ If an app keeps sends you Force Close messages, uninstall it by touching its Uninstall button (refer to Figure 16-6, earlier in this chapter). A lot of apps are out there, and you'll probably find one that runs better.

Performing a Forced Reboot (aka Hard Reset)

If your Xoom freezes like a car radiator in a North Dakota winter, don't worry too much: It may just need a little more time to think. When the wait becomes unbearable, though, terminate your Xoom's thoughts with a forced reboot.

A forced reboot kills only information you haven't saved, which includes any information sitting in currently opened programs (your current game's high score, for example, or unfinished e-mails).

To reboot your Xoom, press and hold the Power button *and* the Up volume key. Let go after a second or two when the screen goes dark. After a moment, your Xoom wakes back up, usually feeling much better.

Don't confuse a forced reboot with a factory reset, described in the next section. A factory reset erases all your Xoom's files, forcing you to start from scratch. A forced reboot, by contrast, only restarts your Xoom when it's frozen or acting erratically.

Starting Over with a Factory Reset

You may want to wipe your Xoom clean and start over for several reasons. Perhaps you're selling it or giving it to a friend. Maybe you want to give your Xoom a fresh start, knowing all the tips and tricks you know now. Maybe you want to wipe it clean before sending it back to Motorola for repairs or for the free 4G upgrade.

The official channels

Both Motorola and Verizon offer support through their websites. Here are the sites, and what you'll find:

✔ Motorola offers software updates, software, Xoom drivers, downloadable user guides,

and online help at `www.motorola.com/myxoom`.

✔ Verizon offers Xoom support at `http://support.vzw.com`.

On a less happy note, perhaps you've encrypted it (as described in Chapter 2) but forgotten the password. Or maybe your Xoom's just not working right, and you don't know what else to do.

No matter what your reason, you can easily wipe your Xoom completely clean, returning it to the state it was in when you first removed it from its box.

A factory reset erases all the data you've created on your Xoom, including photos, videos, and music that you've added to it. Don't do this unless you've backed up your data, described earlier in this chapter, or you have no alternatives.

To perform a factory reset on your Xoom, follow these steps:

1. **Touch Apps⇨Settings⇨Privacy Settings⇨Factory Data Reset.**

2. **Touch Reset Tablet.**

   Depending on how you've set up your Xoom, you may need to enter your password to approve the action.

   Your Xoom will wipe itself clean and then turn itself off.

3. **Turn your Xoom back on.**

If you tried this drastic step as a cure, the factory reset should have fixed the problem, and the Xoom should behave just as it did when you first removed it from its box.

✔ When your Xoom wakes up from a factory reset, it still knows its serial number, so you can still activate it with your carrier. And no, your carrier won't charge you a fee, as you never cancelled your plan.

✔ For a step-by-step guide on what to do when a new Xoom wakes up, flip back to Chapter 2.

✓ When you enter your Google account username and password after a factory reset, your Xoom automatically restocks itself with your Google Contacts and Calendar information, as well as any apps you've downloaded or purchased.

✓ To restore your Xoom from the files you've backed up, connect your Xoom with a USB cable to your desktop computer. Then copy all the files from your desktop computer's Backup folder back to your Xoom.

✓ If you previously told Google to back up your Xoom, as described in Chapter 15, your Xoom also restocks itself automatically with your settings, Wi-Fi passwords, and other information.

17

Customizing Your Xoom

In This Chapter

▸ Putting your stamp on your home screen

▸ Hanging wallpaper

▸ Rearranging apps and widgets

▸ Setting custom notification sounds

*S*ome people love to customize their cars, adding flashy rims, racing stripes, and woofers that make the vehicles bounce to the beat. Others limit their customization to hanging up a new air freshener after a car wash.

People treat their Motorola Xooms differently, too. You can truly make your Xoom your own, for example, by adding fun new backgrounds to your home screens and sprinkling in shortcuts to the apps you use most frequently. Or you can flip past this chapter, leaving everything pretty much the way it looks now.

Whether you love to fiddle with your home screen or figure that you'll customize it when you get around to it, this chapter's always waiting for you.

Customizing Your Home Screens

When you turn on your Motorola Xoom, you see your home screen — the desktop where you do most of your work. I explain in Chapter 3 how to work with your home screen, as well as how to see your two extra home screens off to each side. (Just slide your finger across the screen, and the other home screens come into view.)

You can customize your home screen with anything from the frivolous to the practical.

 To start spiffing up a home screen, tap the plus sign in its top-right corner. This icon, known as the Add button, fetches a miniature view of all five home screens, plus a salad bar of items you can toss onto them (see Figure 17-1).

Figure 17-1: Drag widgets, app shortcuts, or wallpapers to the five home screens at the top.

As shown in Figure 17-1, your five home screens stretch across the top, with your main home screen in the middle. Below the home screens sit four categories of items. Touch any of the following categories to see the goodies inside:

- **Widgets:** These tiny windows sit on your home screen, constantly updating their display with new information. One widget can show your latest e-mail, for example; another can show the latest news, stock updates, or weather changes.

- **App Shortcuts:** Sprinkle a few apps onto your home screens for one-touch access. A shortcut to your Settings app comes in handy, for example, providing quick access to the items you change most often.

- **Wallpapers:** Just like the backgrounds on a Windows desktop, these cosmetic niceties decorate your home screen's background.

✔ **More:** These icons offer customized shortcuts to various items, such as a specific page of your Settings app (Chapter 15), a favorite Music-app playlist (Chapter 12), an often-accessed Browser-app bookmark (Chapter 6), or a link to a particular person or place in your Contacts app (Chapter 8).

Changing your wallpaper

The easiest way to add a personal touch to your Xoom is to add your own *wallpaper* — an image that rests across all five of your home screens.

Your Xoom offers three wallpaper options:

✔ **Gallery:** This option opens the Gallery app, where you can select any photo or graphic on your Xoom, including photos you snapped on the Xoom, downloaded from the Internet, or transferred from your computer.

✔ **Live Wallpapers:** This option places constantly changing, swirling colors, lights, or animations on your home screen. (Depending on the complexity of their movements, Live Wallpapers consume slightly more battery power than regular wallpaper.)

✔ **Wallpapers:** This option lets you choose one of the stock images that came with your Xoom.

To slap some new wallpaper across your home screen, follow these steps:

1. **Touch the Add button in the screen's top-right corner (shown in the margin), or hold your finger down on the home screen.**

   No matter which method you choose, the home-screen customization window appears (refer to Figure 17-1, earlier in this chapter).

2. **Touch the Wallpapers option.**

   The three types of wallpapers — Gallery, Live Wallpapers, and Wallpapers — come into view.

3. **Touch the type of wallpaper you want and then touch one of the images.**

   The image fills the screen, with a cropping window surrounding part of it (see Figure 17-2).

   If you choose Live Wallpaper, you'll see a settings screen for adjusting the way that the wallpaper changes.

4. Drag the edges of the cropping window in or out until you've framed the portion you want to keep.

The cropping window frames your image in a 4-by-3 ratio. Drag the edges in or out with your fingertips. Note how the cropping window shows how the wallpaper will look both in landscape and portrait modes.

Try to crop the image so that the most interesting portion is in the middle, because that's the part you'll see most often.

5. Touch the OK button in the top-right corner to save your new wallpaper.

Figure 17-2: Drag the edges of the cropping window in or out to frame your new wallpaper.

Your new wallpaper spans all five of your home screens, and it fits on the screen whether you're holding your Xoom in landscape or portrait mode.

✔ To create your own wallpaper images, use a resolution of 1920x1280 pixels, but keep most of your subject within the 1280x800 portion. That resolution gives allows a little room for fudging when you rotate the tablet or switch home screens.

✔ Plenty of wallpaper and live-wallpaper apps are available at the Android Market.

✔ To delete live wallpaper that you've downloaded from the Android Market, open your Apps area, touch and hold your Live Wallpaper app, then drag and drop the unwanted wallpaper app onto the Uninstall icon in the top-right corner.

Adding apps or widgets to your home screen

Wallpaper (described in the preceding section) stretches across all five of your home screens. Apps and widgets, by contrast, stay put on the home screen you place them on.

If you put certain apps on certain pages, you can devote each page to a single activity. The items you use most frequently can stay on your main home screen, for example, and a screen to the immediate left or right can be reserved for work, filled with apps relating to your work e-mail accounts and projects. Another screen can be reserved for your weekends, complete with shortcuts to maps, navigation, restaurant reviews, and similar fun activities.

No matter why (or how) you're organizing your home screens, follow these steps to add an app or widget:

1. **Open any home screen, and touch the Add button in the top-right corner.**

   The home-screen customization area appears (refer to Figure 17-1, earlier in this chapter).

2. **Touch the category you're interested in: Widgets, App Shortcuts, or More.**

3. **Drag a widget, app shortcut, or wallpaper to the home screen you want to customize (see Figure 17-3).**

   As the item you're dragging reaches one of the home screens, that screen suddenly appears full size, as shown in Figure 17-4.

4. **Position your finger where you want to place the incoming item; then lift your finger off the glass.**

   Your newly placed app or widget remains in its new home.

Your main home screen

Two more home screens to the left   Two more home screens to the right

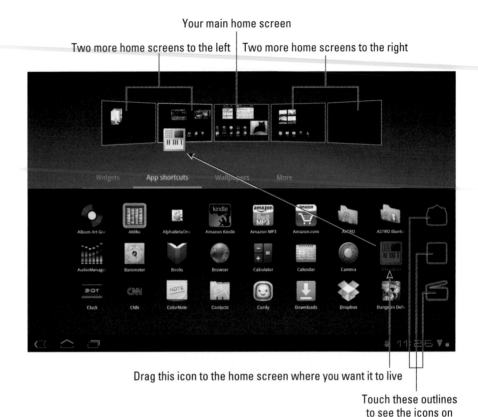

Drag this icon to the home screen where you want it to live

Touch these outlines
to see the icons on
the adjoining page
to the right

Figure 17-3: Drag an icon to the home screen where you want it to live.

As your finger moves to the home screen in Step 4, little grid markers appear. Each grid marker represents one square — just the right size for an icon. When you position your incoming icon in a square and lift your finger, the icon stays in place, and the grid disappears.

✔ Shortcuts to apps and items in the More category always consume one square. Widgets, by contrast, often use a 2-by-3 grid. (Each widget's space requirements are listed below its name as shown in Figure 17-1.)

✔ If you didn't drop the app in quite the right spot, touch and hold it. When it sticks to your finger, move your finger to the right spot — or even to a home screen off to the side. Let go when the app is positioned correctly.

✔ You can place the same app on several home screens. If you use the Maps app all the time, for example, place it on each home screen for one-touch convenience.

✔ Place a shortcut to your Settings app on your home screen. You'll be adjusting the settings regularly to make your Xoom accommodate your work habits.

✔ If your home screen's too full to hold any more items, you won't be able to drop any items there. Delete some of that page's unnecessary items to make room (as described in the next section); then try again.

✔ Are you always navigating to the same destination? Head for the More section, and add a shortcut to that destination.

Lift your finger when you've placed the icon where you want it to live

Figure 17-4: Lift your finger after positioning the icon in its new destination.

Removing apps and widgets from your home screen

Maybe you're tired of an app or widget on your home screen. You may not like the ones that came preinstalled. Or perhaps you've mistakenly dropped an errant app. No matter how the app arrived on a home screen, it's easy to scrape it off by following these steps:

1. **Touch the unwanted item, keeping your finger pressed against the screen.**

   After a second, the app icon attaches itself to your fingertip.

2. **Drag the unwanted item to the Remove icon in the screen's top-right corner.**

   The Remove icon, shown in Figure 17-5, appears when the app sticks to your fingertip. When your dragged app hovers over the Remove icon, both icons glow red.

3. **Lift your finger to drop the app on the Remove icon.**

   The app disappears from your home screen.

Removing an app from your home screen doesn't uninstall the app, which remains in your Apps area. You're deleting only a shortcut to the app, not the app itself. To delete an app, head for the Android Market, which I cover in Chapter 9, or touch the Apps button and drag the unwanted apps' icon to the trashcan in the top-right corner. (You can't delete any apps that came bundled with your Xoom.)

Figure 17-5: Remove an app from the home screen by dropping it on the Remove icon.

Changing the Sounds

Because it's not a phone, the Motorola Xoom doesn't offer ringtones, but you can still tinker with one sound: the notification sound that plays when you receive a new e-mail or other update.

To change your notification sound, touch Settings⇨Sounds⇨Notification Ringtone. In the resulting screen, you find a plethora of robotic murmurs. Touch any sound title to hear it, and when you've found the one you like, touch OK.

If you're adventurous enough to want to add your own sounds, connect your Xoom to your desktop PC, and drop the sound files in your Xoom's `media\audio\notifications` folder.

Part V
The Part of Tens

In this part . . .

The eyes of wild animals search continually for potential threats, mates, and food sources. Human eyes, by contrast, search continually for potential parking spots, free drinks, and neatly organized lists of items. That's why everybody in a grocery-store line winds up reading tabloid headlines like "Ten Best Holiday Gifts," "Twelve Hottest Vacation Spots," and "Ten Celebrity Train Wrecks."

To satisfy your innate urge for lists, this part of the book lays out catchy lists of ten items suitable for any checkout aisle: Ten Essential Free Apps, Ten Essential Tips 'n' Tricks, and Ten Handy Accessories.

18

Ten Essential Free Apps

Flash Player 10.2
ADOBE SYSTEMS

★★★★★ 198,37

Free

OPEN

MANAGE

*S*mall programs called *apps* await you in the sprawling aisles of the Android Market: a huge virtual warehouse stuffed with several hundred thousand of the things.

The Android Market offers a plethora of productivity enhancers: organizers, schedulers, reminders, and managers for your time and tasks.

Plenty of productivity killers await as well: games, music makers, bar tricks, comics, and movie trailers.

Yet the best part of the app-shopping experience comes at the checkout counter. The Android Market offers more free apps than pay apps — a ratio not enjoyed by iPhone or iPad owners who shop at the iTunes Store. For some reason, Android programmers like to give their work away, either for the good of society or a nerdy ego boost.

Here's a list of ten essential free apps you should grab right now.

All the apps listed in this chapter are free. You have nothing to lose by trying them.

Flash Player

One of the most-talked-about differences between the Motorola Xoom and Apple's iPad boils down to this one piece of add-on software: Adobe Flash. Flash excels at displaying videos and graphics on websites. In fact, most of the little ads you see on the web are created through the pseudomagic of Flash.

Nearly everybody could live without the ads, but many websites build themselves entirely around Flash. When you try to read a restaurant's website on an iOS device, only to find that it's created in Flash, you'll realize that having Flash adds a lot of power to a tablet.

Download Flash Player from the Android Market (see Figure 18-1), and your Xoom has access to nearly every website that your desktop computer can reach.

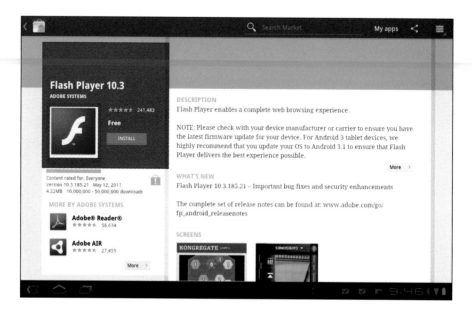

Figure 18-1: Download Flash Player to add Flash support to your Xoom.

If only Flash came with a built-in toggle for shutting off the ads . . .

Motorola's Help Center

Are you a little disappointed by the thin pieces of paper that Motorola tossed into your Xoom's box as an afterthought? Then download Motorola's Help Center app, shown in Figure 18-2. Once on your Xoom, the app offers help in four ways:

Figure 18-2: Motorola's Help Center app offers a direct link to the help forum.

- ✔ **Videos:** The 15 videos walk you through tasks like setting up e-mail, video chatting, and web browsing.

- ✔ **Guide:** This slightly larger version of your Xoom's slim manual offers basic guidance.

- ✔ **Tips:** Although basic, these tips warrant a read.

- ✔ **Support:** This section — the hidden gem — dishes up continually updated answers to frequently asked questions left on Motorola's website. While you're here, visit the Motorola Support Forum, where dozens of Xoom enthusiasts hang out, ready to help you with esoteric problems that aren't covered in manuals.

Oddly enough, Motorola's Help Center app doesn't come bundled with the Xoom; neither is it available from the Android Market. To download it, point your Xoom's browser to www.motorola.com/xoomhelp, and follow the onscreen instructions. (After downloading the app, touch Apps⇨Settings; deselect Unknown Sources; and then touch your downloaded app to install it, as described in Chapter 15.)

Do I need an antivirus program?

Viruses thrive in the Windows platform, with its millions of potential targets. Mobile phones haven't reached those numbers, but they carry data often sought by the thieves who write malware: essential information like contact names, site passwords, and sometimes credit-card numbers.

Viruses have already spread to mobile phones, but your Xoom is relatively safe. In fact, some Android antivirus programs don't yet work on the Xoom, because its version of the Android operating system is new, and the antivirus programmers need a few months to fine-tune their programs.

Also, be wary of antivirus programs that offer to kill your device remotely if it's stolen. Those programs probably won't work on your Xoom, as they usually send a specially worded text message to your Xoom to wipe it clean. A Xoom can't accept text messages, so the remote-kill message will never arrive.

Until new antivirus apps arrive, it's your responsibility to check apps before you download them. Look carefully at each app's ratings and comments before you install it. The bad apples won't have many downloads or good feedback.

If you're not sure about an app, don't install it. You can always go back and install it a few weeks later if nobody reports anything terrible about it.

Google's Apps

Because Google created your Motorola Xoom's operating system — Android — it's only natural that Google has also created a variety of Android apps. Google's apps run very smoothly on the Xoom, and I've installed nearly all of them.

Give these Google creations a try first.

Google Body

A bonanza for medical students, doctors, and physical therapists, Google Body shows a detailed 3D model of the human body (see Figure 18-3). You can break it down into five anatomical layers: muscles, organs, bones, blood vessels, and nerves.

By zooming in and out and rotating with your fingertips, you can examine your body's internal parts in vivid detail without any mess.

The app lets you search for specific body parts, letting you see exactly what your doctor means when he says that your enlarged piriformis muscle irritates your sciatic nerve.

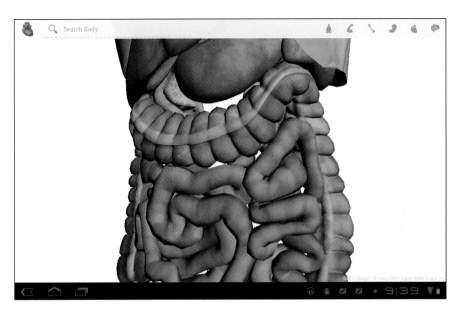

Figure 18-3: Google Body lets you explore the human body, layer by layer.

Google Earth

Just like its desktop predecessor, this app shows the globe sitting idly in outer space. Enter a location, and you fly there. The Xoom's big screen makes for a fantastic armchair tourist experience, letting you fly from exotic locale to exotic locale, scouting out possible future vacations.

Google Finance

Google Finance lets you enter your stock portfolio — real or imagined — and then watch in real time during the day as your wealth drops or rises.

When you're tired of watching the numbers change, enter any stock to delve in to its history and financial statistics.

Google Sky Map

Curious about which star twinkles o'er yonder? Or could it be a planet? Fire up Google Sky Map for the answer. The map turns your screen into an astronomer's star chart that comes alive. As you raise your Xoom skyward, moving it slowly in different directions, the screen displays the stars you see behind it.

Google Sky Map also displays the names of stars, constellations, nebulas, clusters, and galaxies.

Touch Settings and switch to night mode so you don't lose your night vision.

Amazon Kindle

Any books that you've purchased for an Amazon Kindle, you can read on your Xoom by downloading the Amazon Kindle app (described in Chapter 13). The app works much like an Amazon Kindle itself, opening to the page you last read. Also like a Kindle, the app lets you shop for new digital books, including bestsellers.

At the very least, download the free app and then download a few free classics, just to familiarize yourself with both the Kindle app and digital books in general. You'll be seeing more and more digital books in the future.

Amazon MP3

Amazon's been selling digital music for quite some time, yet its MP3 app offers some additional fun:

- ✔ **Buy MP3s:** Did you hear a song on the radio that you *must* buy now? Buy it straight from Amazon, served up as an unprotected MP3. When you buy an MP3, Amazon offers two ways to save it: directly on your Xoom or saved on Amazon's Cloud Drive.

- ✔ **Amazon's Cloud Drive:** Amazon offers you 5GB of storage on its Cloud Drive, which basically is a personal storage spot on the web. You can store not only purchased music there, but also music that you already own and have stored on your computer's hard drive.

When your Xoom starts running out of room, upload some of your MP3 files to Amazon's Cloud Drive, thereby freeing more storage space on your Xoom. You can still listen to your music whenever you have an Internet connection.

If you need more than 5GB of storage, Amazon lets you pay for up to 1,000GB of space.

ASTRO File Manager

Unlike Windows, your Xoom doesn't rely much on the folder storage system. Open your Gallery app, for example, and you see your pictures and movies in a single group, no matter how many separate folders you've stored them in. The same goes for music you're viewing through your Music app.

Sometimes, though, you want to poke around inside your Xoom's folders, deleting unused ones and poking around in others. In those times of need, ASTRO File Manager (see Figure 18-4) works wonders.

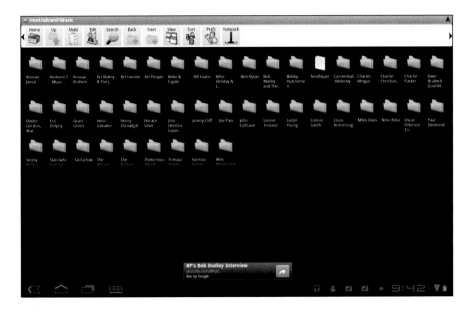

Figure 18-4: ASTRO File Manager lets you explore your Xoom's files and folders.

This app works much like Windows Explorer, letting you touch your way through trees and branches of folders, viewing them as lists or icons. It even lets you browse connected networks or swap files via Bluetooth, if the need arises.

TuneIn Radio

"Those sirens are getting closer," you say to yourself in your hotel room in a strange city. "What's up?"

To find out, fire up your TuneIn Radio app. The program quickly finds your location and then lists all the nearby radio stations, including the city's police scanners.

If you tire of police chatter, the app also offers local music, as well as just about any radio station streaming over the Internet. With access to thousands of radio stations worldwide, the app indexes them all, letting you tailor your sounds to meet any taste in any location.

I describe TuneIn Radio in detail at the end of Chapter 12.

Angry Birds

Sometimes, the simplest games hold the most power over us — a point well-proven by the runaway success of Angry Birds (see Figure 18-5). In this game app, you launch little birds on a slingshot, stretching your finger back and then lifting it to see the bird soar to the far end of the screen.

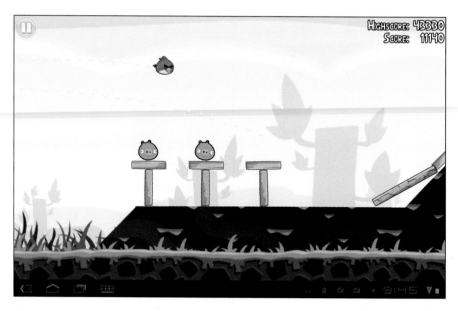

Figure 18-5: Angry Birds lets you sharpen your virtual-slingshot skills.

If you've aimed just right, you knock down a ramshackle house inhabited by evil pigs who stole the birds' eggs. You can easily lose an afternoon or three playing this game. Even cats like it.

USA Today

USA Today, which was kicked around by the old-school media when it launched, has soundly beaten the tablet news offerings of both *Time* magazine and *The New York Times.* Its USA Today app is a stunner. Bright and colorful as its print counterpart, the app fills the Xoom's screen with large photos, thoughtfully designed menus, and news to boot.

You won't find in-depth news coverage in this app, of course, but it gives you enough of a news bite to fill your craving while you're wolfing down a bagel or dashing out to the office.

Pulse

Most websites offer news feeds — continually updated lists of their latest stories. By subscribing to your favorite websites' news feeds and reading them in a newsfeed-reader program, you can read them in one batch, saving delays as you point and click through the web to read them all.

The Xoom's best newsreader so far is Alphonso Labs' Pulse (see Figure 18-6). Unlike many apps built for smaller displays, Pulse stretches luxuriously across your Xoom's full screen, flashing thumbnail photos and headlines from the stories on all your favorite sites.

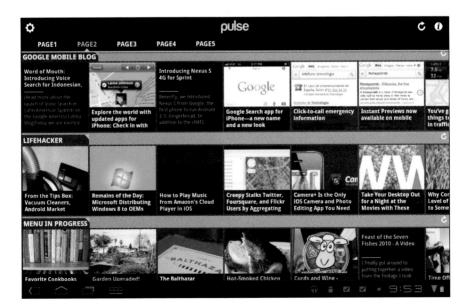

Figure 18-6: The Pulse newsreader app presents content from your favorite sites into one place.

I describe how to set up Pulse in Chapter 13. After you begin reading news with this app, you'll see the problem facing print newspapers and magazines. Nowadays, readers can easily create customized magazines built entirely around their own interests — for free.

Ten Essential Tips 'n' Tricks

In This Chapter

- Taking notes with your voice
- Keeping your Xoom quiet
- Personalizing the home screen
- Using the Recent Apps button
- Remembering things with Stars
- Customizing your home screens
- Entering text in portrait mode
- Doing nonstupid browser tricks
- Making Google Talk video-free
- Housekeeping your home screen
- Shutting an application down

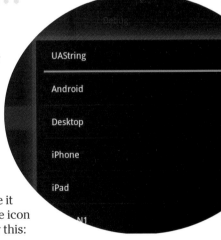

*T*he best tips and tricks are eye-openers, making you think, "Gosh, I should have been doing it *that* way the whole time!"

In that spirit, here are the best tips and tricks I've uncovered while writing this book.

Recording a Quick Note to Yourself

 You've found that million-dollar idea. You've *got* to write it down before you forget. You touch the little microphone icon in the top-left corner of every home screen, and you say this:

> "Note to self: Insulate house with aluminum foil."

You can record your voice, transcribe it, and drop it in a self-addressed e-mail. Touch the Send button, and you'll find both your recording and the transcription waiting in your e-mail.

Even if the on-the-fly transcription mangles a few words, you can make sense of it by listening to your recorded voice.

Silencing Your Xoom

You can set a wake-up time on your Xoom through the Clock app (touch Apps⇨Clock⇨Set Alarm). But how can you get a good night's sleep when your Xoom beeps every time your late-night friends check in on foursquare?

To keep sound interruptions to a minimum, mute the system sounds, but keep the alarm turned on full blast. Here's how:

1. **Touch the Up or Down volume button along the side near the Motorola logo.**

2. **When the sliding panel appears onscreen, touch the sound icon.**

   A line appears through both the System and Notification sound icons, shown in the margin. (By design, your alarm sound can't be muted, so it stays ready to wake you at the appointed hour.)

   Now your Xoom can keep receiving updates through the night, but you never have to hear them.

In the morning, to toggle the sound back on, repeat these steps. The icon's cross-out line disappears, as shown in the margin, and your Xoom is back in action.

I describe the sound settings in more detail in Chapter 15.

Customizing Your Home Screens

Your home screen appears when you first turn on your Xoom. Because it's your desktop, you have the ability to organize it the way you want it.

Dedicating each home screen to a theme

Your Xoom comes with five home screens, each one a blank canvas ready to be customized. Turn one screen into your Work area, for example, by sprinkling in shortcuts to work apps that you use often. Turn another into an Entertainment screen, with apps for playing and downloading music and videos. Yet another can be a Travel screen, with shortcuts to maps, navigation aids, and shortcuts to important reservation e-mails. By turning each home screen into a desktop for a different type of task, you turn your single tablet into five, each ready to handle each situation. I show you how to add and delete widgets and apps in Chapter 17.

Adding essential shortcuts to your home screen

Make your home screen your own by adding shortcuts that take you to the items you use most. (I describe the process of adding shortcuts to your home screen in Chapter 17.) Most people add a few shortcuts from the Apps or Widgets category.

The More category, however, offers some extra-helpful shortcuts that are worth considering:

✔ **Specific settings page:** Are you always traveling to the same Settings page to make some tweaks? Add a shortcut to that page with the More category's Select Settings shortcut.

✔ **Specific places:** If you use your Xoom for navigation, put a shortcut to the Navigation app on the home screen. Even better, create shortcuts to specific destinations by choosing the More category's Directions & Navigation shortcut. When you add that shortcut to your home screen, choose a specific location, be it your home address, your work address, or a city you visit often. Touching that shortcut fires up the Navigation app and guides you straight to the location.

✔ **Weather widget:** Plenty of free weather apps await in the Android Market's free apps section, but I like WeatherBug. Its tiny widget sits on my home screen, automatically updating the current temperature and an icon depicting snow, sun, rain, or something in between.

✔ **Camera:** Remember, when the UFO lands, Sasquatch walks, or the Mayan calendar ends, it's up to you to document the event. A one-touch shortcut to the Camera app keeps you prepared.

Jumping between Programs with the Recent Apps Button

Instead of tapping the Apps button and navigating a sea of app icons to find the one you just used, tap the Recent Apps button (shown in the margin) to see the last five apps you've opened.

After installing the Xoom's 3.1 update, the list becomes scrollable, letting you see dozens of recently opened apps.

By touching the thumbnails of recently accessed apps, as shown in Figure 19-1, you can quickly switch between tasks.

Figure 19-1: Switch between tasks with the Recent Apps button.

Using Stars to Remember Things

We tend to do the same things continually — things we should let our computers take over. To hand that work over to your Xoom, look for frequently accessed items you can mark with a star.

 You can add stars to important e-mails in Gmail, for example, as well as important locations in the Maps app and items that you want to read later in the Google Reader newsreader.

 Whenever you spot something that you know you'll need in the future, touch its adjacent blank star. When the star turns gold, it shows up in that app's shortcut menus.

Typing in Portrait Mode

Experiment with the keyboard. Some people find it easier to type in portrait mode (see Figure 19-2), with the Xoom turned sideways. (You can thumb-type a little easier that way if you're moving up from a phone keyboard.)

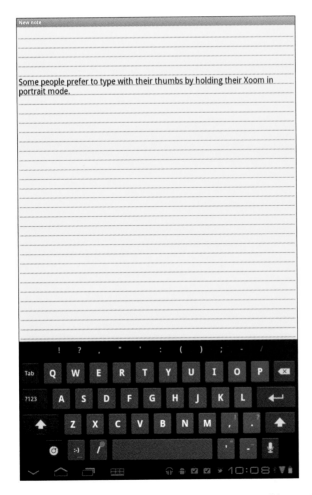

Some people prefer to type with their thumbs by holding their Xoom in portrait mode.

Figure 19-2: Hold your Xoom in portrait mode to type with your thumbs.

If you're a devout thumb typist, you'll also find several alternative keyboard layouts available as free apps in the Android Market.

Turning on Location Tracking in Your Photos

Your Xoom can stamp each photo you snap with your location, using the built-in GPS. That's a fantastic way to categorize your photos, as the Gallery app groups them by location for each access.

To use location tracking, touch Apps⇨Camera; touch the wrench icon in the Settings area; and toggle Store Location on.

If you give away or post a location-tracked photograph on the web, you're also giving viewers a map to the address where it was shot. Turn off location tracking when you take pictures in private homes.

Trying Browser Tricks

All the tips in this section apply to the app that you probably use most frequently: Browser, which lets you stroll through the Internet.

Making websites appear in their full versions

Your Xoom's screen may not be as large as the one on your laptop or desktop computer, but it's much bigger than the screen on a mobile phone. That's why it's an insult when a website formats its text as though you were reading it on a 2- by 5-inch screen.

Web designers will catch on to the problem soon, but until then, here's how to fool websites into thinking that you're visiting on a desktop computer:

1. **Open your Browser app.**

   Touch Apps⇨Browser, and the Xoom's web browser launches.

2. **Type the following text in the browser's address bar and then touch the Enter key:**

   ```
   about:debug
   ```

   Your address bar will look like the one in Figure 19-3.

Figure 19-3: Type **about:debug** in the browser's address bar.

When you touch the Enter key, nothing appears to happen, but you've added a secret setting to your Settings menu.

3. **Touch the Settings menu in the browser's top-right corner.**

   The Settings menu tumbles down.

4. **Choose Settings from the Settings menu, then choose Debug.**

5. **In the Debug menu, choose UA String, and choose Desktop.**

6. **Return to your browser, and touch the Refresh button.**

   Now most websites will display their full-screen selves.

   Unfortunately, you have to repeat these steps every time you turn your Xoom on or off.

Revisiting websites

To see websites that you've visited in the past, press and hold the Back button in the bottom-left corner of the Xoom's screen.

Your browser's History page appears, listing the websites you've visited in the past 30 days, in chronological order.

Touch any site's name for a revisit.

Bookmarking websites

Bookmarks let you revisit favorite pages. To create a bookmark, touch the Browser app's Bookmark icon (shown in the margin); then touch Add Bookmark in the top-right corner.

To see your bookmarks, touch the Bookmark icon; then revisit a bookmarked website by touching its icon.

Touch that bookmark and hold it down with your finger, and a menu appears, letting you do these things:

- ✔ **Open:** Open the website in your browser.

- ✔ **Open in New Window:** Open the site in a new tab (handy when you're comparing information on two sites).

- ✔ **Edit Bookmark:** Change the bookmark's name or web address.

- ✔ **Add Shortcut to Home:** Place a bookmark to this web page on your main home screen.

- ✔ **Share Link:** Send the link to other people, mostly through social-networking sites like Facebook.

- ✔ **Copy Link URL:** Copy the page's address to the Xoom's clipboard so that you can paste it into an e-mail.

- ✔ **Delete Bookmark:** Cross the site off your list of bookmarks.

- ✔ **Set As Homepage:** Make your browser always open to this extraordinary page.

Opening a link in a new tab

Did you spot a link on a web page that you want to read as soon as you're done with the current page? Save it for later by holding your finger on the link until a menu appears; then choose Open in New Tab. The site immediately opens in a new tab. Unfortunately, that new tab jumps to the forefront, diverting your attention from your original page.

To make those additional tabs open in the background, waiting patiently until you get to them, touch Menu⇨Settings⇨Advanced; then select the check box marked Open in Background. Thereafter, when you finish reading the current site, you can move to the other tabs.

Using Google Talk without Video

Google Talk's video chats bring people closer together. They're fantastic for reuniting long-separated family members, for example. But all-revealing video isn't so good when you've just gotten out of bed or when your web connection just can't handle the extra demands of video.

To take Google Talk down a notch to voice-only instead of voice and video, start by sending a text message to your friend; then touch the Microphone icon instead of the Videocamera icon.

Keeping Your Home Screen Free of App Clutter

Each time you download an app from the Android Market, Google tosses a shortcut to that app on your home screen. After you've grabbed a few apps, your home screen starts looking like the area around the office trash can, littered with a few missed shots.

To stop the Market from cluttering your home screen with newly downloaded apps' icons, touch Apps⇨Market⇨My Apps⇨Settings, and clear the Add Shortcuts for New Apps check box.

Closing an Application

There's really no need to close an application. Loaded apps lurk in the memory, waiting until they're called to action again. If memory runs low, those waiting apps disappear automatically as new ones take their place.

If an app misbehaves, though, here's how to kill it manually:

1. **Open Apps by touching Apps in the upper-right corner of any home screen.**

2. **Touch and hold the misbehaving app's icon.**

3. **Drag the icon to the Information icon in the top-right corner of the screen.**

   The app's Application Info page appears.

4. **Touch Force Stop.**

   If an app consistently misbehaves, touch the Clear Cache and Clear Defaults buttons on this page as well. Then you can start the app from scratch without having to uninstall it and then install it again.

Ten Handy Accessories

In This Chapter

▶ External speakers

▶ SpiderpodiumTablet

▶ Bluetooth keyboard

▶ Bluetooth headphones

▶ Micro HDMI cable

▶ External microphone

▶ Auto charger

▶ Padded case

After you've owned a Motorola Xoom for a few hours, you realize that a Xoom would be so much better *if only . . .*

Wouldn't it be nice, perhaps, if you could prop it up for watching movies?

How about watching your own movies during a flight? Wireless headphones would not only be nice for you, but also would be most appreciated by your seatmates.

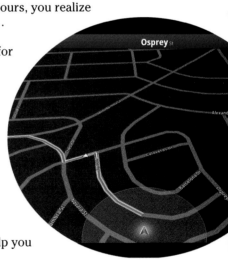

What about getting more storage space? Add a High-Capacity Secure Digital (HCSD) card to your list. Also, heavy-duty typists should check out a Bluetooth keyboard.

This chapter explores the ten best accessories to help you get the most use out of your Xoom.

It's no secret the iPad outsells every other tablet. Luckily, your Motorola Xoom works with almost all of the accessories designed, sold, and marketed for the iPad or iPad 2.

External Speakers

Your Xoom's stereo speakers offer far more stereo separation than cell-phones do. Unfortunately, a Xoom's speakers live on its back side, pointing directly away from you.

For much better sound, pick up a pair of external speakers. Any set of desktop computer speakers will do the trick, although most of them require a wall outlet for power.

For a travel alternative, any speakers made for iPods, iPads, iPhones, or cell-phones will work. Fortunately, a headphone jack is standard for both speakers and headphones.

Don't buy speakers that charge through a USB port unless you plan to recharge them through a desktop computer before taking them on the road.

The larger and heavier the speaker, the better the sound. When you go shopping, then, balance your need for sound quality with your need for portability. Only you know which you value more highly.

For fantastic sound, plug your Xoom into your home stereo. I describe how in Chapter 12.

SpiderpodiumTablet

When you're traveling, versatility is always a plus. That's where the SpiderpodiumTablet excels. Sure, it props up your Xoom on a table in many ways, but that's only half of its talents. With its spiderlike arms, the SpiderpodiumTablet lets your Xoom rest comfortably in these locations as well:

- **Car dashboard:** Drop two arms down your old Dodge's dashboard vent. A dashboard-mounted Xoom's navigation system beats the one you'll find in a Cadillac.

- **Driver's headrest:** Attach your Xoom to the back of the driver's-seat headrest so that it won't tempt you while you drive. The kids can watch movies on it during road trips and hone their navigation skills.

- **Bicycle handlebars:** Google's Navigation app guides you along bike paths as well as roads, and the SpiderpodiumTablet's eight legs let your Xoom cling to your handlebars.

✔ **Tree:** Use the SpiderpodiumTablet as a tripod to mount the Xoom on a branch and take movies of your campsite.

✔ **Plane:** Dangle it from the headrest of the seat in front of you so you can watch a personal in-flight movie. (This arrangement leaves the fold-down tray free for your Bluetooth keyboard if you need to work while you're in the clouds.)

Because the SpiderpodiumTablet folds flat for storage, it's easy to stash under a car seat, in a backpack, or even inside some larger Xoom cases. It's built for an iPad, of course, but works fine with a Xoom. For more information, visit www.breffo.com.

Bluetooth

Meant as a way to replace cables, Bluetooth wireless technology lets gadgets communicate over short distances, usually within the same room.

Your Xoom supports a wide variety of Bluetooth standards, letting it communicate with a wide variety of devices — some better than others, as the rest of this section describes.

Bluetooth keyboard

Typing on glass is like sniffing perfume on a movie character. To bring some reality back to your typing, pick up a Bluetooth keyboard. It connects wirelessly to your Xoom, letting you replace the glass with the real deal.

The Xoom supports what nerds call Human Interface Device (HID) protocol. In plain language, that means you're not stuck with a keyboard sold by Motorola; any Bluetooth keyboard should work, even one from Apple.

Motorola's official Bluetooth keyboard is thin and light, weighing less than a pound (with batteries), but it sacrifices usability for portability. Just like Apple's wireless keyboard, the keys are thin, with no indentations for your fingers to fall into. It sure beats glass, and it packs easily in your luggage or backpack, but it's not the most usable replacement.

You can buy the Motorola Bluetooth keyboard straight from Motorola (www.motorola.com) or from discounters like Amazon (www.amazon.com).

The best features of the Motorola keyboard are its dedicated Android keys, which take you straight to the home screen, Music app, Browser app, Android Market, and e-mail, as well as let you control your music. Touch typists will prefer a more heavy-duty model.

Bluetooth mouse

Your Xoom doesn't work with a mouse — until you install the Android 3.1 update, that is.

After the update, your Xoom recognizes both a Bluetooth and USB mouse. The little onscreen mouse pointer behaves just like your finger, letting you touch, tap, scroll and select items.

Bluetooth USB dongle for your PC

You can pick up a cheap Bluetooth adapter that plugs in to your PC's USB port, bestowing Bluetooth power upon it. Your Xoom can even talk to your PC through Bluetooth. Exchanging files will be slow and laborious, however, especially compared with file swapping through a USB cable.

If you really like the Bluetooth keyboard you picked up for your Xoom, consider paying an extra $10 for a PC Bluetooth adapter. Otherwise, there's not much point.

Bluetooth headphones

Not being able to make a phone call, your Xoom can't use the traditional Bluetooth earpieces that are so popular for cellphones. It *can* use Bluetooth headphones for listening to music, however. In fact, it supports the A2DP (Advanced Audio Distribution Profile) for higher-quality sound than older Bluetooth sound technology.

Still, Bluetooth headphones have their own unique problems. Most of them require batteries (although some of them recharge from a USB port). The extra circuitry involved pushes the price past that of regular plug-in headphones. Finally, unless they cover your ears, they don't sound all that great, which rules out the really portable models.

In fact, because your Xoom will most likely be sitting on a table next to you, you may prefer using standard wired headphones. They cost less and sound better than Bluetooth headphones, and you'll find a wider selection.

Your Xoom comes with a standard ⅛-inch headphone jack, so any pair of iPod or MP3-player headphones will work well.

Micro HDMI Cable

Your Xoom came with a micro USB cable for hitching up to a desktop computer, but it didn't come with a micro HDMI cable for playing back your photos and videos on a high-definition television set.

Don't splurge here. The cables either work, or they don't. A $2 cable works just as well as a $40 cable. I won't name brand names here, but grab the cheapest one you can find via mail order — or online — because most of the ones sold at retail outlets cost way too much.

The ones sold on Amazon.com are so inexpensive, in fact, that you should buy two: one to keep plugged in to your TV set and one to keep with your Xoom while traveling.

Be sure to buy a *micro* USB cable, not a *mini* USB cable, which won't work. You'll find connection instructions in Chapter 5.

External Microphone

The microphone is on the bottom edge of your Xoom, just to the left of all the other ports. See that barely visible hole in the plastic case? All the sound you're recording must pass through that tiny hole. Needless to say, the recording quality isn't top notch.

For better sound, pick up a SwitchEasy ThumbTacks microphone, shown in Figure 20-1. About the size and shape of a pushpin, it slips into your headphone jack.

You can't listen to any sounds while you're recording, which rules out wearing headphones as you record, but the sound quality sure moves up a few notches.

Although the microphone is designed for iPods and iPads, it works well on my Droid X phone as well as on my Xoom. For more information, drop by SwitchEasy's website (www.switcheasy.com).

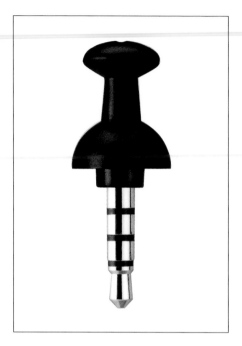

Figure 20-1: The SwitchEasy ThumbTacks 4G microphone improves your Xoom's sound recording quality.

SDHC Card

Your Xoom comes with 32GB of memory and stakes out some of that memory for itself just to keep itself alive. After you toss in some music, apps, and a few movies, it may run out of storage space.

If that happens, buy a Micro Secure Digital (SD) card or Micro Secure Digital High Capacity (SDHC) card, and slide it into your Xoom's memory slot, as described in Chapter 1.

Buying a 32GB Micro SDHC card doubles your memory, bringing your Xoom up to 64GB. Look for your Xoom's SD card slot to begin working after a software update.

Auto Charger

Your Xoom boasts impressive battery life, but it usually depends on the screen's blanking out after a few minutes of idleness. If you plan to use your Xoom for navigation while driving, the screen will be on constantly, showing a map of your progress. Also, your Xoom will need to pick up GPS signals constantly. Both things consume extra battery power.

In short, when you're using a Xoom for navigation, you'll want an auto charger that connects your car's cigarette lighter and your Xoom's charger port.

Because your Xoom doesn't use a standard size for its port, you're stuck with the Motorola version.

Padded Case

Carrying around a Xoom without a case is an exercise in terror. It feels unbalanced, as though it's about to slide from your grasp and shatter on the ground.

To ease the pain, pick up a carrying case for your Xoom. Different people look for different things, so I can't recommend one for everybody. I picked up a padded tablet sleeve at Verizon that works very well, however. The case is a snug fit, comes with a magnetic closure, and includes a little sleeve for headphones and a microphone. It keeps things light while you're traveling, and that's the point of a tablet.

Your Xoom is a wee bit longer than an iPad but not as wide. It should fit into most iPad sleeves and cases, but check the fit yourself at a store or friend's house to make sure.

Index

• *O* •

• *P* •

• Z •